Francis Bacon

Francis Bacon

The Double-Edged Life of the
Philosopher and Statesman

ROBERT P. ELLIS

McFarland & Company, Inc., Publishers
Jefferson, North Carolina

Frontispiece: Francis Bacon.

LIBRARY OF CONGRESS CATALOGUING-IN-PUBLICATION DATA

Ellis, Robert P. (Robert Patrick), 1935–
    Francis Bacon : the double-edged life of the philosopher and statesman / Robert P. Ellis.
        p.   cm.
    Includes bibliographical references and index.

    ISBN 978-0-7864-9727-0 (softcover : acid free paper) ∞
    ISBN 978-1-4766-2052-7 (ebook)

    1. Bacon, Francis, 1561–1626.   I. Title.
    B1197.E45 2015
    192—dc23
    [B]   2015013945

BRITISH LIBRARY CATALOGUING DATA ARE AVAILABLE

On the cover: Portrait statue of Francis Bacon in the Library of Congress Thomas Jefferson Building, Washington, D.C. (Library of Congress)

Printed in the United States of America

McFarland & Company, Inc., Publishers
  Box 611, Jefferson, North Carolina 28640
    www.mcfarlandpub.com

In memory of Anthony L. Ellis
(1967–2014)

Table of Contents

Preface

Francis Bacon became a presence to me when I was a small boy, for he occupied one page in a book called *Minute Biographies* by two authors who hoped that this compilation would attract boys and girls and adults, a wish perhaps more often fulfilled in the 1930s than today. He came fitfully to my attention during school and college and more seriously in my first graduate course, which was supposed to be about English literature of the seventeenth century, but in the hands of the professor became largely about two writers, John Donne, a minor figure in this book, and Francis Bacon. Subsequently I taught Bacon as a relatively small part of my own rather generalized literature courses but never wrote about him.

I read Catherine Drinker Bowen's biography *Francis Bacon: The Temper of a Man* not long after it appeared, and a good deal more about him later. He attracted me as a fine writer and a versatile man who combined a busy and eventually highly important public life as a politician and judge with a powerful desire to promote what the title of one of his books, *The Advancement of Learning*, intimates. Bowen's book remains today the one that a non-specialist reader is likely to encounter first. It is a fine book but a half-century old, and much more has been learned about the man.

Scholarly publications about Bacon are numerous and probably unending, but in this century such works grow very specialized. A large biography that could digest all the facets of Bacon's remarkable life is possible and desirable, but the common reader (to use a term coined by Samuel Johnson, applied by Virginia Woolf in two books of essays, and still serviceable, I believe, to designate serious but unspecialized readers) still awaits such a book. For those readers I have written a smaller book that touches on a considerable number of his aspirations and activities. Many people live what we can broadly call active lives and others live contemplative lives. It is very difficult to do both well, but Bacon did, and both of these lives have a variety of aspects.

I have also rescued Bacon from the many adverse and mostly undeserved criticisms made by subsequent writers. A scholar, Nieves Mathews, has already performed this task impressively on a large scale, but in a book that for various reasons is unlikely to reach very many common readers, and these criticisms continue, frequently in a negligent and offhand way, as if everyone recognizes that Bacon was mean and friendless and dishonored by his contemporaries. Oddly, some honor him chiefly for something he most certainly never did: write Shakespeare's works.

James Spedding remains—more than a century and a half after he edited *The Letters and Life of Francis Bacon* in seven volumes, and with two other men *The Works of Francis Bacon*, also in seven volumes—the father of Baconian studies. Now the Oxford University Press is issuing, with the help of many scholars, new editions of Bacon's works, but Spedding is one editor with a viewpoint of his subject. It is the viewpoint of a Victorian and of a man whose exhaustive research has been supplemented over many decades, but he is still the common reader's editor, and all those volumes are available to anyone with access to the Internet.

I quote extensively from Spedding. References to his seven-volume edition of *The Letters and Life of Francis Bacon* will be signified in this way: "LL1.1," where the numerals signify the volume and page; references to *The Works of Francis Bacon*, also in seven volumes, edited by Spedding and two other men, will be signified by "W1.1." I hope my readers are not distracted by the forest of citations; I suspect that they will disappear, so the speak, from the view of anyone who is not much interested in precise sources, just as the network of poles and wires that bring us electricity disappear for us. This book reproduces spellings and other stylistic features of Spedding's volumes, which are sometimes inconsistent because he was working with a variety of manuscripts and editions. I have included what I think to be the best selection of Bacon's own words that can be found outside editions of his writings.

In a few places I have made references to Shakespearean plays by act and scene only in my text on the theory that readers can easily find the passages to whatever line of whatever edition they happen to have at hand. Some citations from other well-known authors are given without specific references on the theory that these oft-printed works can easily be found. References to secondary sources appear in endnotes. In these instances I have made some stylistic modernizations, such as the elimination of rather distracting spellings and capitalizations in John Aubrey's *Brief Lives*, a book important for all Baconians.

A few acknowledgments are necessary here. This book might be called the product of a cottage industry, for my wife Christine, as early editor and advisor, and son Matthew, who rushes to help his electronically challenged father, have in these ways and also by exercising their boundless patience contributed enormously to this book. They are in no way to be held accountable for any of its defects. As a long-retired professor who now finds frequent attendance at academic libraries difficult, I must also thank the HathiTrust Digital Library, for without that library this book would not have been written.

Introduction

In a period of two decades, from 1552 to 1572, there sprang forth in England an unusual number of boys destined to be ranked among the major English writers: Edmund Spenser, Sir Philip Sidney, Christopher Marlowe, William Shakespeare, John Donne, Ben Jonson. Looking back, we can see that their period was one of the greatest in English literary history. Another boy born in the midst of those two decades, Francis Bacon, belongs on that list. The other men were all poets or playwrights or both, and some of them also wrote distinguished prose. Only Bacon endures primarily as a writer of prose. He gets major credit as an innovator in the essay and the fictional Utopia, and he also displayed his literary gift in works not usually considered primarily as literary works.

Unlike the other writers in the above list, Bacon has also been called a philosopher, a scientist, and a statesman. Partly because of differences between the meaning of *philosopher* and *scientist* in Bacon's day and in ours, it is difficult to classify Bacon's activity precisely. Not everyone agrees that he truly deserves these designations, but the mere fact that they have been emphatically made marks him as an extremely unusual man. Most decidedly, he was a type of person not always appreciated: an intellectual. If we employ one definition of *intellectual*, a person "given to study, reflection, and speculation," however, we realize that we must respect such a person. If we think of the intellectual as a person who does such things because he or she enjoys them, we can see that the intellectuals are like most of us—people who do something because they like to do it.

As an intellectual, Bacon delighted in a good thought the way a sailor delights in making a good knot. A true intellectual, as opposed to a person who merely appreciates being thought of as one, enjoys the ideas he works with, even if the results do not add up unmistakably to a "philosophy." An intellectual doesn't deal merely with one or a small number of thoughts anymore than a sailor deals only with ropes. People who limit themselves to an idea or two or a knot or two are hobbyists, not philosophers or sailors. The things people enjoy are part of larger entities, knot-tying of sailing, for instance. Bacon's major idea was huge. He wanted to master knowledge itself, although he eventually realized that he couldn't possibly do it. One aspect of knowledge that interested him enormously was nature. He did not pursue nature in the way that Wordsworth or Thoreau did—nobody could do that four hundred years ago—but his approach to nature, I shall try to show, foreshadowed the ideas of many thoughtful people today.

Bacon also greatly enjoyed the principles and applications of government and politics. It could hardly have been otherwise. His father held important posts in governments headed by two important monarchs, half-sisters with different ideas of government—Catholic Queen Mary and Protestant Queen Elizabeth—at a time when religious affiliations dominated politics, especially for daughters of a man who had proclaimed himself head of the faith in England.

Francis was devoted to his older brother Anthony; they were the only two children of Sir Nicholas Bacon and his second wife, the former Anne Cooke. Nicholas Bacon's children with his first wife were older and more or less out into the world. Sir Nicholas, Anne and the boys lived at York House in London on the bank of the Thames River, the home and workplace of Sir Nicholas as Lord Keeper of the Great Seal; sometimes they dwelt at Gorhambury, an estate that he constructed in the two boys' early childhood near St. Albans, about twenty miles north of London. In his maturity Francis seldom traveled farther from London than this place, while Anthony developed into a man who worked on and loved the European continent.

Sir Nicholas Bacon believed strongly in education and made sure that even Francis, the youngest of his eight children, received plenty of it with learned tutors at home; additionally, the two brothers could hardly help learning much from their father, and their mother too, who was a gifted translator. Thereafter Francis partook of a trio of intellectual experiences parallel to what some people receive today: college, internship, and professional training. Beginning at age twelve, he spent two years at Trinity College, Cambridge; more than two years as an aide to the English ambassador to France, and most importantly, admission to one of the inns of court, Gray's Inn, where Sir Nicholas himself had learned law. Bacon could not easily have stepped away from such avenues of opportunity. They provided not only the delights an intellectual seeks but a profession to enter, a place into which one could step.

Trinity gave him more of the classical languages than the substantial supply he surely already had. We don't know which authors delighted Bacon most, but based on the later use he made of him let us nominate as one Pliny the Elder, author of a work called *Naturalis historia*, whose two words, *natural* and *history*, became vital in Bacon's vocabulary. He did not stay for a degree, but he learned what mattered most, and he grasped, as bright young people often do, the limitations of a conservative curriculum and thus never suffered the danger of becoming a pedantic professor. At the age of fifteen Gray's Inn admitted but did not receive him, for he was off to Paris and other places with the French Court to work for Sir Amias Paulet, the new ambassador to France. He learned much of practical political life and perhaps heard word of a man who had written a substantial part of a yet unpublished book called, curiously, "Essais," meaning "attempts" or "trials." Early in 1579 Bacon, just turned eighteen, returned and enrolled in Gray's Inn, much more than Cambridge his campus, a place where he could study, meet men of the sort he would work among, and if he wished, continue to live, which he did for considerable periods over the next forty-seven years.

Bacon progressed rapidly as a man of law but not at all rapidly in the court of Queen Elizabeth. Despite the fact that Bacon attempted a number of times to gain her favor and that of her chief advisor, Lord Burghley (his uncle in fact, for Sir Nicholas's second wife was the sister of Burghley's wife), Bacon attained no great honor at court before she died in 1603, by which time he was forty-two. He had made his mark in Parliament, but of course the monarch only summoned Parliament when he or she needed a subsidy, and although Parliamentarians considered themselves more than just financiers, they talked a good deal more than they were permitted to act.

Introduction

After Elizabeth died, Bacon's public career prospered under the new Scottish-born king, James I, but not until 1607 did he gain the post of solicitor general and begin an assent that culminated eleven years later when James named him Lord Chancellor. As for his writing career, in 1597 he had published the first edition of his essays, then only ten short works. In 1605 he issued his first important book, *The Two Books of Francis Bacon: Of the Proficience and Advancement of Learning, Divine and Human.* Three words of this cumbersome title, *The Advancement of Learning*, customarily identify it and express succinctly Bacon's intellectual aim. Dedicated to James, it stood as a new kind of book, "simultaneously a defense, a celebration, and a program for action," as one scholar puts it.[1] In its final paragraph Bacon proclaims that he has "made as it were a small Globe of the intellectual World, as truly and faithfully as I could discover" (W6.412).

As he progressed at court he continued to study "natural history," a formulation that seems to us rather distant from what we call science, on the one hand, or philosophy on another, but accurate nevertheless. His pronouncements on nature jump off the pages of the forever incomplete *Instauratio Magna* (in its English version, *The Great Instauration*), particularly its major component, *The Novum Organum (The New Organon)*. Examining these Latin titles, for Latin was the literary language of educated Europeans, we find that *instaurare* meant "to renew" or "to begin anew," the second of which Bacon was employing, for he believed that scholars to that time had botched the job of explaining nature.

To Pliny, who wrote in the first century AD, *organum* meant "implement" or "instrument," as the corresponding Greek words had meant to earlier writers. From *organum* comes *organ* and a host of other English words. Mainly because of the way Bacon used the word, today it means "a body of principles of scientific or philosophical investigation." Another cognate, *organic*, we now often associate with chemistry, a subject of which Bacon knew nothing, although a man born the year after Bacon's death who became one of his most important followers, Robert Boyle, is often considered its founder. Bacon used his organum or organon to direct the task of renewing the understanding of nature.

The Great Instauration begins with an introduction in which Bacon wonders "whether that commerce between the mind of man and the nature of things, which is more precious than anything on earth, or at least anything that is of the earth, might by an means be restored to its perfect and original condition" (W8.17). What did he mean by *original*? It applies to *commerce*, a word of the marketplace then as now. When did the business between mind and nature rest "perfect and original"? Leaving aside that perhaps insoluble assumption, we can perceive that Bacon was proclaiming that attention to this commerce exceeded any concern with power, money, sex, anything else. One of his qualifications, *of* rather than *on* the earth, reflects an essentially religious conviction; another, which appears later in the sentence quoted above, offers as an alternative to a "perfect and original condition" a "better" one. Even so qualified, the statement conveys a powerful cerebral urge.

In another preliminary section, "The Plan of the Work," Bacon informs his readers that his work will be "a history not only of nature free and at large … but much more of nature under constraint and vexed; that is to say, when by art and the hand of man she is forced out of her natural state, and squeezed and moulded" (W8.48). Most likely we understand this statement much better than did his contemporaries. Four centuries ago would a man felling a tree consider himself to be squeezing and molding? Today we are liable to worry that we have pushed nature too far, felled too many trees, interfered with the flow of too many streams. Despite the fact that many writers in recent decades have suggested that Bacon taught us to do these things, Bacon did not favor prompting nature in a haphazard or domineering way, "For man is but the servant and interpreter of nature: what he does and what he knows is only what he has observed of nature's order in fact or in thought; beyond this he knows nothing and can do nothing" (W8.53). He repeats this assertion in almost the same words at the beginning of Book I of *The New Organon*. The extent of Bacon's squeezing and service we must investigate later.

To form Book I of *The New Organon*, Bacon compiled one hundred thirty instances of his favorite rhetorical device: the aphorism, a short, trenchant, pointed observation. Bacon's prose could not survive entirely aphoristic, and he chose to reinforce his aphorisms with "magisterial" prose, his word for a more ornate, persuasive style. The two modes seem contradictory. An aphorism, he insisted, compelled the reader to think, to examine, to test what is being said. Magisterial prose asked the reader to accept happily what the authority has furnished—but Bacon could not resist a compulsion to combine the two modes. The early aphorisms in this work are short: for example, "Nature to be commanded must be obeyed" (W8.68). At about the point where he introduces his famous Four Idols, he elaborates, he vows to persuade. In the 130th and final aphorism he wishes that others will follow his form of interpretation, but eventually he had to resign himself to the likelihood that other scholars would work in their own way. He concludes with the more general hope "that the art of discovery may advance as discoveries advance" (W8.164).

One cannot compare Bacon and Thoreau very extensively. Both wanted to investigate nature. Both loved to rummage in Pliny. Bacon did not roam the wilds—as close to him in London as they were to Thoreau in Concord. A typical Englishman in this respect, Bacon would rather saunter through his garden than tramp through the woods beyond the London wall. He wanted his gardens (he had them at Gorhambury, at Gray's Inn, and even at the Thames-side York House in London) chock-full of plants, and in his essay "Of Gardens," he demonstrates his capacity to differentiate them thoroughly. As a servant of nature, he was implying a necessity—for even a public man with servants of his own knew that he served, and had to serve, the monarch—to follow a rigorous set of duties and obligations. "All depends on keeping the eye steadily fixed upon the facts of nature and so receiving their images simply as they are," he writes in his preface to *The New Organon* (W8.53).

Bacon's readers, who quickly perceive that he many times urges the "use" of nature, have paid less attention to his commitment to receiving and accepting her gifts. Had he guessed at the possibility of a wholesale exploitation of nature, he would remind such misguided followers that "the subtlety of nature is greater many times than the subtlety of the senses and understanding" (W8.69). He does not say, with Wordsworth, "Little do we see in Nature that is ours," but he recognizes and deplores the sparseness of humans' grasp. To take a specific feature of nature, clearly fascinating to him, that he pursued more thoroughly than any other, he commenced his *Historia Ventorum* (*The History of the Winds*) with some general principles, one being that winds are variable "and compounded as it were of nature and chance.... But yet even in a variable subject, if rules are diligently framed, a prediction will generally hold good." After this brave meteorological goal, he sets forth thirty-three questions: "Are there not winds blowing from every quarter of the heaven?" "What do earthly things and things which take place on earth contribute to the winds?" "Inquire carefully into the height or elevation of the winds." "Do some winds blow above at the same time that others blow below" (W9.382–390)? Thus he anticipates the work that our meteorologists, buoyed by many scientific advances, pursue today. To us they seem like normal questions, not exactly scientific but clearly involving the application of scientific knowledge which Bacon possessed only primitively and crudely. But who besides Bacon was even asking such questions in the early seventeenth century?

To some extent Bacon delved into answering such questions. Consider one of his "articles of inquiry," as he called them: "Diligently collect all kinds of prognostics of winds" (W9.389). This article represents a preliminary to the "use" of wind that even the greenest of thinkers today could hardly oppose. Here is Bacon's comment on one prognostication: "Those who are unwilling to admit that Columbus conceived so certain and fixed opinion of the West Indies from the narrative of a Spanish pilot, and consider it still more unlikely that he derived it from the obscure vestiges and rumours of antiquity, take refuge in this: that from periodical winds blowing to the coast of Portugal, he imagined that there was a continent to the westward. The circumstance is doubtful and not very probable, since the wind could hardly travel so great a distance" (W9.395–96).

But of course winds can travel immense distances. He answered an important question on the basis of a wrong assumption that any contemporary would have shared—that is, if any of them were so proceeding. For centuries after Bacon, no one knew how to answer such questions; most often they saw little point in asking them. Well into the twentieth century no one could predict winds accurately. In September of 1938 a terrible hurricane peppered much of a totally unprepared New England. People out delivering mail or harvesting their crop had no prior notice of forces that suddenly threatened their very existence.

Introduction

Bacon loved to ask questions and pursue their answerability. His wondering took the form of "observations," the aspect of scientific inquiry he was best able to perform. Here are a few of his seventy-eight observations concerning wind: "If the body of the sun appear blood-red at setting, it forebodes high winds for many days." "From long observation, sailors suspect storms on the fifth day of the moon." "Feathery clouds, like palm branches or the fleur-de-lis, denote immediate or coming showers." Even those of us who, unlike the farmers and mariners of Bacon's time, do not observe cloud formations daily can immediately see the problem with this type of observation. People still like to make predictions based on a red setting sun, but meteorologists, knowing the many variables of nature at work, do not. Bacon of course knew that wind is just one of many natural forces, but his method and the investigative procedures of his time forced him to concentrate his approach in that way. Did Bacon provide any measurements? The most precise ones he makes in this instance pertain not to winds but to the dimensions of ships and sails of the British navy, in effect calculations based on various factors of which wind is just one.

He did not restrict his immense curiosity to natural events with or without human intervention. Bacon's career illustrates the fact that philosophical adventurers were beginning to realize the difficulty, if not the impossibility, of an individual's capacity to survey human knowledge. He grew more aware of how much help his intellectual journey would require, but the journey, quite apart from judgments about the extent of his success (matters much argued about) has compelled the imagination of many people. Whether we regard ourselves as living, either positively or negatively, in a Baconian world or in a post–Baconian world, acknowledging the formation of such adjectives from his name also acknowledges his position in a very select category. The two works with the Latin names already mentioned, often thought his greatest, are read in their entirety only by serious students, but the two most often read—the *Essays* and his *New Atlantis*, both written in English—are best appreciated by observing their relationship to these major works.

Even admirers of Bacon's work tend to censure him as a man. Too easily they fall in behind critics who never knew him, magnify his faults, and charge him with frailties for which no substantial evidence exists.

Historically, the first of these men is John Aubrey, born a few weeks after Bacon died but able to obtain some facts of his life from acquaintances. Because Aubrey's *Brief Lives* was not published until the late nineteenth century, he cannot be blamed for early manifestations of dislike for Bacon. He reported important observations by two men who knew him. You will note that Aubrey quite properly here referred to Bacon as "his Lordship," although writers almost unanimously ignore this designation, which meant much to Bacon and to all who respect the dignity of noble rank. "Mr. Thomas Hobbes was beloved by his Lordship, who was wont to have him walk with him in his delicate groves where he did meditate: and when a notion darted into his mind, Mr. Hobbes was presently to write it down, and his Lordship was wont to say that he did it better than anyone else about him."[2]

The assertion that these two great men of the seventeenth century strolled together is a charming addition to Bacon's biography. Aubrey reports that Dr. William Harvey, famous for being the first man to explain the circulation of the blood, "had been physician to the Lord Chancellor Bacon, whom he esteemed much for his wit and style, but would not allow him to be a great philosopher." Many later writers would agree with this summation, but Harvey added a brief physical description of Bacon with a striking simile: "He had a delicate, lively, hazel eye; Dr. Harvey told me it was like the eye of a viper."[3] Harvey spent much time studying the fascinating features of animals, probably including vipers, and may not have intended a comparison as negative as Aubrey's account conveys. It has struck home, however, with many of Bacon's detractors. Aubrey also made a reference to Bacon's sexual habits that will have to be qualified—briefly—later. (Bacon did marry; as we will see, beyond providing for his wife, he displayed no great affection for her.) By and large Aubrey admired Bacon, but since the publication of *Brief Lives*, his presumably less complimentary observations have been much quoted.

Among the attacks on Bacon's character, the most famous is Alexander Pope's in 1733, more than a century after Bacon's death. Because it appears in a famous section of a major poem (*Essay on Man*, IV, 281–282), and because Pope excelled in the making of memorable rhymed couplets, who could forget it?

Introduction

> If Parts allure thee, think how Bacon shined,
> The wisest, brightest, meanest of mankind.

Here are two positive superlative adjectives—but no one knew better than Pope the force of rhymed finality. If Bacon was the meanest of all men, he could not be trusted. A plenitude of moralistic interpretations has arisen for this mean man with the viper's eye. Bacon could not have had friends, for instance, because who could befriend such a person? History declares, however, that his many friends included people both good and great. The one book of more than six hundred pages that defends Bacon against his detractors, many people, probably his detractors *en masse*, have never read.[4]

As Bacon advanced as a judge and advisor to King James, he retained his place in the House of Commons, a blending of governmental powers that undoubtedly seems strange to those of us who have been taught the importance of their separation. Yet it was then possible, although probably never as successful as what Bacon accomplished in the first and second decades of the seventeenth century. This multiple role became more difficult for him as time went on and honors increased. Despite his rise under James—he turned solicitor general, clerk of the Star Chamber, attorney general, Lord Keeper of the Great Seal, and finally, in 1618, Lord Chancellor—he long persisted in Parliament because he was a great orator and a man with the capacity to understand the psychology of motivation that could bring men to an agreement. This included the difficult task of bringing Parliamentarians into agreement with King James, who tended to consider his own opinions unassailable. Bacon also possessed superb analytical skills and a trait appropriate to, but not always practiced by, legislators: a decent regard for the common people.

He did not perceive that in newly-unified Britain, including James's Scottish realm, a quest for a more authoritative role was rising in Parliament. At the time it mainly took the form of a suspicion that perhaps a group of competent men like themselves deserved a task more advantageous, more significant, than meeting only at the king's request and only for the purpose of voting him money to pay his bills and fund his favorite initiatives. They certainly could do more than occasionally wangle a minor concession from the monarch in return for the essential funds. Bacon, however, trusted the monarchy. Kingship was sacred; God, who conferred sacred things, conferred political power. To put it baldly, what could a rational subject expect, beyond this semi-divine kingly power? In common with his contemporaries, Bacon hoped that the monarch, clearly an imperfect person like everybody else, respected the divinity of his power and proceeded accordingly. Despite his foresight, Bacon could not foresee democracy.

Bacon fell from grace, both the king's and the nation's, at the age of sixty. With few exceptions he had spent the earlier decades working honorably and writing notably on intellectual and moral issues. He strove for a fine balance between his Parliamentary and royalist stances. Five years after his appointment as solicitor general, he wrote King James that "no man can say but I was a perfect and peremptory royalist, yet every man makes me believe that I was never one hour out of credit with the lower house" (LL4.280). A political biographer agrees: "His parliamentary career had been spent entirely in the Commons, and he had always maintained the trust and respect of that house…. His tenure in Parliament had been anything but tranquil, and yet it had been dignified. Bacon had been respected as a gifted orator and his eloquence had won him general recognition. Moreover, his patience and skill as he conducted joint conferences and generally attempted to work out difficult compromises, had gained the praises of even those who often opposed him."[5]

His duties included making critical judgments invariably unfavorable to some defendants. A judge in his time and place could accept gifts that did not influence legal decisions, but this possibility did not stop people from trying to influence him with gifts—and Bacon was a man whose lifestyle often thrust him into awkward financial situations. The gifts were proffered precisely to facilitate favorable decisions. Under such circumstances it was easy for opponents to attack the reception of such gifts (although no convincing evidence established that Bacon had judicially favored anyone from whom he had accepted such gifts). Propped on the edge of a moral cliff like many other judges in his time, Bacon tumbled off. When he confessed to acting imprudently, if not illegally, his opponents—including men whose aspirations he had stung in and out of court and one legal rival with whom he had a long record of conflict, Sir Edward Coke—did what opponents always do in such circumstances: they rose in numbers against him.

His judicial power was taken away, he was fined (although little, if any, of the fine was ever collected), and he was banned from the royal verge, an area that included his London haunts. He retained his title of Viscount St. Alban, but the House of Lords did not permit him to sit among them. Like important political figures today, he contemplated and longed to perpetuate his legacy, but his efforts to regain respectability failed. He desperately wanted to return to public life; still, he now had more time than ever to pursue his intellectual career. He could retire to Gorhambury and pursue knowledge full time.

Of the seven great writers named at the beginning of this introduction, only Bacon and Ben Jonson lived into their sixties, and of these two, only Bacon published major works in his last six years. In fact, if we include the late expansion of *The Advancement of Learning* into nine books, all of his important works appeared between 1620 and 1627. He published the important third edition of his *Essays* in 1625, and *New Atlantis* came out the year after his death. It would be difficult to find among English writers—or for that matter, among any writers—another whose major works all appeared after he turned fifty-nine.

It is now time to go back to the beginning of the career of Francis, Lord Verulam and Viscount St. Alban, or, as modern tradition obliges us to call him, Francis Bacon.

1

Now Somewhat Ancient

As principal advisor and thus gateway to Queen Elizabeth, Lord Burghley received many letters. Most likely he did not often need to read or acknowledge the efforts of many correspondents inexorably seeking patronage. If he read the one in hand, he probably chuckled at the following sentence: "I wax now somewhat ancient; one and thirty years is a great deal of sand in the hour-glass" (W1.108). In this year of 1592 Burghley could count more than forty additional years in his own hourglass. This correspondent, his nephew, was again emphatically proclaiming his ambitious and restless nature.

If he read on, he came to an even better example of this dreamy aspiration. "I confess that I have as vast contemplative ends, as I have moderate civil ends: for I have taken all knowledge to be my province" (W1.109). Thus did this youngest son of the late Sir Nicholas Bacon proclaim his goal.

Sir Nicholas, the Lord Keeper of the Great Seal, had taken as a second wife Burghley's sister-in-law, Anne Cooke, who had also served Queen Elizabeth significantly as a gentlewoman of her privy chamber. Burghley knew his nephew well enough to suspect the assertion about his "civil ends," probably intended to assure his reader most humbly that he did not expect be assigned too glorious a mission at the present time. On some levels Francis had moved along swiftly. Throughout the 1580s, from the age of twenty, he had served in Parliament. He had studied at Gray's Inn, where Burghley himself had learned the law, had been chosen bencher six years ago, and reader, a man who lectured on the law, only two years after that. He had risen in a profession important to a monarch. But Burghley could not believe "moderate civil ends," for further on in his letter Bacon alluded to "the meanness of my estate." This man did not merely want knowledge but power to go with it.

Young Bacon's father had served in Parliament in the time of Henry VIII and held posts under Edward VI and Mary before Elizabeth's reign. As Attorney of the Court of Wards and Liveries in 1547 he drew up plans for the welfare of the children who became wards of the Crown when their fathers, tenants-in-chief designated as knights of the Crown, died. The lands and any minor children of such men fell into the custody of the monarch. His plans did not move forward under Mary, but Elizabeth, taught by Roger Ascham, who wrote *The Schoolmaster*, a great educational treatise, agreed with Sir Nicholas on the importance of educating these children properly. Writing to William Cecil, the future Lord Burghley, then Master of the Court of Wards, in 1561, Sir Nicholas recommended the establishment of a school for wards that would include not only Latin and Greek, but French and other modern languages, music, physical education, and Christian devotion. Broadly speaking, his educational ideas derived from humanist educational theory, and he chose eclectically from the works of such earlier humanist scholars as Erasmus, Sir Thomas More, and Thomas Elyot. In his letter to Cecil he recalled "diverse gentlemen that gave gladly great wages to their horsekeepers and huntsmen than to such as taught their children, whereby they had very ready horses and perfect dogs, so they had very untoward children."[1] When the school was established at Redgrave in Sussex, where Sir Nicholas had lived with his first wife, Sir Nicholas saw to it that it would admit worthy students from poor families. His humanism and interest in educational reform tempered the puritanical streak that also colored his behavior.

In that early Elizabethan year of 1561 he had to be thinking also of the educational future of his two youngest sons. Anthony turned three that year, and on January 22, Francis was born. They benefited also from the educational distinctions of their mother. A woman could be educated only by a rare father who believed in schooling for at least some women. One year after Nicholas Bacon's first wife, the mother of his first six children, died in 1552, he married the daughter of Anthony Cooke, who had educated his daughters thoroughly. Anne also enjoyed tutoring by the highly-respected Roger Ascham and by John Cheke, who taught Greek at St. John's College, Cambridge. She proved to be the brightest of her father's unusual cluster of daughters. Her husband wrote a number of unremarkable poems, but one, to Anne, heaps scorn on the many women who desire only vain things, whereas "for you I could not find / A more deep thing than fruits of mind."[2] Presumably he gave her books; one of her activities was reading to him. But she did more than read.

Anne could claim membership in the small company of women like Queen Elizabeth, who continued studying with Ascham after her coronation at age twenty-five, and Mary Sidney, sister of Sir Philip, who took up one of the literary tasks he left unfinished at the time of his death from an injury in the Battle of Zutphen in 1586. Mary Sidney's completion of the verse translation of the Psalms her brilliant brother had begun exceeded his in quality. Her brother had dedicated his romance, *The Countess of Pembroke's Arcadia*, to her. Mary's niece, Mary Wroth, also benefited from the Sidney legacy and composed the first romance by an Englishwoman. Not many young women shared their advantages.

Few professions beckoned even to these rare women, for the literary world encouraged them primarily only in such things as the translation of religious writings. Anne translated the *Ochines Sermons* of Bernardino of Siena, a fifteenth-century Franciscan priest who had a following in England. Her best-known work is a translation of the *Apologia Ecclesiae Anglicanae* (*Defense of the Anglican Church*) by Bishop John Jewel. In his history of sixteenth-century English literature, C. S. Lewis writes: "Anne Lady Bacon who translated his Apologia in 1564 deserves more praise than I have space to give her. Latin prose has a flavor very hard to disguise in translation, but nearly original.... If quality without bulk were enough, Lady Bacon might be put forward as the best of all sixteenth-century translators."[3]

At the age of three or so Francis would have exuded curiosity about what his mother was doing when she bent over a desk in her study for hours. He hoped, perhaps, that she would let him see for himself, as few male writers, then or now, would. It seems more likely that she would have let him have a peek than that Sir Nicholas would have allowed Francis or Anthony to pester him in the part of the house where he worked.

Home for these boys was York House in the Strand near what is today the Thames Embankment. Named for the Archbishop of York, who briefly owned this now three-centuries-old building which later constituted the London home of the Bishops of Norwich, it stood as one of the many medieval Catholic properties seized by King Henry VIII. In 1558 it was leased to Sir Nicholas Bacon as a home and office for the Lord Keeper, near the Court and at riverside a handy exit place for any longer trip. Francis Bacon knew it in his earliest years and again a few decades later, when it became his workplace and home.

An important London official needed a country home—especially at times of the outbreak of the bubonic plague. Nicholas Bacon began the construction of an estate near St. Albans in Hertfordshire, about twenty miles northward, around 1563, one of the plague years, and over the next five years completed it. He built it on the site of an old Bene-dictine abbey, later sold to a Norman, Robert de Gorham, in the twelfth century, who naturally called it Gorhambury. Two centuries later the Benedictines re-acquired the property, but King Henry VIII appropri-ated it and passed it on to a man named Ralph Rowlat. Eventually it came to Nicholas Bacon as a suitable retreat for a court official.

Any boy would long to see such a sight, and surely Sir Nicholas took his two sons, both less than ten years old, there on occasion. They would have seen a large, asymmetrical building chiefly in an English style but featuring a neo-classical, two-story porch, brick faced with chalk rubble and limestone, some of which came from Normandy, and with Doric columns. After some repair the porch still stands; otherwise, only a few pieces of original construction remain. In the 1560s the boys would have been able to race around through thirty rooms on the ground floor. In the center they would gape at a mall, with a chapel on the left, with three walls enclosing a courtyard beyond.[4]

During Francis's early years events took place that would affect the realm and himself in particular. Elizabeth, the last surviving child of King Henry VIII, had become queen in 1558. Robert Dudley, the fifth son of a duke who had planned to put his sister-in-law Lady Jane Grey on the throne, had, after spending some time in the Tower of London as part of that conspiracy, gained stature by serving in a military cam-paign in France and became a favorite of the queen. He desired to marry her, for a royal husband might win his way to a position grander than mere consort of a monarch. He was, after all, a man, and a ruler should he a man, he would have thought. But the years went by, and Elizabeth refused to marry him or anyone else. Her younger cousin Mary Stuart, as a descendant of Henry VII, appeared to be the next in line. Unlike Elizabeth, Mary proved a marrying woman. At sixteen she wed a man about to become King Francis II of France. She had already been queen of Scotland from the age of six days in 1542, when her father, James V, died. Mary's mother administered the kingdom during Mary's childhood. Her time as queen consort of France ended in 1560, when Francis II died; five years later she wed a man disliked by nearly everyone else, Henry Stewart, Lord Darnley. This marriage produced a son, James, whose future mattered a great deal to Sir Nicholas Bacon and to his brother-in-law Cecil, both advisors of Elizabeth, for James would then be second in line. James's parents were Catholics, and England had not been happy with Mary Tudor, Elizabeth's half-sister, as queen, and longed to see James reared as a Protestant.

Darnley's many faults included a suspicious nature. His suspicions of David Rizzio, his wife's secretary, led to plotting his murder. The following year Darnley himself was murdered, probably by the Earl of Bothwell, whom Mary soon thereafter married. With Scotland enraged, Mary, finding few friends left, French or Scottish, was forced to abdicate and fled, without her latest disgraceful husband, south of the border. England had James's mother, but they did not have him, for he had been sworn in as an infant monarch, just as she had been. Sir Nicholas and Cecil failed in their attempt to bring James to England, but Presbyterians now ruled Scotland; therefore, the young king received a Protestant upbringing, different from Anglicanism but preferable to Catholicism and the authority of the pope, which English persons had learned to dread.

The English kept this woman of dangerous tendencies confined, as the elder Bacon and Cecil advised Elizabeth to do. In the spring of 1570 negotiations for her release took place in York House. Sir Nicholas opened the discussion with what his biographer called "a lengthy and belligerent harangue"[5] directed at the Bishop of Ross, who was pleading for Mary's release. This event must have fascinated Francis, now nine years old. Would he not have longed to be part of it? Would it have been possible for him to sneak to some secret spot from which he could overhear it? We can only speculate; history has not given us a word on this matter. Ross, Bacon claimed, had libeled Elizabeth. Ross defended his treatise, argued that justice demanded her return to Scotland, and assured his listeners that Mary would behave. Cecil contended that Mary could not be trusted and again urged that James be brought to England. Scotland kept James; the English kept Mary. James learned Presbyterianism; Mary retained her fervent Catholicism. In 1587, Mary, suspected of complicity in plots to assassinate Queen Elizabeth, was executed. Sixteen years later James came to England as James VI of Scotland and James I of a realm that included both England and Scotland. From this point Francis Bacon's career, as we will see, prospered.

Anthony and Francis Bacon would have spent summers in Gorhambury at least until 1573. It must have struck the young Bacons as sufficiently huge, but a few years later Sir Nicholas's brother-in-law would complete a grander house called Theobalds. When the queen visited Gorhambury in 1572 she is alleged to have teased her Lord Keeper: "My Lord, what a little house have you gotten." To which Sir Nicholas prudently answered, "Madam, my house is well, but it is you that have made me too great for my house."[6] He went to work later to build a great gallery for her next visit in 1577. It may have been much earlier than the first visit to Gorhambury that the queen noted the alertness of her Lord Keeper's youngest son. Asked his age, Francis replied that he was "two years younger than Her Majesty's happy reign." This story comes from William Rawley, Francis Bacon's chaplain and, after his death, the compiler of a short life and some of his yet unpublished works (W1.136). Rawley alleges that she often referred to him as "the young Lord-Keeper." The mature Bacon could remember this tribute only with bitterness; he would not hold the position his father had notably fulfilled until fourteen years after her death.

At the age of twelve he went, very young even for his time, to Trinity College, Cambridge, with his older brother, commencing at fifteen, closer to the average age. The two boys were continuing, and would continue, a close relationship. They had little contact with their father's six older children by his first wife, by this time well into their adult lives.

Sir Nicholas decided that two years under the master of Trinity, John Whitegrift, future Archbishop of Canterbury, sufficed as the first installment of Francis's three-part higher education. Withdrawn from Trinity in December of 1575, Francis soon learned of the next two parts.

In June he was entered at—but did not attend—Gray's Inn, where his father and half-brothers had learned the life of the law. Now he prepared to join Sir Amias Paulet, scheduled in September to leave for duty as the new ambassador to France. First he would learn something about diplomacy. According to William Rawley, "Sir Nicholas resolved that his son, who had seen at home the efficacy of a good regimen in keeping the body politic sound, should go with him [Paulet], and see the symptoms of disease produced in a similar subject by a bad one" (LL1.6). One sentence in Bacon's essay "Of Dispatch" suggests that he also absorbed some practical work habits while working with Paulet: "I knew a wise man that had it for a by-word, when he saw men hasten to a conclusion, *Stay a little, that we may make an end the sooner*" (W12.162).

Little evidence remains concerning what Bacon did when not assisting the ambassador. We can trace two aspects of French life important to him in his service with Paulet from September 1576 to March 1579. Following the death of the French king, Francis II (Mary Stuart's first husband), in 1559, religious intolerance burst forth, reaching a bloody peak in 1572, when on St. Bartholomew's Day—August 24, the time of the wedding of the French king's Roman Catholic sister, Margaret of Valois, and Henry of Navarre, a Protestant—Catholics massacred many French Protestants called Huguenots, who had gathered for the occasion. Charles IX, dominated by his mother, Catherine de Medici, continued instigating religio-political conflict until his death in 1574, and another of Catherine's sons succeeded as Henry III when Bacon was arriving in Paris. Those anxious to end the religious conflict strove to formulate a peace plan, but the plans of Henry and his mother predominated. Paulet, the English ambassador, was of course a staunch Protestant and thus a fit guardian for his young assistant, whose mother's puritan conscience, by the way, outdid that of her husband. Their youngest son, observing the threat of Catholic power and aware that it could happen likewise in England, but also contemplating the disorder arising from all intra–Christian conflict, was garnering a dislike of it that he would display in future years. He would rely on the diplomatic skill he was developing in dealing with religious as well as political conflicts.

He also absorbed a literary lesson, or at least the basis for one. A Frenchman in his early forties, already retired from a court life that he could not appreciate, was composing a number of prose compositions, many of them only a few pages in length, which he called "essays." If Bacon did not learn of these yet-unpublished works of Michel de Montaigne in France, he absorbed enough of the language and culture—especially those aspects of it that had driven Montaigne into early retirement—to appreciate this new literary form upon its publication in 1590, a year after his return to England.

Bacon's father also had to concern himself about the health of his two youngest sons, which looked precarious. After a few months of service, in July of 1577, Paulet wrote to Sir Nicholas, assuring him of Francis's fitness.[7] Later, apparently having begun to doubt his original conviction that Francis might profit from living in a "diseased" place, he again asked about his son's safety in this uncertain political situation, but Paulet assured him that he was "safe, sound, and in good health."[8]

Sir Nicholas was approaching the age of seventy. In his will he specified that he wished to be buried at St. Paul's rather than at Gorhambury, which would go to Anthony as the older of his two sons by Lady Anne. (Francis's later wishes would be strikingly different.) As befitted a man twice married with eight children, Sir Nicholas exhibited great prudence in financial matters, spent modestly and saved a considerable sum in his late years, traits that Francis would not emulate. He did not, however, succeed in preparing his youngest son's financial future, although it is thought that he might well have been planning to do so with the money left in his account at his death.[9]

He surely recognized Francis's mental acuity and talent for a legal career and a disposition like his own to labor tirelessly at the tasks at hand. He might have hoped that Francis would imitate his work for educational reforms, but he hardly could have expected it to happen as profoundly as it did, moreover in a far more ambitious and elaborate manner. Sir Nicholas does not seem to have been a man who would have dreamed of "vast contemplative ends." In common with many fathers, he could see resemblances between himself and his sons but also divergences, some of which inevitably he might have pondered anxiously.

After more than two years of working for Paulet, Francis surely expected that the third stage of his education could not be far off. Soon Sir Nicholas wrote to Paulet, informing him that his now eighteen-year-old son should come home and take up residence in Gray's Inn. Paulet assured the senior Bacon that he loved the young man and would have continued to take good care of him, but that he understood this decision by a "happy father of a towardly son."[10] In his short biography, Rawley relates that while still in Paris, on February 17, 1579, Bacon "dreamed that his father's house in the country was plastered all over with black mortar" (LL1.7–8). Home again in England, he learned that his father had died on February 20. Presumably Francis Bacon, not generally a man given to morbid or prophetic dreams, had conveyed this story to Rawley.

So in that year Bacon began his close and profound association with Gray's Inn, his late father's favorite of the four inns of court where a young man could learn the law, gather with lawyers, and take up quarters. Although the inns of court have changed, their locale has changed much more. Gray's Inn Road at Holburn is well within the London of today; in 1579 it stood outside the city's western wall, north and west of London proper, legally part of Middlesex County. A short walk would take a dweller into open fields. One of the first men to write on English law, Sir John Fortescue, asserted in a fifteenth-century work: "The place of study is not in the heart of the city itself ... but in a private place in the suburbs."[11]

In Bacon's time and for a good while thereafter Gray's Inn continued to retain this suburban setting. The property had belonged to the Grey (usually so spelled) family for many generations. By 1547, perhaps a little earlier, it became the property of a society of lawyers.

As the inns of court existed in Fortescue's time, they were law schools only on a part-time basis. "There is both in the inns of court and the inns of Chancery a sort of an academy or gymnasium fit for persons of their station; where they learn singing, and all kinds of music, dancing and such other accomplishments and diversions, which are called revels, as are suitable to their quality, and such as are usually practiced at Court. At other times, out of term, the greater part apply themselves to the study of the law."[12]

Revels continued as important features in Bacon's time, mainly at Christmas as we will see, but by the time the sixteenth-century lawyers took possession, they found the old buildings inadequate and began rebuilding in earnest. Bacon would have come into a hall seventy feet long, thirty-five feet wide and forty-seven in height, apparently begun under Queen Mary and finished in 1559 by Queen Elizabeth. At one end the chief table stood on a raised dais. To the right a characteristically Tudor oriel window would, on a sunny day, cast a colorful glow. Other windows bore armorial designs of past members of the Society of Gray's Inn. At the other end of the hall a richly designed oak screen concealed the vestibule. Tradition holds that Queen Elizabeth donated the screen and dining tables.

Bacon would soon have learned that the society required his presence in the chapel on appropriate occasions. Information on the appearance of the chapel, which may have gone back at least to the time of Henry VIII, is scattered and somewhat contradictory, but the rules required that he attend "divine service" and partake of communion. Surveyors made the rounds, we learn in a document of the mid–1580s, and reported anyone lying in bed at the time.[13] Although an old manuscript alleged that Bacon founded the Gray's Inn library, it certainly existed before his time. No doubt his later fame led to this promotion of an undue claim, but we will see Bacon does deserve credit for later improvements at the inn.

Members had to respect strict laws of dress. Beards could not be too long. In Mary's reign members of the Inns of Court, with some exceptions, were "forbidden to wear in their Doublets or Hoses any light colours, except Scarlets or Crimsons; or wear any upper velvet cap, or any scarf or wings in their gowns. White jerkins, buskins, or velvet shoes, double cuffs on their shirts, feathers or ribbons in their caps." Penalties? The first time a fine, the second, expulsion.[14] Elizabeth may have been a valuable donor, but she also imposed her rules. She rejected "bringing into the Realm such superfluities of Silks, Cloths of gold, Silver, and other most vain devices."[15] This prohibition, which extended far beyond the inn, reflected her view of the expense of such importable items.

As a legal institution an inn of court could establish rules of its own, but its legal precedence proved complex and confusing. It could impose penalties on its members—although if it had to go to court, it might find its authority ineffective. One doubts that Gray's Inn fledglings would have dared to move legally against it, but in other ways young men then as now could be difficult to manage. As one member commented about the newcomer, "He is roaring when he should be reading, and feasting when he should be fasting."[16] That a house of prostitution could operate nearby we learn from Shakespeare's play *The Comedy of Errors*, performed at Gray's Inn as we will see. More licit activities also abounded. A young man could learn to dance, to fence, to take part in musical activities. After about 1600, when Bacon continued to have chambers at the inn, a man at law could go bowling nearby. Although Bacon exhibited no practice of the sporting life, he later can be found giving advice on proper bowling form.

One cannot doubt that visiting one of the theaters, flourishing by the 1570s, attracted students. We can suppose he was familiar with theater, for like most English writers of his time, Bacon mentions it frequently. Educated men learned Latin by reading the plays of Terence and Plautus, but contemporary theater thrived; everyone agreed with the powerful metaphor best expressed by Jaques in *As You Like It*: All the world's a stage. Young men-of-law, even those as serious as Bacon, would feel absolutely obliged to shoulder into the pit at the Theatre or the Curtain after hearing preachers say such things as "Will not a filthy play, with the blast of a trumpet, sooner call thither a thousand than an hour's tolling of the bell bring to the sermon a hundred?"[17]

Before his son returned from France, Sir Nicholas had assigned a Gray's Inn lawyer named Richard Barker the task of watching his sons. Had they shown signs of slacking, of roaring and feasting, he doubtless would have intervened. Of the two, Anthony showed much less interest in the law, and with the help of his uncle, Lord Burghley, he began, as an assistant to the queen's principal secretary, Sir Francis Walsingham, a career in England's intelligence service in France, doubtless more exciting to him than his younger brother's closely-monitored tenure in the same country. Anthony thus came to know people destined for prominence in his brother's life such as Robert Devereux, the 2nd Earl of Essex.

Francis Bacon was made an utter barrister in 1582, a bencher in 1586, and a reader in 1588. A barrister was someone who could be called to the bar while still studying, which technically made him eligible, but perhaps not likely, to practice in court. He also could teach students. A bencher was part of the governing body of the institution, and a reader would lecture on particular legal topics. By what process did Bacon advance? First of all by bolts, "conversational arguments addressed to or put to a student by a bencher and two barristers in private."[18] The term *bolts* may have been peculiar to Gray's Inn, for this definition cannot be found in the *Oxford English Dictionary*. The typical beginning student could hardly relish facing these three gentlemen "in private." But a student as adept as Bacon found it a challenge and went forth bravely, as adept students do.

Subsequently, when the student had become sufficiently expert at bolts, he was admitted to the moots, where questions upon legal matters were debated by the students in the presence of the benchers of the Society of Gray's Inn.

> The object of these exercises promotes the faculty of ready speaking, and, in order to secure this end, the disputants were kept in ignorance of the topic to be argued and called upon to discuss it.
> The case, drawn up by the Reader, was laid upon the salt-cellar before meals; none were permitted to look into it under pain of expulsion from the Society.
> These discussions were strictly legal, and the proceedings were conducted as nearly as possible in the manner to those of the Courts themselves. About the end of the 17th century.... Moots fell into disuse, and they have now entirely ceased.[19]

Students in Bacon's time argued that with printed texts from which they could study now available, these traditional and harrowing experiences among benchers and readers were unnecessary. One would expect, however, that it may have taken decades for the society to agree to such a change. At any rate, Bacon discovered that he could advance rapidly through the system. Lord Burghley assisted Bacon in gaining access to the company of readers in 1586, though not with full status. Bacon wrote to his uncle: "Indeed I find in my simple observation that they which live as it were *in umbra* [under a shadow] and not in public or frequent action how moderately and modestly so ever they behave them selves yet *laborant invidia* [they labor grudgingly]. I find also that such persons as are of nature bashful [as my self is] whereby they want that plausible familiarity which others have are often mistaken for proud. But once I know well and I most humbly beseech your lordship to believe that Arrogancy and overweening is so far from my nature as if I think well of my self in any thing it is in this that I am free from that vice."[20]

Many readers of Bacon, including partial ones, find his self-assessment inaccurate, for he later proved more bold than bashful and quite capable of "Arrogancy and overweening." At twenty-five, however, he may only have been awkwardly trying to establish that he does not labor grudgingly, that he hopes not to be misunderstood by the compatriots among whom he now will labor. Most likely he also worries that because his prestigious uncle has helped him take his place among men who were for the most part considerably older, they may resent his presence among them. A look at a Gray's Inn historian's list of readers shows that usually they required more than twice as many years of preparation as Bacon needed to attain that status. In one sense Bacon was proud—proud of joining the company of these older men. The concerns and awkwardness he displays in this letter he will overcome, but not perhaps his capacity for the faults of which he feels himself free.

Aside from his remarkable progress at Gray's Inn, we have few specific facts about Bacon as he passed through his twenties in the 1580s. Clearly some of the major events of that decade affected him profoundly. Many of them pertained to the sea. In December of 1577, while Bacon was working for the English ambassador in Paris, another Francis, surnamed Drake, had set off from Plymouth (the English Plymouth, of course) with five ships and 164 men and boys to sail around the world. On September 26, 1580, while Bacon labored at the law, Drake returned in one ship, *The Golden Hind*, accompanied by fewer than sixty men. He sailed in with treasure, chiefly extracted from Spanish ports in Mexico, Chile, and Peru. Some Englishmen, concerned about future troubles with Spain, thought that the gems, gold, and silver—the last bulking the largest in the holds of *The Golden Hind*—should be returned. Elizabeth thought differently. She came out on New Year's Day 1581 wearing a crown Drake had given her. The newly knighted Sir Francis Drake loomed as a hero on the English horizon.

Sir Walter Raleigh, whom Bacon would encounter several times, also made his name. Like Drake, Raleigh had the golden urge that normally brought England into abrasive contact with Spain and its own distinctive colonial urge. He did not fulfill either urge to his satisfaction, but his two attempts to colonize "Virginia," a name expressive of England's presumably virgin queen, culminated on Roanoke Island, far north of the territory dominated by Spain. Preoccupation with the Spanish Armada had much to do with England's failure to defend the interests of the second group of Virginians. Drake's treasure-hunting had crimped relations with Spain, for some years less of a threat to the realm than France, but conflicts flared in the 1580s, culminating in 1588, a date every English schoolboy knows, when a combination of the English navy under Admiral Lord Charles Howard of Effingham, with Drake as vice admiral, and some helpful winds (Bacon's favorite subject in nature) would tumble Spain's reputation and signal the emergence of a new preeminent sea power. (Only a landlubber, Bacon developed an additional fondness for ships.)

Because of the exploring expeditions—not only of Drake and Raleigh but also Martin Frobisher, Sir John Hawkins, Sir Humphrey Gilbert, John White, and others, and particularly because their exploits came together in the works of Richard Hakluyt—tales of travel enchanted the English people. Hakluyt published his first important book in 1582, *Diverse Voyages Touching the Discovery of America*, and actually helped Raleigh plan his first colonial project. He reached his publishing peak in 1589 when the first edition of *The Principal Navigations, Voyages, Traffics, and Discoveries of the English Nation* appeared. If we look ahead in Bacon's life for a moment, we can estimate the impact of these explorations and the work of Hakluyt. In *The New Organon* he wrote, "In our times ... both many parts of the New World and the limits on every side of the Old World are known, and our stock of experience has increased to an infinite amount" (W8.104).

Again, in the same work: "I reject all forms of fiction and imposture; nor do I think that it matters any more to the business at hand, whether the discoveries that shall now be made, were long ago known to the ancients ... than it matters to mankind whether the new world be that island of Atlantis with which the ancients were acquainted or new discovered for the first time. For new discoveries must be sought from the light of nature, not fetched back out of the darkness of antiquity" (W8.154).

Bacon, it must be admitted, consulted antiquity frequently and actually wrote a Utopian piece of fiction, the first of this genre in the English language, not an old but a *New Atlantis*. For Bacon, discoveries come from nature, but nature resides all over the world revealed by the voyagers and their literary champion.

If, as seems likely, Lady Anne wrote to Francis in his early years at Gray's Inn, he probably did not keep the letters. When, some years later, the brothers lived together, she addressed Anthony but clearly intended the letters for both of them. Some letters survive from the early 1590s. Considering the tone of these letters, we can judge what the earlier ones must have been like. The following is from an undated letter she probably wrote early in 1592, after Anthony had returned from Europe and was lodging with his younger brother.

> This one chiefest counsel your Christian and natural mother doth give you even before the Lord, that above all worldly aspects you carry yourself ever at your first coming as one that doth unfeignedly profess the true religion of Christ, and both the love of the truth now by long continuance fast settled in your heart, and that with judgment, wisdom, and discretion, and are not afraid or ashamed to testify the same by hearing and delighting in those religious exercises of the sincerer sort, be they French or English.... Be not speedy of speech nor talk suddenly, but where discretion requireth, and that soberly then. For the property of our world is to sound out at first coming, and after to contain. Courtesy is necessary, but too common familiarity in talking and words is very unprofitable, and not without hurt-taking *ut nunc sunt tempora* [as times now are]. Remember you have no father. And you have little enough, if not too little, regarded your kind and no simple mother's wholesome advice from time to time [LL1.112–13].

Although Lady Anne lived for a further eight years, this highly intelligent woman already seems to be living hopelessly in the past. The sons have had thirteen years of experience of life without a father. They have surely read and heard this advice for well over a decade. The fact that Anthony has returned from a long stay in France with its plenitude of Roman Catholics does not justify the intensity of her religious counsel to a man in his mid-thirties. After reading a dozen or so of the extant letters to her elder son over the next few months, Spedding finds in them the same piety, the same jealous as well as zealous exercise of her authority, "curiously mixed," he notes, "with little solicitudes about his physic, his diet, his hours of sleeping, waking, and going abroad, and all his smaller household arrangements" (LL1.113).

By 1591 the officials of Gray's Inn made Bacon surveyor of the grounds; his initiatives would follow in the years to come. Although he would often reside at the inn, he felt the need of another place. Gorhambury belonged to Anthony, and although the latter was often abroad and undoubtedly would have welcomed his brother, Bacon clearly wanted a place of his own. No one else in the family now needing Twickenham, an old Bacon summer residence, he moved there in 1593. This move brought up a household matter that may seem familiar to today's readers.

On February 14, 1593, he wrote to his mother: "I can fain, as they say, between Gray's Inn and Twick[en]ham to rob Peter and pay Paul, and to remove my stuff to and fro, which is chargeable and hurteth the stuff. And therefore, Madame, they would do wondrous well if you thought so good; and if your Ladyship would give me leave to see what I want, the rest may remain where it shall please you. But herein I refer myself to your Ladyship's good pleasure" (LL1.271). He is asking that his extra stuff be stored at Gorhambury, where his mother was living. We have no answer to this request but suspect that he knew that she would oblige, as good parents, even nagging ones, normally do.

2

Like a Child
Following a Bird

Perhaps because Bacon's hopes for royal favor were not prospering, particularly because Lord Burghley was ignoring his pleas, he decided that his chances might profit from an application to Burghley's son, Sir Robert Cecil, who as his father aged, grew more important at court. Writing to Cecil from Gray's Inn on April 16, 1593, Bacon, confident of his "good opinion, good affection, and readiness," suggested to his cousin that he might be able "to deal more effectually for me than otherwise," with whatever implications about his father Cecil might suspect (LL1.237).

Bacon wished to be considered for the position of attorney general, as the present one was being promoted. Since Burghley was patronizing Sir Edward Coke, a leading candidate, Bacon's chances of Cecil coming out in opposition to his father must have seemed dubious. Moreover, Cecil, who hoped to become his father's successor, feared the influence exerted upon Elizabeth by a brazen friend of Bacon, Robert Devereux, 2nd Earl of Essex.

The contrasts between the heir apparent to the position of queen's first secretary and the young lord could hardly have been more striking. Both had looked delicate in their childhood, but Cecil remained diminutive and hunchbacked; Essex, having received the benefits of military training, had overcome his childhood delicacy and attained some stature as a soldier. Cecil served as a polite administrator for Queen Elizabeth; Essex played cards with her. Elizabeth respected Cecil's ability but called him her "pygmy"; Essex fascinated this unmarried queen, as had his stepfather, the Earl of Leicester. The queen found Cecil reliable; Essex overcame his reputation for impetuous and erratic behavior with his charm. Cecil had to mind his manners; Essex could get away with insulting her, although, as we will see, not with total impunity.

Bacon saw in Essex an audacious man who needed the kind of prudent advice that he considered himself able to give. Essex regarded Bacon as a man of wisdom and discernment. These two could assist each other, and Essex proved willing to promote eagerly Bacon's candidacy for attorney general. Bacon needed the impetus a court insider could provide. His opponent, Coke, nine years older than Bacon, had far more practice in courts of law, and he harbored no impractical philosophical agenda to distract him from the task at hand. Unsurprisingly, Robert Cecil joined his father in recommending Coke's promotion; Essex's support of Bacon meanwhile sharpened the Essex-Cecil aversion.

Bacon's chances for preferment also suffered from a parliamentary speech he had made in March of 1593. The queen, after several years of rivalry with Spain, whose armada her navy had beaten off five years earlier but still proved formidable, needed subsidies that required an increase in taxation. Bacon agreed with providing them but spoke against her timetable. She wanted the subsidy paid in four years, but because of its size, Bacon, along with some other members of Parliament, opted for six. To complicate the rift, Lord Treasurer Burghley asked for a conference between the two houses of Parliament. This proposal threatened the authority of Commons. Bacon, always ready to support the privileges of the lower house, rose to his feet to argue that "the creation and privilege ... of this House hath always been first to make offer of the subsidy from hence unto the Upper House" (LL1.216). He stirred Commons to vote against any such conference. The Lords politely disagreed. Could not a conference be held without the Lords actually "confirming"? Sir Robert Cecil suggested a "general conference" about the subsidy that avoided the ugly word *confirmation*. In a two-house legislature, then as now, no agreement can be allowed to threaten the power and position of either.

At this point Bacon offered an amendment, which, it has been commonly believed, set the queen against him and thus hindered his chances of climbing the courtly ladder. He loved to divide an issue; now he gave three reasons for establishing six years as the payment minimum: difficulty (if not impossibility), danger and discontent, and the possibility of a change in the manner of supply. He proceeded to develop his points carefully, as he always did. We can guess that the queen and her advisors judged this performance an unnecessary irritation. The bracketed additions to the manuscript are the nineteenth-century editor's.

> For impossibility, the poor men's rent is such as they are not able to yield it, and the general commonalty is not able to pay so much upon the present. The gentlemen must sell their plate and the farmers their brass pots ere this will be paid. And as for us, we are here to search the wounds of the realm and not to skin them over, wherefore we are not to persuade ourselves of their wealth more than it is.
>
> The danger is this: we [shall thus] breed discontentment in the people. And in a cause of jeopardy, her Majesty's safety must consist more in the love of her people than in their wealth. And therefore [we should beware] not to give them cause of discontentment. In granting these subsidies thus we run into [two] perils. The first [is that] in putting [two] payments into one [year]. We make it a double subsidy; for it maketh 4s. in the pound a payment. The second is, that this being granted in this sort, other princes hereafter will look for the like; so we shall put an ill precedent upon ourselves and to our posterity; and in histories it is to be observed that of all nations the English care not to be subject, base, taxable, etc.
>
> The manner of supply may be by levy or imposition when need shall most require. So when her Majesty's coffers are empty, they may be imbursed by these means [LL1.223].

As it turned out, Parliament rejected Bacon's amendment and granted the queen's request for a four-year subsidy, Bacon probably shaking his head sadly and hoping that pot and plate could somehow prevail. Unlike the majority of his colleagues, who apparently declined to worry excessively about economic effects or possible pillages by a future monarch, he demonstrated for neither the first nor the last time a conservative financial resolution—although he often failed to practice it personally. He often expressed a concern for the pocketbook of both gentlemen and laborers; one should sense that conviction and not mere political expediency motivated him. His own financial difficulties continued over the years, for he lacked an internal House of Commons to restrain him.

Did his contrary position in this matter impede his chances of rising on the courtly ladder? Did the queen perhaps suspect an implication that she was being accused of skinning the populace? Most likely, she could not accept his financial restraint as an honest fear of establishing a bad precedent for future monarchs—or the further danger that she, plagued by a long record of living within a tight budget, might discover, to the horror of Parliament, other unpleasant sources of income. In an attempt to patch matters up, Bacon wrote to Lord Burghley, but his effort suffered, as such efforts often do, by sounding more like justification than the expected apology: "I spake simply and only to satisfy my conscience, and not with any advantage or policy to sway the cause." He hoped that his uncle would "continue me in your good opinion" (LL1.234). For his unsatisfactory position and his unsuccessful attempt to explain it, Bacon, it appears, paid a heavy price. He soon wrote to Cecil in hope of what by now must have seemed an impossible appointment to the post of attorney general, soon to open up. The Earl of Essex also put in an emphatic endorsement, at which Cecil most likely sneered privately.

Here is part of an exchange between Essex and Bacon near the end of March in 1594 with the legal position still unfulfilled but Essex still hopeful.

> Sir,
>
> I have now spoken with the Queen and I [see] no stay from obtaining a full resolution of that we desire. But the passion is in by reason of the tales that have been told her against Nicholas Clifford, with whom she is in such rage for a matter which I think you have heard of, it doth put her infinitely out of quiet; and her passionate humour is nourished by some foolish women; else I find nothing to distaste us; for she doth not contradict confidently, which they that know the minds of women say is a sign of yielding. I will tomorrow take more time to deal with her, and will sweeten her with all the art I have to make *benevolum auditorem* [an obliging hearer] [LL1.290].

Essex's reference to Nicholas Clifford is of no consequence to us except as a reminder that Queen Elizabeth angered easily. His tone suggests that he expected no trouble with her, for she is a woman and can be expected to act like one. This supposition is a dangerous one, for the queen had proved entirely capable of supposedly male virtues. Here is Bacon's reply in full:

> My Lord,
>
> I thank your Lordship very much for your kind and comfortable letter, which I hope will be followed at hand with another of more

assurance. And I must confess this very delay hath gone so near me, as it hath almost overthrown my health. For when I revolved the good memory of my father, the near degree of alliance I stand in to my Lord Treasurer, your Lordship's so signalled and declared favor, the honourable testimony of so many counselors, the commendation unlaboured and in sort offered by my Lords the Judges and the Master of the Rolls elect; that I was voiced with great expectation, and (though I say it myself) with the wishes of most men, to the higher place; that I am a man that the Queen hath already done for; and princes, especially her Majesty, loveth to make an end where they begin; and then add hereunto the obscureness and many exceptions to my competitors; when (I say) I revolve all this, I cannot but conclude with myself that no man ever received a more exquisite disgrace. And therefore truly, my Lord, I was determined, and am determined, if her Majesty reject me, this to do. My nature can take no evil ply; but I will by God's assistance, with this disgrace of my fortune, and yet with that comfort of the good opinion of so many honourable and worthy persons, retire myself with a couple of men to Cambridge, and there spend my life in my studies and contemplations, without looking back. I humbly pray your Lordship to pardon me for troubling you with my melancholy. For the matter itself, I commend it to your love. Only I pray you communicate afresh this day with my Lord Treasurer and Sir Robert Cecil; and if you esteem my fortune, remember the point of precedency. The objections to my competitors your Lordship knoweth partly. I pray spare them not, not over the Queen, but to the great ones, to show your confidence and to work their distaste. Thus longing exceedingly to exchange troubling your Lordship with serving you, I must

> Your Lordship's, in most entire and faithful duty,
>
> F. B. [LL1.290–91].

Here we see an urge to resign himself to the scholar's life, but whenever he asserts it, he is fired also by his ambition for a public life. The letter also exudes a great depth of disgust with his lady queen. Bacon knows that Essex, more than anyone else in the realm, can talk frankly and confidently with England's ruler. He is asking the earl to convey the intensity of his desire for the office and his qualifications—not judicial ones, for they as yet looked weak, but the prestige of his admirers. We know that he is overrating Burghley and Cecil as possible champions, but they are the path to the monarch, and they will read his letters before she does. He remembers his father, who moved up judicially at a young age. At this time, however, he learns that he is expecting too much. A few months later he tries for a position that often leads upward, solicitor general, but she rebuffs him again. Bacon justifiably thought well of his capacities and had not the temperament capable of accepting defeat dispassionately.

In a letter to his mother in June he may be seeking whatever help she might give in his quest of the post of solicitor general, but he also acknowledges that her failing health concerns him.

> My humble duty remembered, I was sorry to understand … that your Ladyship did find any weakness; which I hope was but caused by the season and weather, which waxeth more hot and faint. I was not sorry, I assure your Ladyship, that you came not up, in regard that the stirring at this time of year, and the place where you should be not being very open nor fresh, mought rather hurt your Ladyship than otherwise…. I purpose, God willing, to run down, and it be but for a day, to visit your Ladyship and to do my duty to you. In the meantime I pray your Ladyship … that you enter not into further conceit than is cause, and withal use all the comforts and helps that are good for your health and strength…. Thus I commend your Ladyship to God's good preservation. From Gray's Inn, this 9th of June, 1594.
>
> Your Ladyship's most obedient son,
>
> Fr. Bacon [LL1.300].

Now in her 60s, Lady Anne demonstrated fits of temper beyond the ordinary. In the same month, Bacon learned from Anthony, now lodging with him at Gray's Inn, that Edward Spencer, a servant of his brother designated to work for her at Gorhambury, had complained that "nobody can please her long together" (LL1.310). In another letter Spencer reveals that Lady Bacon had accused him of breaking hedges and of "ill-will." He had apparently come home too late to suit her, and she had sent him to bed without his supper! "There is not one in the house but she fall out withal," wrote Spencer, who described her as "not in charity one day a week; but with her priests, which will undo her" (LL1.312).

It seems unlikely that the brothers could do much about Spencer's situation. Writing to Francis in August, Anne complained that she was "full of back pain" (LL1.312). She also revealed that she was sending her sons some pigeons. Were they intended as messengers? Bacon's writing makes clear his fondness for birds. She closed with her usual advice:

"Sup nor sit not up late. Surely I think your drinking to bedwards hindreth you and your brother's digestion very much. I never knew any but sickly that used it; besides ill for head and eyes. Observe well yet in time" (LL1.313). She would live on at Gorhambury for many more years, but her letter-writing seemingly diminished. One that she managed to get out on December 5, 1594, pertains to one of the more famous episodes of life at Gray's Inn, the Christmas revels of that year.

These revels were an old institution at the Inn that its inmates apparently had neglected for a few years, but now they vowed to bring back with a bang. As far back as the reign of Henry VIII, the gentlemen of the inns of court produced elaborate masques on festival occasions. Musicians, dancers, and actors would enact a world of monsters, heroes, fauns, satyrs, faeries and witches. Puritans like Lady Bacon despised such entertainments, and the revolution of Puritans in the 1640s would end them. Discovering Gray's Inn's elaborate plans, Lady Bacon anticipated trouble: "I trust they will not mum nor mask nor sinfully revel," she wrote Anthony (LL1.326). Their standard of sinfulness surely did not match hers; mumming and masqueing would not condemn their souls. An older Bacon discussed masques rather disdainfully as "toys," but he participated in their staging at Gray's Inn in 1594 and at other times.

The men of law had another form of theater in mind. Modern concern with the drama of Bacon's day focuses not on the masque, which appealed to an upper crust, but on the popular theater, which flourished under the support of lords and ladies and probably attracted those who could hurtle themselves into rubbing elbows for a few hours with the hoi polloi. For who could ignore the drama in late Tudor or early Stuart England? Bacon could, on occasion, abuse the five -act play as well as the masque. The fourth of his famous "idols" or impediments to understanding he relates to the theater "because in my judgment all the received systems [of philosophy] are but so many stage-plays, representing worlds of their own creation after an unreal and scenic fashion" (W8.78). In *The Advancement of Learning* he dismisses poetry as one part of learning creditable for "the expressing of affections, passions, corruptions, and customs," but not in his mind substantial: "It is not good to stay too long in the theater"

(W6.206). As we will see, he could also speak more generously of the dramatic arts.

During the Christmas season of 1594, Gray's Inn would become a seat of drama—and also a miniature kingdom. Its members would elect a Prince of Purpoole, for Gray's Inn stood on the site of a property once called the Manor of Purpoole, associated with the founding Grey family.[1] A contingent arrived from the Inner Temple to help celebrate the event, the two inns having maintained a long relationship. Gray's welcomed the leader of the visitors as "ambassador." A company of performers would entertain them and various other prominent guests. When all assumed their places, however, the hall, including the staging area, spilled over with various "lords, ladies, and worshipful personages," leaving no room for the invited actors. Obviously disgusted by this lack of planning, the men of the Inner Temple withdrew. In an effort to restore order, the hosts urged a session of dancing among the guests while the team of invited players, their vast social inferiors, waited impatiently but probably resignedly and the hosts, probably wishing they could remember how these things had been done in the old days, scurried about. The players, no doubt, were used to putting up with such conditions when performing in places not constructed for thespian purposes.

This theatrical company had been established in the spring of that year by Lord Hunsdon, whose duties as Lord Chamberlain included the organization of functions, principally among them entertaining the queen. An actor with a knack for playwriting had joined the company. The first documentation of William Shakespeare's membership is payments that he received, along with Will Kemp and Richard Burbage, one for the performance of comedies for the queen at Greenwich very recently, December 26, and one for a play called *The Comedy of Errors* at Gray's Inn two days later. Given the common supposition that all of Shakespeare's plays from this time on were performed by the Lord Chamberlain's men and the further supposition that Shakespeare regularly acted in these plays (it has been suggested that he played Egeon, the first speaker in *The Comedy of Errors*), we may hope that this was how he occupied himself on December 28 before an audience that included a man from a quite different sector of London life, Francis Bacon.

It must have been a busy week for them if they played, as the records say they did, at these two prestigious places. Fortunately for the actors, *The Comedy of Errors* is Shakespeare's shortest play. Its chief model, *The Menaechmi*, written sometime around the year 200 B.C. by Plautus, the greatest Roman comic dramatist, appealed to the young Shakespeare, as it did centuries later to Rodgers and Hart, who called their version *The Boys from Syracuse*. The officials of Gray's Inn no doubt wanted it played on the first day of Christmas, but Queen Elizabeth had to be accommodated. Shakespeare's familiarity with legal language and procedures has been often noted, and some scholars believe that he actually wrote it with the Gray's Inn audience in mind.[2]

Misidentifications, common in Shakespearean comedy, bring about its "errors." In this play two states, Ephesus and Syracuse, are at war. Certainly the lawyers at the inn would note that as the play begins, Duke Solinus of Ephesus is confirming for Egeon what he expects: incarceration. "Merchant of Syracusa, plead no more; / I am not partial to infringe our laws." Already a case has developed! Although his presence here is his death warrant, Egeon, worrying more about his personal troubles, tries to concern the duke with them also. They emanate from the loss long ago of his wife and one of his twin sons in a shipwreck. The error that renders all other errors in the play possible was Shakespeare's decision to give both twins the same name, Antipholus, and to add two more twins, each named Dromio, to serve as attendants, one for each Antipholus. For most of the play, action focuses on the confusions generated by the numerous possibilities of mistaken identities. Finally Egeon is saved from death by an abbess, who just happens to be his long-lost wife. A happy ending thus prevails.

The dramatic errors scarcely justify a conclusion in the *Gesta Grayorum*, a book printed in 1688 based on a manuscript describing the proceedings: "So the night was begun and continued to the end, in nothing but confusion and errors; whereupon it was ever afterwards called The Night of Errors."[3] It almost seems that the non-dramatic errors were also staged. On January 3, the revels continued, the Gray's Inn men having concocting satires on the failings in the Night of Errors. The Inner Temple men were brought back, given seats by the Prince of Purpoole, and propitiated by an elaborate demonstration of friendship, populated by such friendly pairs as Theseus and Pirithous, Achilles and Patroclus, Pylades and Orestes, and such, all guided by the Goddess of Amity and an arch-priest. The last two friends, Graius and Templarius, make the point most explicitly.

The *Gesta Grayorum* insists that Bacon "certainly had a hand" in preparing this entertainment. Spedding sees his hand particularly in a series of closing speeches by six of the Prince's councilors, especially in one that deals with the study of philosophy. The second councilor recommends "the exercise of the best and purest part of the mind, and the most innocent and meriting conquest being the conquest of the works of nature; make this proposition, that you bend the excellency of your spirits to the searching out, inventing, and discovering of all whatsoever is hid and secret in the world; that your Excellency be not as a lamp to shineth to others and yet seeth not itself, but as the Eye of the World, that both carrieth and useth light" (LL1.334). Thus the great Baconian message—knowing and appropriating nature. Had any other bencher been familiar with this concept, he would presumably have had to acquire it from Bacon.

The fifth councilor, speaking for virtue, opens: "I have heard sundry plats [plots] and propositions offered under you severally; one to make you a great Prince, another to make you a strong Prince, and another to make you a memorable Prince, and a fourth to make you an absolute Prince. But I hear of no invention to make you a good and virtuous Prince....Wherefore, first of all, most virtuous Prince, assure yourself an inward peace, that the storms without do not disturb any of your repairers of state within" (LL1.339).

If asked, Bacon would hardly have been the man to turn down the job of either councilor *or* counselor. Indeed, these passages are Baconian in their rhythms, the parallelism, and the patterns of repeated sounds, as well as the careful subdivision of a proposition. Of course this elaborate attempt to conciliate the Inner Temple does not prove the Night of Errors a deliberate attempt to reinforce the comedic point about the dangers of misrule. Creating chaos seems to be an imprudent way to demonstrate the perils of error.[4] The Night of Errors continues to be something of a puzzler.

Essex's continuing efforts for Bacon notwithstanding, the bid for the solicitorship failed. Writing to his brother in January of 1595, Bacon, clearly worried about prodding a woman difficult to prod, suggested to Anthony "that if I continue this matter, she will seek all England for a Solicitor rather than take me" (LL 1.346). In a letter to Fulke Greville, Bacon lamented that he felt "like a child following a bird, which when he is nearest flieth away and lighteth a little before, and then the child after it again, and so *in infinitum*, I am weary of it" (LL 1. 359). A trio of troubles boxed him in: lack of a position, lack of money, and a lack of leisure to get on with his pursuit of knowledge. Burning as were these first two, the last may have vexed him most. How many people thought as did Sir Robert Cecil, who in Spedding's words considered his cousin "a speculative man indulging himself in philosophical reveries calculated more to perplex than promote public business" (LL1.355)?

Essex, writing to Sir Thomas Egerton on May 17, 1596, while trying to advance Bacon's prospects, confessed his inability to understand Bacon's philosophical soul. Seeing his own mission as trying to save Bacon from an idle life, he judged it one "not spent in public business" (LL 2. 34). At the same time, Essex seemed truly sorry that his proposals for Bacon to the queen had not helped but actually may have hurt his chances. He gave Bacon a piece of land that may have adjoined that on which Bacon's Twickenham Park lodge stood. Land representing money, Bacon soon sold it to lessen his distress. He continued to realize how thoroughly the favor of the sovereign keyed success. On one of his more hopeful, yet pathetic, days he wrote Anthony that "the Queen saluted me today as she went to chapel" (LL2.37).

Opportunities continued to flare up and then to fade. In April of 1596, Sir John Puckering, the Lord Keeper of the Great Seal—the position Bacon's father had held—died. First in line stood a considerably older man, Sir Thomas Egerton, to whom Anthony Bacon, long close to Essex, wrote, suggesting that the position of Master of the Rolls could be obtained for Egerton's brother as a reward for declining Lord Keeper and thus giving Francis his chance, but Egerton did not comply. Bacon-Essex mutual assistance peaked in this year, and Bacon advised Essex to avoid five different ways of undermining his own opportunities with the queen. Pointing them out in one sentence, he used the rest of the letter to explain them. The Queen (and to a considerable extent Bacon also) saw Essex as "a man of a nature not to be ruled; that hath the advantage of my affection, and knoweth it; of an estate not grounded to his greatness; of a popular reputation, of a military dependence: I demand whether there can be a more dangerous image than this represented to any monarch living, much more to a lady, and of her majesty's apprehension" (LL2.41).

Essex had to downplay all these tendencies on which he prided himself. He had to convince her that he was not ungovernable, merely dissatisfied with his achievement to date. He must not appear too military, for the queen was a woman of "peace." Essex welcomed Bacon's advice on each point but soon proved incapable of following it when he sat at tea with the queen. Essex also understood better than Bacon that much as Elizabeth loved peace, she was inclined to honor warriors for their victories. An older woman of complexities, she found her young companion's unruliness charming—but in some of its applications infuriating and insufferable.

March 12, 1597, marked an event that could conceivably solve one of Bacon's principal problems. Sir William Hatton died, leaving a widow who was young, beautiful, and extremely well provided for. Bacon, knowing that he would have to outshine his friend Fulke Greville, a man reported to be a favorite, sent Essex on an exploratory mission. In this year he was preparing for publication the first edition of his essays, and although "Of Marriage and Single Life" would not appear in this edition, he had perhaps already formulated something equivalent to its opening sentence: "He that hath wife and children hath given hostages to fortune: for they are impediments to great enterprises, either of virtue or mischief."

In seeking a wealthy wife Bacon was attempting what many impoverished men did. Of Bacon's sexual life a little more remains to be said, but it is safe to agree with his best modern biographer, Catherine Drinker Bowen, that women did not attract him particularly. To send Essex to plead his cause lacked assertiveness, to be sure, but Bacon seemed to shake off the attempt by his lordly viceroy—despite the fact that Lady Hatton married Sir Edward Coke, who had beaten him out of the post of attorney general. We will see Lady Hatton entering Bacon's life again in a context that might be called romantic, although more in the manner of adventure than love-making.

In the summer or autumn of 1597, Bacon, having been granted the clerkship of Star Chamber, a post he did not crave, proposed to the new Lord Keeper, Egerton, who also held the post of Master of the Rolls, that if Bacon might play that role, Egerton could appoint someone else (again, perhaps his son) to Star Chamber. Egerton preferred to retain the masterchip—a judicial one of considerable importance—himself. Egerton had the knack of impressing the queen, who made him her counsel, solicitor general, and attorney general, before she had appointed him Keeper of the Great Seal. Thus his office was York House, Bacon's birthplace. In the same year Elizabeth gave Bacon the merely honorary title of Queen's Counsel Extraordinary. Bacon had increasing business with Egerton and must have encountered the young clerk this great man employed as a secretary in 1598, John Donne. Bacon surely saw him at work, no doubt in a room he knew intimately. Thus again Bacon encountered one of the other great writers of his age—but to Bacon the young man was a mere secretary, while to Donne the visitor probably represented another of the tiresome attorneys who frequently came upon the scene. He may have become acquainted with him. No evidence exists to establish that Bacon ever knew Shakespeare, but by 1598, he must have recognized him as the author of several plays about English kings, although not one whose life Bacon would someday write, Henry VII.

Because Donne published his poems only by distributing them among friends, Bacon may never have read one. The varied careers of Bacon and Donne would not have drawn them together, but they shared several experiences. Donne had also studied the law, and now was working for a distinguished judge, although entertaining no serious thoughts about the profession, he did not persist in it. Henry Wotton, who the next year would work as secretary for Bacon's friend Essex, was Donne's friend and Bacon's cousin. Donne himself had taken part in two expeditions against Spain, on the second of which Essex had commanded one of the ships. Bacon's and Donne's modern biographers do not write of any significant relationship between the two men. In most respects Donne's and Bacon's writings differed radically. Instead of nature and learning, Donne wrote of love and religion. They share one distinctive literary trait: a habit of launching many of their works in forceful—even impetuous—ways. Donne could begin poems with lines like:

> For God's sake, hold your tongue and let me love
> or
> Kind pity chokes my spleen, brave scorn forbids
> Those tears to issue which swell my eyelids
> or
> Batter my heart, three-personed God.

Bacon, a few months before he saw Donne laboring at York House, had published the first spare edition of his *Essays*. He too drove at his reader from the start:

> Studies serve for pastimes, for ornaments, and for abilities
> or
> Costly followers are not to be liked, lest while a man maketh his train
> Longer, he make his wings shorter
> or
> Riches are for spending, and spending for honour and good actions
> [W12.291–297].

Donne exclaimed, Bacon asserted, but neither needed to fear an editor who judges writers by their first sentences. For those Baconians who might be wondering about the first example above—yes, Bacon did improve it later, and some of his other striking initial statements had not yet been written.

In 1597 Bacon was thirty-six, more than halfway to the Biblical threescore years-and-ten that most people never reached, and his public and philosophical accomplishments so far fell far short of his aspiration. He had long been a Parliamentarian, which only met, of course, when the monarch needed it. He had been passed over for several important positions, suspected of being less than fully cooperative by the queen, and of being too philosophical for effective pursuit of public business.

The first thing about Bacon's 1597 book is its abrupt title, which he would expand later. Readers of the first two essayists, Montaigne and Bacon, always notice the sharp contrasts in style and tone, but both thought of the essay as an attempt, a "trying out" of a topic. In both French and English the word had a considerable earlier history of use as a verb, and that use persists, although we are more likely to say that we are "trying" or "testing" than that we are "essaying" something. To essay something was to put it to the proof, to test the fitness or excellence of the thing under consideration. Earlier writers like Cicero and Seneca made things that we might call essays, but we do not see them thinking of their efforts as tests. Montaigne and Bacon both spent a considerable amount of time revising, adding to these things that they called essays. Montaigne, it has been said, was trying to form a self-portrait, a basically Renaissance invention. Bacon was trying out ideas, as if with a notion that many commonplace ideas had not been truly tested before, not sufficiently thought-out.

One of Bacon's best-known initial eruptions marks "Of Studies": "Studies serve for pastimes, for ornaments, and for abilities." Bacon loves to divide his subjects into portions, especially in a series of grammatically parallel elements. The version I have just quoted for the second time, however, is not the version that most people read: "Studies serve for delight, for ornament, and for ability." Bacon realized that *delight* is vastly superior to *pastimes*, and that the plural forms of the noun, along with the *s* sounds at the beginning, turned the initial first sentence into something of a hiss. His decision to issue a series of versions of his essays enabled him to make improvements—often in style, usually in development, sometimes to reflect changes in his conception of his subject.

Bacon delighted in aphorisms, which he thought produced "broken" thoughts or fragments of thought. He expected his aphorisms—short, compact, pithy expressions—to provoke the reader into thought. He wanted what we today call "interaction." *Studies*, not *college* or *education*, as we would be more inclined to say today, keyed this active process. "Read not to contradict, nor to believe, but to weigh and consider." A later version, while longer, is still sharply aphoristic: "Read not to contradict and confute; nor to believe and take for granted; nor to find talk and discourse; but to weigh and consider." He mounts the reader a challenge. You are not to simply slap up his aphorisms on your bulletin board. His ideas are not the final ones on the subject. Theoretically, at least, your version may efface his. Only the reader's inclination to participate, to reconstruct a "broken" statement, can justify Bacon's theory.

Bacon's early essays display few metaphors, and he does not use them to be "poetical." In "Of Discourse": "A good continued speech without a good speech of interlocution sheweth slownesse: and a good reply or second speech without a good set speech sheweth shallownesse and weaknes, as wee see in beastes that those that are weakest in the course are yet nimblest in the turne" (W12.293). In "Of Honour and Reputation" he has a striking metaphor, if we observe that one meaning of temper is "to tune" or "to bring into harmony," as in *Well-Tempered Clavier*. "If a man so temper his actions as in some one of them hee doe content everie faction or combination of people, the Musicke will be the fuller" (W12.300). Some of these quotations also exemplify Bacon's fondness for giving advice. At this point he had little expectation of counseling the queen, who did not admit him to her presence, and Cecil displayed little desire to pass Bacon's advice forward, while Burghley, probably better disposed toward him than was his son, had turned seventy-seven and would die the following year. Bacon concentrated on advising Essex, also a discouraging non-follower. The time when England must expect a new ruler edged closer. Bacon may have been wondering whether the next king would recognize competent advice when he heard it. A degree of public approval may well have suggested the composition of more essays by which he could counsel the world.

The modern reader probably finds a row of short aphoristic nuggets of general advice less compelling than did his contemporaries. Today we examine the qualifications of the helpers, rather expecting them to justify their effort by having overcome vice or misfortune. Bacon's audience may not have been impressed, however, to discover that the offerer of several bits of wisdome in "Of Expense" had recently run up a debt of £300, and that when the lender threatened him, Bacon responded by sending off notes to Cecil and to Sir Thomas Egerton to complain of this insult—to which, it appears, they paid little attention. He could give advice, but if, like the rabbit in *Alice's Adventures in Wonderland*, he neglected to follow it, we might seek an advisor who had emerged from debt and made a killing on the stock market—but emergence from failure impresses us more than it did Bacon's contemporaries, who probably had less chance of such a reversal.

3

Not in the Proportion I Hoped

Renewal of the on-again, off-again war against Spain supplied Bacon's friend Essex with chances for military glory. Reasonably successful in a 1596 expedition against Cadiz, he led what became known as the Islands Voyage, its mission the following year to waylay Spanish treasure ships returning from Asia in the Azores, but the effort failed, partly because of storms, partly inadequate leadership. In another continuing irritation the situation in Ireland needed attention in 1598, for Hugh O'Neill, 2nd Earl of Tyrone, inclined to negotiate with Philip II of Spain, had subsequently professed loyalty to Elizabeth, been pardoned by her—and then attacked an English force under Sir Henry Bagnal, killing him and much of his army.

Bacon urged Essex to redeem himself in the Irish situation, pointing out the honor that could flow to him "if the principal persons employed come in by you and depend upon you" (LL2.95). His basically diplomatic advice contrasted sharply with Essex's desire to lead a military force against Ireland. After English conferees debated the situation through the second half of 1598, Essex emerged as the prospective champion early the following year.

From Bacon we have only an account written several years later. "Touching his going into Ireland it pleased him expressly and in a set manner to desire mine opinion and counsel. At which time I did not only dissuade but protest against his going: telling him with as much vehemency and asseveration as I could that absence in that kind would exulcerate the Queen's mind, whereby it would not be possible for him to carry himself so as to give her sufficient contentment, nor for her to

49

carry herself so as to give him sufficient countenance: which will be ill for her, ill for him, and ill for the state" (LL2.127).

Did Bacon really believe that he could bring the impetuous Essex around by such arguments? Essex had already provoked the queen's ulcers on several occasions; her "contentment" he probably did not often take the trouble to contemplate. *The First Part of King Henry IV* was playing about this time. A play about war, it became also a play about honor. Essex would of course despise Sir John Falstaff's words and deeds, especially his words in Act 5, Scene 1: "Honor pricks me on. Yes, but how if honor prick me off when I come on? ... What is honor? A word. What is that word, honor? Air." Falstaff inevitably proves cowardly; yet, Essex's concept of honor may have been dangerously close to that of the reckless Hotspur in Act I, Scene 3:

> By heaven, methinks it were an easy leap
> To pluck bright honor from the pale-faced moon,
> Or dive into the bottom of the deep,
> Where fathom line could never touch the ground,
> And pluck up drownèd honor by the locks.

Honor was not an easy leap. For Bacon honor could proceed proudly from the wise counseling of political leaders. "I am sure," Bacon summed up his own role, "I never in anything in my lifetime dealt with him in like earnestness, by speech, by writing, and by all means I could devise" (LL2.127). Unlike Essex, Bacon perceived the Irish not as foreigners but as subjects who had perhaps gone astray but might be recovered. He undoubtedly knew that Tyrone had grown up in London, that the admirable Sir Henry Sidney had been his protector. The court rang with undercurrents, however, of doubts concerning the competence of Elizabeth's young favorite, for he had never exhibited great qualities of leadership, and his motives hardly coincided with Bacon's prudent counsel.

While Elizabeth and her advisers pondered Essex's reliability, Bacon busied himself with Parliamentary speeches, one an anti-enclosure speech setting out four points: "Foreclosure of grounds brings depopulation, which brings forth idleness, secondly decay of tillage, thirdly subversion of houses, and decrease of charity and charge to the poor's maintenance, fourthly the impoverishing the state of the realm" (LL2.82).

It stands as one of Bacon's numerous expressions of concern for the poor. Almost a century earlier a discussion of the problem had permeated Sir Thomas More's *Utopia*. A great market for wool encouraged sheep farmers to seek land long tilled by poor peasants. As we see today machines replacing people in the labor market, in the sixteenth century sheep replaced people as occupiers of the land. Bacon's speech illustrates this longstanding issue in a basically agricultural nation, but his argument looked not just old but old-fashioned to some of his colleagues.

Meanwhile he remained in touch with Essex, advising him to contribute to the discussion of Irish affairs sullied by Tyrone's unpredictable leadership. In a letter to Essex in March, Bacon recommended a "commission of peaceable men … to plant a stronger and surer government" (L2.100). Essex sent Anthony Bacon, whom he had known longer than he had his brother, an "apology," in short, a defense of his militaristic spirit, for he saw the situation in Ireland as one admitting no possibility of peace while Tyrone disingenuously negotiated with King Philip of Spain. On July 2, Essex took part in an argument that involved Sir Robert Cecil, Lord Admiral Howard, and the queen. Apparently thinking that she was rejecting his suggestion as to which man might best be sent to Ireland, Essex turned scornfully from her. The queen reacted sharply, "gave him a box on the ear and told him to go and be hanged. As Essex laid his hand on his sword, the Lord Admiral [Lord Charles Howard] stepped between them."[1] At this point neither could stand the other; one can only speculate as to what a reckless use of this sword might have occasioned, had the Lord Admiral not prevailed. The outraged Essex stomped out of the room. Even this misbehavior Elizabeth forgave him— while she apparently continued to resent Bacon's interference with the timing of her tax plan.

Other men besides Bacon labored to calm Essex down. He not only escaped punishment but received quick attention from the queen's physician when he fell ill in September. Before the year ended she appointed him commander of the force in Ireland. By March of 1599 she granted him a larger army than any deputy to that troublesome dependency had ever been given. Before Essex left on his mission, Bacon tried once more to guide the wayward lord. "Your Lordship is designed to a service of great merit and great peril … so the greatness of the merit includes no small consequence of peril, if it be not temperately governed" (LL2.129–130). In those last six words he expresses, politely in the passive voice, his thesis. His insistence on the cardinal virtue of temperance leaps out of the letter several times. He closes—more hopefully than expectantly, perhaps—with "my best wishing" (LL2.133).

When Essex arrived in Ireland, he began a series of moves which Queen Elizabeth and her advisors—and for that matter later scholars—found difficult to understand. Tyrone lurked in the north; Essex spent a lot of time in the south. He may have been stationing garrisons at various points in the countryside, but if he did, he went too far. He had gone forth with sixteen thousand men and in July he had requested and received two thousand more, but when he caught up with Tyrone's forces in Ulster on September 3, his men numbered only half of Tyrone's. A few days later he drew up a six-week, renewable truce with the Irish leader. A question that has persisted ever since: did Essex ever intend to attack Tyrone? Surely he had not suddenly adopted Falstaff's version of honor.

Originally his orders permitted him to return to England if necessary, but when the queen sent him the extra troops she specified that he must remain with them. He also infuriated the queen by commissioning fifty-nine knights—more, some thought, than to date existed in the realm. On September 28, 1599, weary from his long trip, he charged into Queen Elizabeth's bedchamber at her court in Nonesuch. As one biographer expressed it: "No living man had ever seen her undressed before."[2] Amazingly, it seems, she greeted him warmly. After she had prepared herself for the day as a working ruler, they met, she still apparently happy to see her wayward commander, but upon further questioning the queen's good mood faded. That evening he was told to stay in his chamber.

The next day Bacon learned of his arrival. The letter he sent off, however, indicates that although he knew little of his friend's recent activities, he realized that a *nubecula*, a little cloud, had formed.

> Conceiving that your Lordship came now up in the person of a good servant to see your sovereign mistress, which kind of compliments are many times *instar magnorum meritorum* [a sign of great merits], and therefore that it would be hard for me to find you, I have committed to this poor paper the humble salutations of him that is more yours than any man's and

more yours than any man. To these salutations I add a due and joyful gratulation, confessing that your Lordship, in your last conference with me before your journey, spake not in vain. God making it good, that you trusted we should say *Quis putasset?* [Who would have believed?] Which as it is found true in a happy sense, so I wish you do not find another *Quis putasset* in the manner of taking this so great a service. But I hope it is, as he said, *Nubecula est, cito transibit* [It is a little cloud, it will speedily pass]: and that your Lordship's wisdom and obsequious circumspection and patience will turn all to the best. So referring all to some time that I may attend you, I commit you to God's best preservation [LL2.150].

With Essex's home now his prison, Bacon obtained passage for a fifteen-minute conversation with him, which he later described thus, using the same cloud image:

He asked mine opinion of the course that was taken with him. I told him, My Lord, *nubecula est, cito transibit.* It is but a mist. [It will pass quickly.] But shall I tell your Lordship it is as mists are: if it go upwards, it may perhaps cause a shower: if downwards, it will clear up. And therefore, good my Lord, carry it so as you take away by all means all umbrages and distastes from the Queen: and especially, if I were worthy to advise you, as I have been by yourself thought, and now your question imports the continuance of that opinion, observe three points. First, make not this cessation or peace which is concluded with Tyrone as a service wherein you glory, but as a shuffling up of a prosecution which was not very fortunate. Next, represent not to the Queen any necessity of estate whereby as by a coercion or wrench she should think herself enforced to send you back into Ireland; but leave it to her. Thirdly, seek access, *importune, opportune*, seriously, sportingly, every way. I remember my Lord was willing to hear me, but spake very few words and shaked his head sometimes, as if he thought I was in the wrong—but sure I am he did just contrary in every one of these three points [LL2.150–51].

Soon Essex faced confinement in the house where Bacon had spent his early years, York House, the base of the Lord Keeper, Sir Thomas Egerton, now obliged to keep an eye on this difficult man. Another difficult man, Tyrone, busily issued the queen twenty-one propositions—repulsive to English ears but deeply desired by most Irish—including recommendations "that the Catholic religion be openly preached," "that Oneale, ODonnel, Desmond, and their partakers, shall have such lands as their ancestors enjoyed two hundred years ago," and "that all Irishmen shall freely traffic as Englishmen in England" (which means, of course, as freely as Englishmen traffic) (LL2.154–55). To all who accepted Henry VIII and his successors as heads of the English church, proposals that lands now legally the property of English lords and gentlemen be given away and that the Irish need not remain in their hovels could be better laughed at than seriously considered.

Bacon, probably still unaware of many of his friend's misdeeds, recommended to the queen that Essex be given a chance to divulge his own version of his Irish adventures, and that she should "restore him to his former attendance, with some condition of honour to take away discontent" (LL2.158). Bacon tended to assume that his own discontent must afflict others as well. The magnetic Essex retained friends who hoped that if he confessed his sins, Elizabeth would, as she had often done, forgive him, but his proponents were diminishing. In the weeks that followed, the prisoner lapsed into illness, and the queen delayed making any decision about his political fate. By the end of 1599, after a life-threatening period, he recovered his health.

Early the next year preparations commenced for a trial before the Star Chamber; then it was postponed. In March he was allowed to return to his home. At that time the queen ordered several people who lived in the Essex household to remove themselves. This group included Anthony Bacon, a man with a record of high praise for his intelligence work abroad, which had investigated and helped prevent any number of plots against the queen. Since then, Anthony Bacon had been managing Essex's political correspondence. He would not participate, however, in upheavals soon mounted by other followers of Essex, who had to return to York House for an inquisition led by Attorney General Coke: Why, for instance, had he spent weeks in places like Munster while his enemy remained up north in Ulster? Why had he made an unauthorized treaty with Tyrone? Why had he left Ireland against the queen's instructions? And so on.

Despite the prospect of taking part in the judicial examination of Essex, Bacon continued to try to alleviate the rift between Elizabeth and her recalcitrant warrior. On July 19 he wrote: "I desire your Lordship also to think that though I confess I love some things much better than your Lordship, as the Queen's service, her quiet and contentment, her honour, her favour, the good of my country, and the like, yet I love few persons better than yourself, both for gratitude's sake, and for your own virtues, which cannot hurt but by accident or abuse" (LL2.191).

Essex responded in the manner of a philistine. "I am a stranger to all poetical conceits, or else I should say somewhat of your poetical example." He signed the letter "Your retired friend, Essex" (LL2.192). His retirement would not long prevail. On August 26 the queen set him at liberty, though he had to stay away from court—quite likely because she still feared the force of his personality. Away from him, she could impose such sanctions as refusing to renew for him a grant of a farm of sweet wines. As the year ended Essex's still substantial core of friends gathered at Essex House to plan rebellion. Essex determined, though with little evidence at hand, that Sir Robert Cecil, the son of and successor to the now deceased Lord Burghley, was plotting his ruin. As the year went on, followers of Essex, some at odds with Elizabethan officials, continued to flock to his house, while Bacon tried to alleviate the rift between Essex and the monarch. He framed sample letters of reconciliation which Anthony Bacon took to him.

Meanwhile, Essex's friends plotted, with or without his advice and approval, for on this matter scholars disagree. Spedding describes the development thus: "By the end of January 1600–1 [the editor preserving first the Elizabethans' calendar, then the one we reckon by], all these intrigues and secret consultations had ripened into a deliberate and deep-laid plot for surprising the Court, mastering the guard, and seizing the Queen's person, and so forcing her to dismiss from her counsels Cecil ... and others, and to make such changes in the state as the conspirators thought fit" (LL.208).

On February 6, to provoke Essex's known interest in a previous monarch repugnant to Elizabeth, his friends visited the Lord Chamberlain's players at the Globe Playhouse to urge a performance of *Richard II*, which they had not performed for some time. For a donation, the company agreed. Why this request? Queen Elizabeth and the inept king deposed in 1399 had few traits in common, but it loomed large for the conspirators that she, like Richard, had failed to produce an indisputable heir to the throne. The Essex supporters gathered the next day. It has been speculated that Shakespeare himself played the role of Richard.[3] In Henry Bolingbroke, the man who assumed the crown in 1399, Essex's followers recognized their hero. Even King Richard's courtiers had, so to speak, agreed with them in Act I, Scene IV, for they "observed his courtship to the common people, / How he did seem to dive into their hearts / With humble and familiar courtesy." Perhaps they even believed that Essex, whose father had been Viscount Hereford (Henry Boling-broke had been Duke of Hereford), could in the position or ruler, as Richard noted in the same speech, be "our subjects' next degree in hope." Thus the Bard, as it were, goaded these disaffected men into treasonable acts.

Essex is reputed to have uttered such abominations as that the queen "was as crooked and distorted in mind as in body."[4] Such evidence as survives shows him acting rashly, as usual, but with no more aptitude for command than the historical or dramatic Richard displayed. He symbolized, but cannot be said to have led, the brewing discontent, for time and time again Essex, captivating as he was, could not guide others. By Sunday evening he and his supporters were all confined, and in the next few days charges piled up against them.

The evidence showed that on that Sunday morning (hardly a suitable day for rebellion) a gathering at Essex House had attracted suspicious onlookers, causing Lord Keeper Egerton, a friend of Essex, to make an inquiry, presumably under orders from the queen. Essex then bounded off to gain support from the Lord Mayor and the sheriffs, but upon his return he was intercepted, pistol fire broke out, and several men died. Eventually the Lord Admiral and forces from the Tower arrived on the bloody scene. By evening Essex and his men had surrendered. The royal forces charged Essex with various crimes, among them detaining a queen's officer, bringing forces of the city to counteract her forces, and failing to control the shooting that erupted.

When the prisoners were brought to trial, the procedure adopted by Attorney General Coke dismayed Bacon. Essex bore a legacy of troublesome behavior, but Bacon pointed out that many of the present charges and replies were irrelevant to the case at hand. What mattered most was that an armed group had gathered, had been warned by the Lord Keeper, and yet persisted. "The Earl of Essex answered that if he had purposed anything against others than those his private enemies, he would not have stirred with so slender a company. Whereunto Mr. Bacon answered: 'It was not the company you carried with you, but the assistance which you hoped for in the city which you trusted unto.... But the end was treason, as hath been sufficiently proved'" (LL2.230).

Essex and four of his companions faced execution. One man clearly involved in the plot, the Earl of Southampton, escaped with life imprisonment and degradation of his title. The life turned out not to be his, however, but Queen Elizabeth's. Among later achievements, he induced a performance of *Love's Labour's Lost* for Queen Anne after her husband ascended to the throne as King James and freed him. His rank restored, Southampton lived nearly as long as James, dying in 1624.

After Bacon aided in the prosecution of his friend, the queen chose him to write a narrative account of the crimes of Essex and his accomplices. The queen edited this document, making alterations which show that Bacon continued to maintain a certain regard for a man he now, along with other judges, branded a traitor. The queen, for instance, altered Bacon's "My Lord of Essex" to "the late Earl of Essex" or simply "Essex."

The spring of 1601 brought two disconcerting events to Bacon, the first exemplifying the hostility between Bacon and Edward Coke, the other a family tragedy. It is best here to let Bacon speak for himself:

A true remembrance of the abuse I received of Mr. Attorney General publicly at the Exchequer the first day of term; for the truth whereof I refer myself to all that were present.

I moved to have a reseizure of the lands of Geo. Moore, a relapsed recusant, a fugitive, and a practicing traytor; and shewed better matter for the Queen against the discharge by plea, which is ever with a *salvo jure* [sound law]. And this I did in as gentle and reasonable terms as might be.

Mr. Attorney kindled at it, and said, "Mr. Bacon, if you have any tooth against me; pluck it out; for it will do you more hurt than all the teeth in your head will do you good." I answered coldly in these very words; "Mr. Attorney, I respect you. I fear you not: and the less you speak of your own greatness, the more I will think of it."

He replied, "I think scorn to stand upon terms of greatness towards you, who are less than little; less than the least"; and such other strange light terms he gave me, with that insulting which cannot be expressed.

Herewith stirred, yet I said no more but this: "Mr. Attorney, do not depress me so far; for I have been your better and may be again, when it pleases the Queen" [LL3.3].

This exchange does not resemble an emotional outburst of two men who might later apologize and shake hands. In Bacon's time some men would have challenged each other to a duel and risked being shot down. Bacon and Coke, however, were primarily men of words rather than physical reactions. Bacon and his brother were both physically frail (Francis less so than Anthony), and Bacon opposed dueling absolutely. Coke lived a long life and seemed to be a healthy man for his time, but his biographer found no violent streak in him. Bacon used language more adeptly; Coke possessed what he had no need to talk about: that at the moment he stood greater in the mind of the queen. Perhaps unjustly but prudently, Bacon blamed his judicial opponent, rather than the queen or her advisors, for his long exclusion from a powerful position. The exchange shows Bacon still hoping that she would prove mindful of him, still, at the age of forty, *Mr. Bacon*, not *Sir Francis*.

Nor did his barbed rejoinders to Coke at the Exchequer satisfy Bacon, who later wrote Coke a polite letter, no doubt laboring long over it, for it displays many of the stylistic features readers of his essays will recognize. It attempts resolution but not reconciliation.

> Mr. Attorney,
>
> I thought best, once for all, to let you know in plainness what I find of you, and what you shall find of me. You take to yourself a liberty to disgrace and disable my law, my experience, my discretion. What it pleaseth you, I pray, think of me: I am one that knows both mine own wants and other men's; and it may be, perchance, that mine mend, and others stand at a stay. And surely I may not endure in public place to be wronged, without repelling the same to my best advantage to right myself. You are great, and therefore have the more enviers, which would be glad to have you paid at another's cost. Since the time I missed the Solicitor's place (the rather I think by your means) I cannot expect that you and I shall ever serve as Attorney and Solicitor together: but either to serve with another upon your remove, or to step into some other course; so as I am more free than ever I was from any occasion of unworthy conforming myself to you, more than general good manners or your particular good usage shall provoke. And if you had not been shortsighted in your own fortune (as I think) you might have had more use of me. But that tide is passed. I write not this to show my friends what a brave letter I have written to Mr. Attorney; I have none of those humours. But that I have written is to a good end, that is to the more decent carriage of my mistress' service, and to our

particular better understanding one of another. This letter, if it shall be answered by you in deed, and not in word, I suppose it will not be worse for us both. Else it is but a few lines lost, which for a much smaller matter I would have adventured. So this being but to yourself, I for myself rest [LL3.4–5].

A greater blow than the contemptuousness of his rival fell upon him. Bacon's great editor explained the death of Anthony, his only full brother, as a result of "gout and the stone." Much of Spedding's characterization of Anthony Bacon suggests how similar the two men were. He called Anthony "a grave, assiduous, energetic, religious man, with decided opinions, quick feelings, warm attachments, and remarkable power of attaching others; a gentleman of high strain, open handed and generous beyond his means; but sensitive and irritable; a little too apt to suspect, feel, and resent an injury; a little too hasty to speak of it, and occasionally, I dare say, driven by the perplexities of pecuniary embarrassment into unreasonableness and injustice; but generally fair, tolerant, and liberal" (LL3.6–7).

Francis Bacon did not lack the power of "attaching" others, but Anthony's skill probably exceeded his. No doubt this quality came in handy in his investigative work.

He asserted his power in several Parliamentary bills that were argued in 1601, including one against abuses in weights and measures, and one of his own, a motion that a committee be established to repeal superfluous laws. "Laws be like pills all gilt over, which if they be easily and well swallowed down are neither bitter in digestion or hurtful to the body.... The more laws we make the more snares we lay to entrap ourselves" (LL3.19). Bacon frequently looked at laws philosophically, a habit not always characteristic of legislators. The fact that this motion failed should not surprise us; lawmakers are fond of their achievements as parents are fond of children, even those who may not turn out as well as hoped. In addition, Bacon possessed an ability to sniff out imperfections in laws of the sort a majority of his colleagues might have found expedient to retain.

In a short undated letter, probably in August of 1601, Bacon wrote to a friend that "the Queen hath done somewhat for me," but quickly added, "though not in the proportion I hoped" (LL3.14). Perhaps he was wondering if she would ever alter that proportion. In that year she seemed healthy, but her sixty-seven years provoked the old worries about the succession. A correspondence began between the principal secretary, Sir Robert Cecil, and representatives of the man regarded by many as the likeliest successor, King James VI of Scotland, the son of Mary Stuart. By provisions of the will of King Henry VIII, if his son Edward should die without issue (which of course happened) the crown would pass to the House of Suffolk through Henry's niece Frances. Henry did not favor a crown for his daughters, but a Suffolk male would presumably be available. Sir Nicholas Bacon, as Lord Keeper, who like many Englishmen feared Catholicism rearing its head through Queen Mary of Scotland or her successor, had favored this outcome.[5]

The reign of Henry's daughters Mary and Elizabeth, as well as Mary Stuart's death, had in many minds obviated Henry's will, and the next most likely candidate was James, Mary Stuart's son, but not a Roman Catholic. Did Elizabeth, who had never proclaimed a successor, know what Cecil was up to? If she knew, she remained quiet. Although she always suspected that acknowledging a successor might cause her endless trouble, she presumably would not object to such negotiations as a trusted subordinate might be conducting in behalf of the realm.

On the Irish question, Bacon eagerly offered advice to whoever would listen. Under Charles Blount, Lord Mountjoy, the English had achieved a victory over Irish dissidents and driven a Spanish force off the coast, but issues remained with respect to the future relationship of Ireland and its English masters. In 1602 Bacon wrote to his cousin Cecil to urge the establishment of "civility" in that rambunctious possession. Typically, he subdivided his plan into "the extinguishing of the relicks of the war," "the recovery of the hearts of the people," "the removing of the root and occasions of new troubles," and "plantations and buildings" (LL3.46).

Cecil most likely found such advice naïve and impractical. We might call Bacon a social planner well before his contemporaries found such an occupation a quintessential element in administering a sovereign nation. Coupled with these proposals, of course, stood stout measures of Anglican bias, such as the necessity of revamping "their barbarous laws" and of countering their religion by sending good preachers (non-scholastic, but also not too puritanical) to them. He of course thoroughly opposed Tyrone's brand of independence. Such proposals as Bacon was making had no chance without the queen's acceptance, and Bacon did not know whether Cecil even brought his plans to her attention. Evidence suggests that she did not share Bacon's hope of recovering Irish hearts; neither would many succeeding monarchs.

Early in the year 1603 the queen began to fail. Although he would write a tribute to her later, at this point Bacon was addressing himself to Scottish people of his acquaintance to establish his relationship with James VI of Scotland, soon to come south as James I of England. After Elizabeth died on March 24, 1603, James's peaceful arrival relieved many anxious hearts and raised Bacon's hopes for an advancement he strongly believed was long overdue.

4

The Corner-Stone Laid

Consider *advancement* the key word for Bacon in 1603. After writing to several people, English and Scottish, as resources for an introduction to the new monarch, he sent, by twenty-one-year-old Toby Matthew, son of Dr. Tobias Matthew, a prominent churchman and future Archbishop of York, a letter to James himself. Matthew, whom Bacon had met when the young man took up residence in Gray's Inn in 1599, would remain his friend throughout life. In the letter Bacon reminded the king of his father's and brother's services to Queen Elizabeth, pledged his own, and predicted that "the corner-stone is laid of the mightiest monarchy in Europe" (LL3.63).

James, concentrating on establishing his own position, quickly reminded his new subjects of his lengthy experience, thirty-five years as king of Scotland, twenty as its actual ruler, in a life of thirty-six years. He probably recognized that this impressive monarchical record would not necessarily make his new one easier. In moving south several decades after Sir Nicholas Bacon and others attempted to bring him into England and the prospect of plenty of time to learn English ways, James was bringing such habits as a Scottish burr and, more importantly, a record of relationships with Catholic Spain that looked like intrigues to English eyes. Bacon, invariably more candid in his essays than in addressing rulers, had not yet written "Of Travel," which begins: "Travel, in the younger sort, is a part of education; in the elder, a part of experience. He that travelleth into a country before he hath entrance into the language, goeth to school, and not to travel" (W12.137). Traveling to a new land to settle in and rule it complicated James's schooling.

Learning that he would continue on the Learned Counsel that had advised Elizabeth, Bacon could hope to gain the political stature that had always eluded him in Elizabeth's long reign. At the same time, his philosophical urge was growing. As he had once written to Lord Burghley, Bacon now addressed his influential son, who soon would be raised to the peerage. In a letter of July 3, 1603, he retold one old message and added one new one. "My ambition now I shall only put upon my pen, whereby I shall be able to maintain memory and merit of time." Perhaps Cecil might be interested that now, for the first time since his cousin's lackluster pursuit of Lady Hatton, "I have found out an alderman's daughter, an handsome maiden, to my liking" (LL3.80). Bacon had recently found it necessary to congratulate three colleagues at Gray's Inn as new-made knights; he would not mind, and certainly a new bride and her family would not mind, the same status for himself. We do not have Cecil's immediate reply, if any, but he responded in his way by including Bacon among no fewer than three hundred new knights at the coronation ceremony. For reasons that are not clear but probably involved financial arrangements of the sort that usually dominated such unions, marriage with Alice Barnham, it turned out, would not take place for three years. Nevertheless, he had become, if only in a vast crowd of knights, *Sir* Francis Bacon.

If he contributed little to the work of the king's Learned Counsel in 1603, he did compose *A Brief Discourse Touching the Happy Union of the Kingdom of England and Scotland. Dedicated in Privacy to His Majesty.* Bacon drew a parallel between James and ancient Persian kings, "for the Persian magic, the secret literature of these kings, was an observation of the contemplation of nature and an application thereof to a sense politic" (LL3.90).

Why Persian? Perhaps Persian kings seemed particularly royal; western Europeans acknowledged the importance of Persian history and culture. After defeating Persia, Alexander the Great became in his own mind virtually a Persian. Bacon goes on to trace historical unifications among nations. He downplayed the linguistic dissimilarities that so often trouble new neighbors and pointed out the benefits. "Both your Majesty's kingdoms are of one language, though of different dialects; and the difference is so small between them, as promiseth rather an enriching of our language than a continuance of two" (LL3.97), a linguistically sound judgment. Not everyone shared Bacon's optimism about the junction of the two contiguous lands of England and Scotland, but he wrote as a man cognizant of the value of a positive endorsement of a perhaps troublesome but necessary process of unification.

Many English subjects worried more about the religious situation than he did. Bacon prepared a paper for the king on the "better pacification and edification of the Church of England." *Pacification* meant the containment of separatists and immoderate Puritans whose religious excesses threatened Anglicanism and its latest royal head. Bacon's mother ranked among intemperate Puritans, but he tended to see them as contemporaries of hers—people of advanced age unable to represent a threat. He did not seem to perceive or credit the growing strength of English dissidents. Now the realm included Scottish dissidents, mainly Presbyterians with no fondness for powerful bishops, although King James, as James VI of Scotland, had managed to endure prelates and restrain the Presbyterian fervor when necessary.

Bacon upheld a "golden mediocrity," a balance between reform and tradition. Bacon proved conventional on such topics as preaching. "God forbid, that every man that can take unto himself boldness to spend at hour together in a Church upon a text, should be admitted for a preacher, though he mean never so well" (LL3. 119), but for preachers who strayed, he recommended brotherly advice from a body of colleagues. Bacon noted such deficiencies as "nonresidents and pluralities," that is, ministers who did not even live within their parishes and those who were rewarded for nominally serving parishes that they did not even visit, but they continued to abound, as novelists as late as Anthony Trollope exemplify.

King James, displaying little trace of Bacon's subtlety, proclaimed, "I will have one doctrine, one discipline, one religion, in substance and ceremony" (LL3, 128), a simplistic solution for a thornily complex ecclesiastical situation. The tenth of the fifteen reforms to which King James's name would be permanently attached stands as the most memorable: "One uniform translation to be made, and only used in all the Churches of England." The work not named in the document is of course the Bible, the one baptized *King James* and ultimately "authorized" rather than the heavily annotated Geneva Bible (which, interestingly, James had authorized in Scotland).[1]

Other matters interested James more. He chose Bacon to monitor the discussions—they would prove lengthy—of the practical difficulties facing the unifiers of the two kingdoms. One was wardship, for all sons of even prominent fathers could, under certain circumstances, become wards of the monarch. Older fathers and those troubled by illness had to wonder what a monarch from the north might be contemplating in the way of favorite sons. The matter was discussed, the resolution deferred.

Providing the monarch with all the supplies of life fell to purveyors, many of them notoriously corrupt. Their abuses, everyone agreed, had to end. In a speech before the king at Whitehall, Bacon fashioned an analogy: "It is of the leaves and roots of nettles; the leaves are venomous and stinging where they touch, the root is not so, but is without venom or malignity, and yet it is that root that bears and supports all the leaves" (LL3.183). The purveyors oppressed the common people, taking shares of their produce and even hacking down trees that they needed. Bacon, who loved to develop contrasts sharply, wrote, "I am a little to alter their name; for instead of takers they become taxers" (LL3.184). James agreed wholeheartedly: corrupt purveyors needed to be disciplined—so long as supplies rolled in.

The question of whether Scots would accept decisions formulated in England bothered James not at all. He confidently promised that he would compel their assent. Bacon reported that the king's wants were simple enough: the union must be acknowledged, its name must be agreed on, and a commission should be formed to deal with other details. But as the days of the unification conference continued, the mere discussion of the name required several sessions. One proposal—that the name *England* be abandoned ("Great Britany," the favorite alternative)—Parliament struck down. The king, invited to participate but bored by meetings at which he did not prevail, insisted that he did not want to interfere with his subjects' duties. He told a committee that "he wished his heart were of crystal, that all might see his cogitations" (LL3.207).

Presumably rewarding Bacon for his efforts in moving the unification process along, the king on August 18, 1604, confirmed in writing his membership, previously given orally, in his Learned Counsel and gave him a £60 pension for life. These were not enormous bestowals, but they signaled a promising start for him in the new reign. The process of forming the union continued until November 24, when Bacon and the Lord Advocate of Scotland reviewed the articles. Their task had to be completed in three days. It was "to reduce and join them together in such form and method as was sweet and agreeable in coherence of matter and would be fit to set down in the instruments themselves to be propounded to the Parliaments." They acceded and succeeded (LL3.24). They presented the articles to Lord Tivye, the president of the Council of Scotland, and Lord Cranbourne, as Sir Robert Cecil could now sign himself. Bacon wrote a preface to the report, which went unused, as the two lords took over that task. Parliament, facing such catastrophes as the plague breaking out in 1603 and the Gunpowder Plot (an attempt to murder the king and his family, foiled in 1605, thus giving the country a famous annual holiday), did not act on the unification document until 1606. But by that time, unification, in the mind of the king, had already happened.

While working for unification of the two realms, Bacon busied himself philosophically, composing in Latin, the language of educated men, his upcoming *The Advancement of Learning* and, for immediate contemplation, shorter discussions of topics that revealed aspects of his thinking. In "Experientia Literata" he speculated as follows: "Believing that I was born for the service of mankind, and regarding the care of the commonwealth as a kind of common property which like the air and the water belongs to everybody, I set myself to consider in what way mankind might be best served, and what service I was myself best fitted by nature to perform" (LL3.84).

A prospective statesman might say much the same thing about such matters as unification, but Bacon would revitalize both the nation and the process of learning. In the process he would have to destroy much of what passed for learning. Before he could do that, however, he had to defend learning. The full title of the work he would issue in 1605, *The Two Books of Francis Bacon of the Proficience and Advancement of Learning*, in its English version, seems to present us with synonyms. Both *proficience* and *advancement* have to do with "moving forward." Yet it is impossible to believe that, even in an age that did not mind concocting long titles, Bacon would have used two words meaning the same thing. *Proficience* is a word of his own invention, but *proficiency* existed earlier and seems to have signified mainly skill—something one must have before moving very far forward.

Defending comes first, however, because most topics, including learning, have their enemies. One might compare Bacon's endeavor with that of a book posthumously published a decade earlier under two titles, *An Apology for Poetry* or *The Defense of Poesy*, and written earlier yet, for Sir Philip Sidney died earliest of the great writers mentioned at the beginning of this book from a war injury in 1586. Sidney was defending poetry, as the second of its alternate titles makes clear, an art that he himself practiced with great distinction. In our time the literature of the late Tudor and early Stuart era needs no defense, but Sidney, observing in particular the growth of narrowly puritanical attacks on imaginative literature, felt impelled to make it, and Bacon just as clearly needed to defend learning or, more precisely, defend the importance of pursuing learning comprehensively, and also "advancing" it. Some of these anti-intellectual trends pervaded Christianity. In the view of some preachers, humanist scholars, in their reliance on ancient counterparts, were countenancing atheism. The same could be said about post-medieval scholastics with their heavy Aristotelian bias. Un-Christian pagan images abounded in poetry.

For Bacon, the study of nature meant the study of God's handiwork. God, he wrote, "*hath placed the world in man's heart*" (The italics are in Spedding's edition [W6.93]). Yes, a little learning could be a dangerous thing. "It is an assured truth and a conclusion of experience, that a little or superficial knowledge of philosophy may incline the mind of man to atheism, but a farther proceeding therein doth bring the mind back again to religion" (W6.96). Bacon saw no conflict between Christianity as he understood it and the pursuit of knowledge, as he would practice it. He also recognized a political threat to learning from men who thought that impractical knowledge impeded practical accomplishment, especially in that common human activity, warfare. Were soldiers and scholars compatible? Sidney, who died from a war wound, had certainly proved that a poet could be a hero. Bacon was beginning to prove that as a scholar, he could participate effectively in government, but he had no military experience. He pointed out that certain well-known military men were scholars.

Despite some later efforts to raise forces to protect his daughter Elizabeth, the wife of Frederick V of the Palatinate and Bohemia, James's record as a man who preferred peace to war holds up well. By dedicating his book to King James, a ruler who preferred striving for peace to pursuing costly and futile wars, Bacon was making a further point against the militarists. In addition to such attacks from without, intellectuals could, by falling into rhetorical and logical errors, damage their own cause. Defending learning therefore demanded a critical attitude to avoid self-imposed absurdities. Bacon excelled at skewering philosophers gone astray.

Like Sidney, he divided knowledge into history, philosophy, and poetry. Sidney of course preferred poetry, Bacon history and philosophy (both of which included aspects of another body of knowledge eventually called science). Sidney, one of the earliest great Elizabethan poets, recognized that one poet of great stature, Edward Spenser, had already risen, and that others could be expected to ascend. To be sure, Shakespeare and Marlowe, very young men when Sidney died, soon would flourish. Bacon resembled Sidney as an early bird in his field of study. Galileo was three years younger than Bacon; René Descartes, often coupled with Bacon as early voices of what came to be called *science*, nine; Johannes Kepler, ten; Thomas Hobbes, who worked for Bacon for a while, seventeen. William Harvey, in his twenties, had not yet blossomed; Locke, Leibniz, and Newton did not yet exist. In assessing the new learning, Bacon had a small and mostly undistinguished school of intellectuals to observe.

In *The Advancement of Learning*, Bacon does not merely address the king and then, getting him out of the way, so to speak, proceed on his work; he mentions him many times in the text, even referring to James's own writings, which he touted as worthy, although later generations have tended to neglect them. James even preceded Bacon in composing essays, for his *Essays of a Prentice in the Divine Art of Poesie* appeared seven years before Bacon's epochal work. Bacon was praising a man essential to his own success, but in lauding James, he was acknowledging one of the few monarchs who reflected literary glory on his teachers, one of whom, George Buchanan, ranked as Scotland's greatest humanist scholar of that era.

Bacon often quotes another kingly scholar. Solomon had warned "of making many books there is no end; and much study is a weariness of the flesh" (Ecclesiastes.12.120). Solomon, the wise king, counteracted the long list of deficient monarchical intellects. Bacon, always assuming the necessity of monarchic structure in reputable government, clearly appreciated an erudite monarch. King James surely would not only accept but read a book like *The Advancement of Learning.*

Having defended the scholar, Bacon set to work categorizing the errors that led men astray, the first being men studying "not matter but words." One principle of religious scholarship, close attention to the language of eminent divines, threatened to generate such errors. Men of Luther's time had not sinned in offering "an affectionate study of eloquence and copie [expressive fullness] of speech" (W6.119). Subsequent writers, however, had overdone the process, falling in love with words, Bacon notes, much as Pygmalion fell in love with the statue he had made. The legend finds its full complement in George Bernard Shaw's *Pygmalion* and in Alan Jay Lerner's *My Fair Lady*, where the Cockney girl can fool a roomful of socialites not with the sense but with the mere pronunciation of the words she is speaking.

The second disorder is worse, the substitution of "vain matter" for "vain words." Here the scholastic philosophers provided examples. Their errors, several centuries old, still tripped people up.

Surely, like as many substances in nature which are solid do putrefy and corrupt into worms, so it is the property of good and sound knowledge to putrefy and dissolve into a number of subtle, idle, unwholesome, and (as I may term them) vermiculate questions, which have indeed a kind of quickness and life of spirit, but no soundness of matter or goodness of quality. This type of degenerate learning did chiefly reign amongst the schoolmen; who having sharp and strong wits, and abundance of leisure, and small variety of reading, but their wits being shut in the cells of a few authors (chiefly Aristotle, their dictator) as their persons were shut up in the cells of monasteries and colleges; and knowing little history, either of nature or time, did out of no great quantity of matter and infinite agitation of wit, spin out unto us those laborious webs of learning which are extant in their books [W6.121–22].

Along with its devastating congeries of adjectives, this passage illustrates Bacon's habit of employing animal images. His keenness for nature focuses his attention on specific creatures, often small ones. The *wormi-ness* is intense, both in Anglo-Saxon and the Latin *vermiculate*. Worms, and thus schoolmen, are *quick*, *lively*, and full of *agitation*. They also resemble spiders. These wormy, spidery fellows sometimes make sense but inevitably "they end in monstrous altercations and barking ques-tions" (W6.124). Here they have turned also into dogs. Even his literal phrases—"abundance of leisure," and "no great quantity of matter"—stick in the memory.

Worse than contentious learning, although not described so color-fully, is "fantastical learning," which depends upon two-fold deceit: the determination to mislead and, on the part of the receiver, a willingness to be deceived. This "foulest" vice of learning differs from the other two in the importance of the role of recipients, who will be seduced into adding fantasies of their own. Famous for condemning Aristotle as a "dictator" in his section on "vain words," in this part Bacon cites Aristotle as a man of "wisdom and integrity," who knows better than to practice this deception. Bacon offers astrology, natural magic, and alchemy as examples of fantastical learning.

Before commencing positively on the dignity of knowledge, Bacon lists ten "peccant humors." As pursuers of medieval and Renaissance studies know, the blending of the four humors (fire, air, earth, and water) explained many aspects of human physiology and psychology—what we sometimes call temperament or disposition. When an adjective like *peccant*, which means "sinful" or at least "disorderly," is applied to it, we are talking about not just natural temperament but the unwise exercise of it. Among peccant humors are such things as relying too much on the extremities of "antiquity" and "novelty" and failure to trust a new discovery because if it really mattered it would have long since been rec-ognized. But the most important error—the tenth of these humors, of course—is "mistaking or misplacing of the last or furthest end of knowl-edge," a failure to recognize that knowledge is "a rich storehouse, for the glory of the Creator and the relief of man's estate" (W6.134). He was suggesting to his readers that they actually possessed an "estate" that learning could promote. Life, Bacon kept insisting, could be improved.

Solomon (whose name Bacon spells Salomon) was not merely a wise man who warned against making too many books, for he—like

James—was a king, and "the glory of God is to conceal a thing, but the glory of the king is to find it out," for kings are "God's playfellows in that game" (W6.141). Bacon then provides a few pages of divine testimony in favor of learning in such figures as Moses, Solomon, Christ, the Apostles, and even, despite their villainous reputation in England, the Jesuits. The human embodiments of learning included such stalwarts as Queen Elizabeth, "endued with learning in her sex singular, and rare even amongst masculine princes" (W6.152), and Alexander the Great, a great warrior-king but also the pupil of Aristotle. "The images of men's wits and knowledges remain in books, exempted from the wrong of time and capable of perpetual renovation" (W6.168–69). Presumably Bacon would have responded favorably to such things as E-books and other electronic marvels, but only if they served as a medium of perpetual renovation. *Renovation*, it should be noted, is a vital word because it simultaneously calls attention to the importance of reclaiming what is valuable and presenting what is new.

Book Two of the *Advancement* is an extremely ambitious review, classification, and evaluation. Unlike Book One, patterned upon the classical oration and thus allowing Bacon opportunities for colorful denunciations of the errors of others, the second book comprises simple judgments as to whether the state of knowledge on a given subject is sufficient or deficient. As has often been pointed out, he did not complete it as neatly as Book One, but he made a brave sally into the state of human and divine learning in 1605. A number of its assertions touch on matters that occupy us today.

He begins with references to places of learning such as colleges. "I find it strange," he says, "that they are all dedicated to professions, and none left free to arts and services at large" (W6.174). Indeed, colleges were dedicated to professions—medicine, law, and the ministry—as today to a greatly increased number of professions. An opponent might argue that many contributions to the arts were made by those physicians, ministers, and lawyers, and later by the colonial administrators who graduated from the colleges at Oxford and Cambridge. "There is no education collegiate which is free," Bacon pointed out (W6.175). By *free* he means what we call *liberal*.

How many people today enter a "liberal arts" college to prepare for a specific profession, and how many of them find themselves heading, often by necessity, into some other way of life? On the basis of his later work Bacon may already have been thinking of what we call "vocational education," not free at all and guided by a technological or mechanical urge, an education that would not encourage a person to be philosophical. He may already have been thinking of a place of learning like Salomon's House, the epicenter of his late work *New Atlantis*.

Having divided knowledge into the subjects of history, poetry, and philosophy, he partitions the first of these into natural, civil, and ecclesiastical. Under civil history he proposes the subject of lives, meaning biographies. Another strange thing, he finds, is the infrequency of biography. He cites Ariosto's *Orlando Furioso*, which he probably knew in Sir John Harrington's 1591 translation. In the thirty-fourth and thirty-fifth cantos of this translation the poet "feigneth that at the end of the thread or web of every man's life there was a little medal containing the persons's name, and that Time waited upon the shears, and as soon as the thread was cut, caught the medals and carried them to the river of Lethe" (W6.194). These medals would be delivered by swans, which would carry them to a temple. As Harrington puts it,

> But as the swans that here are still flying are
> With written names unto the sacred port,
> So these historians learned and poets rare
> Preserve them in clear fame and good report.[2]

Ariosto's and Bacon's point here seems to be the desirability of preserving the reputation of good people, but later in Book Two he makes another point about biography, uncommon in its time, however familiar today. In discussing business, a subject he treats at some length, he argues that "histories of Lives is [*sic*] the most proper for discourse of business" (W6.359–60). His explanation is psychological, for it concerns the importance of the inner life, an uncommon emphasis in biographies up to Bacon's time, although visible in some of John Aubrey's *Brief Lives* and operative in both Montaigne's and Bacon's essays. Writing long before the terminology and procedures of psychology were devised, Bacon seems to be anticipating, if only dimly, a type of biography that did not come to fruition for about three centuries. Bacon would write a biography of King Henry VII, a worthy anticipation of biography offered not as a mere source of moral instruction but as a revelation of a person. As he told Prince Charles in his introduction, "I have not flattered him ... but took him to life as well as I could" (W11.25).

Bacon does not discuss poetry at any length. Most of his commentary would have been acceptable to Sidney. In poetry, he points out: "There is agreeable to the spirit of man a more ample greatness, a more exact goodness, and a more absolute variety, than can be found in the nature of things.... Poesy serveth and conferreth to magnanimity, morality, and to delectation. And therefore it was ever thought to have some participation of divineness, because it doth raise and erect the mind, by submitting the shows of things to the desires of the mind; whereas reason doth buckle and bow the mind unto the nature of things" (W6.203). Important as the desires of the mind are, ultimately, Bacon is more interested in the nature of things.

For Bacon and his contemporaries, philosophy encompasses many preoccupations. The study of the body he divides into four parts: medicine, cosmetic, athletics, and the sensual arts, with the first drawing the most attention. Cosmetic he associates with "artificial decoration," which he disparages as "being neither fine enough to deceive, nor handsome to use, nor wholesome to please" (W6.252). It would be interesting to know what he would think of this art as practiced in the twenty-first century. Athletics are not important, "for the Olympic Games are down," and in the sensual arts, "the chief deficience in them is of laws to repress them" (W6.253).

He divides reason into invention, judgment, memory, and tradition, the last important because it encompasses for him the transfer or delivery of knowledge. Although he makes a firm distinction between two highly contrasting types of delivery, he never resolves their use in his own practice. These two rhetorical devices he calls "magistral" and one of "probation." (He does not use "probational," so I will avoid the adjectival form.) He introduces them thus: "For as knowledges are now delivered, there is a kind of contract of error between the deliverer and the receiver: for he that delivereth knowledge desireth to deliver it *in such form as may be best believed and not as may be best examined;* [the italics are mine] and he that receiveth knowledge desireth rather present satisfaction than expectant inquiry; and so rather not to doubt than not to err; glory making the author not to lay open his weakness, and sloth making the disciple not to know his strength" (W6.289).

There is a "contract of error" because knowledge should be delivered in the same way that it was invented. A magistral writer, then, wants to sweep the reader off his feet, impel acceptance, while the writer who urges his reader to examine prose critically uses probation. As we know from Bacon's early essays, his favorite device for achieving probation is the aphorism: "Aphorisms, except they should be ridiculous, cannot be but of the pith and heart of sciences, for discourse of illustration is cut off; recitals of examples are cut off; discourse of connexion and order is cut off; descriptions of practice are cut off; so there remaineth nothing to fill the Aphorisms but some good quantity of observation" (W6.291).

Bacon sums up the matter thus: "Aphorisms, representing a knowledge broken, do invite men to enquire further" (W6.292). Both *probe* and *prove* derive from the Latin *probare*, meaning to *try*, *test*, or *examine*, and the two words are closely related. One probes in order to prove. But as Bacon would have it, a person probes in order to provoke a process which might lead interactively to proof. You or I might complete a proof by carefully examining and amending one of Bacon's broken bits of knowledge.

Was Bacon correct in his judgment of the utility of aphorisms? When a reader comes upon "He that hath wife and children hath given hostages to fortune" or "Studies serve for delight, for ornament, and for ability," does a process of analysis, of trying out, of testing, begin—or do we merely nod at these nuggets of wisdom? When we examine the numbered aphorisms in *The New Organon*, we find that they start concise and pointed, as an aphorism presumably should be, and later shade into a more magistral tone. What we are talking about, perhaps, are two contending sides of Francis Bacon: the one who gave us trials to question and work upon and the advisory one who enjoyed sweeping us along rhetorically.

One of his observations might be chewed on today. Some of the best books, he says, "are of so little effect towards honesty of life, because they are not read and resolved by men in their mature and settled years, but confined almost for boys and beginners" (W6.341). Unlike today's world, with the content and style of teaching materials whittled down to a presumed learning level (a level often adjusted to expectations of mediocrity), the boys of Bacon's time studied the classics, written for mature people. They studied the works of men like Virgil and Cicero, who wrote for adults. Did they turn away from these writers when through with formal education? The evidence suggests that older people—older writers, at least—did not discard these writers as pabulum for beginners; they continued to love "sweet Tully," as they might call Marcus Tullius Cicero, in their maturity. Bacon does not deny the great classics to "boys and beginners," however, nor does he analyze the reasons why mature people do not maintain an intellectual pace.

In the course of *The Advancement of Learning* Bacon quotes Machiavelli frequently. In his discussion of the will he approves of the author of *The Prince* for writing "what men do and not what they ought to do" (W6.327). The will for Bacon is primarily the organ charged with determining good and evil. A person must focus on what he calls the culture of the mind. "For if these two things are supposed, that a man set before him honest and good ends," he writes,

> and again that he be resolute, constant, and true unto them, it will follow that he shall mould himself into all virtue at once. And this is indeed like the work of nature; whereas the other course is like the work of the hand. For as when a carver makes an image, he shapes only that part whereupon he worketh; ... but contrariwise when nature makes a flower of living creature, she formeth rudiments of all the parts at one time; so in obtaining virtue by *habit*, while a man practiseth temperance, he doth not profit much to fortitude, nor the like; but when he dedicateth and applieth himself to *good ends*, look what virtue soever the pursuit and passage towards those ends doth commend unto him, he is invested of a precedent disposition to conform himself thereunto; which state of mind Aristotle doth excellently express himself, that it ought not to be called *virtuous*, but *divine* [W6.343].

The realm of social knowledge he divides into "the three summary actions of society; which are Conversation, Negotiation, and Government" (W6.348). Here he surprises us, writing much more about negotiation than government. Negotiation, that is business dealings, had interested him for a long time, being the subject of one of his first ten essays. "Business hath not been hitherto collected into writing" (W6.350), he notes, but of the writers who had touched upon it, he cites Solomon extensively. Actually, Proverbs and Ecclesiastes, Biblical books attributed to Solomon (although scholars consider them as dating over a period centuries longer than Solomon's lifetime) actually do offer much advice that, as one modern Biblical commentator observes of Proverbs, "shows 'what really works' and how to achieve success in the business of living a full life," a somewhat Machiavellian conclusion.[3]

Bacon emphasizes, in his discussion of negotiation, the "discerning of a man's self," which he compares to a "well setting forth of a man's virtues, fortunes, merits; and again in the artificial covering of a man's weaknesses, defects, disgraces" (W6.372)—in short, all the virtues and defects that you would like to know about the other person if you were trying to negotiate a successful deal. In business one must operate from strength. As in war, according to Machiavelli, "the true sinews of the wars are the sinews of men's arms," in business, Bacon argues, success is in "the sinews and steel of men's minds, wit, courage, audacity, resolution, temper, industry, and the like" (W6.381).

In one of the letters sent to important people with copies of his book, Bacon wrote, "I have led my life in civil causes; for which I was not very fit of nature, and more unfit by the preoccupation of my mind" (LL3.253). Had he known the future as well as he did the past, would he have given up the causes for which he found himself "unfit"? As things stood, civil duty required him to spend his time writing reports on such things as the commission's conclusions concerning the purveyors, who now, much to his liking, no doubt, discovered themselves banned "forever" from taking down any trees. Working people, the reader will remember, loved those trees "above ten times their value," because they represented "the beauty, countenance, and shelter of men's house," as Bacon had elegantly expressed it (LL3.184). When he was performing feats for which he was not "fit by nature," one feels that he felt an immense pride in accomplishing such things. He may have misjudged himself as a scholar out-of-place, or perhaps merely pretended to scorn his capacity for an activity—public service—which he knew he could and did practice successfully. This was an aspect of the art of rejecting artfulness described in Baldassare Castiglione's *Il Cortegiano* (*The Courtier*), a Renaissance handbook known to all courtiers of Bacon's time, as *sprezzatura*, a word for which English seems to have no equivalent.[4]

On May 10, 1606, Dudley Carleton, the recipient of many letters from one of the era's great letter writers, John Chamberlain, gave his friend a short description of the ceremony of Bacon's marriage to Alice Barnham (presumably the "handsome maiden" he had described three years before): "Sir Francis Bacon was married yesterday to his young wench in Maribone Chapel. He was clad from top to toe in purple and hath made himself and his wife such store of fine raiments of cloth of silver and gold that it draws deep into her portion. The dinner was kept at his father-in-law Sir John Packington's lodging over against the Savoy, where his chief guests were the three knights Cope, Hicks, and Beeston; and upon this conceit (as he said himself) that, since he could not have my lord of Salisbury in person, which he wished, he would have him at least in his representative body."[5]

This passage deserves a few comments. Can we determine Carleton's attitude toward the bride? Is a *wench* a young woman of no great moral distinction? Yes and no, now and in Bacon's time. Generally, however, the noun signified a young woman, sometimes a rustic young woman, which Alice was not, being the daughter of an alderman. Definitions of the term include "female servant," "mistress," and "prostitute." However Carleton judged her, he saw her as a very young woman, and the sight of a fortyish man with persistent financial problems marrying a teenaged daughter of a wealthy man would hardly have surprised him.

Today we would expect the dress of a bride to be more fetching than her husband's costume, but Bacon was clearly the star of the show; thus his full-length purple, financed by his father-in-law, caught the guest's eye more clearly than Lady Bacon's "raiments." Carleton's supposition that their purchase was eating into the "portion" on which Bacon was no doubt relying is an interesting point, but it does not disclose to us Bacon's own attitude. The three named guests represented Robert Cecil, now Earl of Salisbury, in his offhand way of honoring his cousin by sending three men who probably appreciated cutting in on the available entertainment and viands.

Thereafter Bacon's mate more or less disappears from sight. In his explanation, Spedding fulfills the official mid–Victorian outlook:

"Twenty years of married life in which the gossips and scandal-mongers of the time found nothing to talk about have a right to remain exempt from intrusion" (LL3.292). Bacon does refer to his wife in a letter three months after the wedding acknowledging a friend's "loving congratulation for my doubled life, as you call it, I thank you for it. No man may better conceive the joys of a good wife than yourself, with whom I dare not compare. But I thank God I have not taken a thorn out of my foot to put it into my side. For as my state is somewhat amended, so I have no other circumstance of complaint. But herein we will dilate when we meet; which meeting will be more joyful if my Lady bear a part to mend the music" (LL3.298–99).

Alice was no thorn. That Bacon lacked the qualities of a romantic lover the reader has already guessed. She brought financial assistance to him; in return he gave her a comfortable and prestigious social position. Until an incident very late in his life there is little more to say.

Again passed over for solicitor general, Bacon complains to an old friend, Lord Chancellor Ellesmere, who would understand an aside that might well have fitted into "Of Marriage and Single Life": "A married man is seven years elder in his thoughts the first day" (LL3.295). Marriage had, so to speak, thrust Bacon emotionally into his fifties. The new Lady Bacon would live at Gorhambury where the elder Lady Bacon still lived, approaching eighty and probably infirm. If there existed any conflict between the two ladies, no word of it has come down.

In August of 1606 a friend of Bacon's at Gray's Inn, Jeremiah Bettenham, died, a much more emotional experience than a marriage: "No man knoweth better than yourself what part I bear in grief for Mr. Bettenham's departure. For in good faith I never thought myself at better liberty than when he and I were by ourselves together. His end was Christian and comfortable, in parfite memory and in parfite charity, and the disposition of that he left wise, just, and charitable" (LL3.298).

A historian at the inn where Bacon learned, taught, and often lived informs us that "as late as the year 1754 there was standing in Gray's Inn Gardens on the west side within that space where in 1798 there was a circle of trees, an octagonal seat covered with a roof which had been erected by Francis Bacon (afterward Lord Verulam) to the memory of his friend, Mr. Bettenham." This passage goes on to locate Bacon's place at the inn: "Lord Bacon's chambers were in No. 1, Coney Court, which formerly stood on the site of the present row of buildings at the west side of Gray's Inn Square, adjoining the gardens. The whole of Corey Court was burnt down by fire ... about 1678."[6]

This memorial testifies to three loves of Bacon's life too often omitted by those who write of him: gardens, Gray's Inn, and friendship. We should remember that Bacon had long been exercising his fondness for nature in the establishment and maintenance of gardens. If the idea of a man like him actually rolling up his sleeves and working on the land seems preposterous, we can easily see him at least closely supervising the people who did the work and scrutinizing the results.

We know that his gardening at Gray's Inn goes back as far as 1597. As one historian of the inn puts it, "It is believed on very good grounds that the gardens were originally laid out in the year 1597, under the direction of Lord Bacon [who at the time, of course, was many years short of the peerage], the then Treasurer of the Society, and there is still preserved on the northwest side of the garden a 'catalpa-tree,' which, tradition says, was planted by him. He evidently took great delight in these gardens, and there is an Order of Pension extant in the following terms: '4 July 1597. Ordered that the sum of £7 15s. 4d. due to Mr. Bacon, for planting of elm trees in the walk, be paid next term.'"[7]

There is another such order for more elm trees the following term, no doubt with the same provider. We can guess that Bacon, who wrote much about trees, enjoyed them in his long residences at the inn Gray's Inn, a place that served him well—and that he served well.

On June 25, 1607, King James approved Bacon as solicitor general, the first judiciously important position that he had obtained. Now forty-six years old, Bacon must have felt relief charged by annoyance that the wait had extended so long. His authority would grow, and as it grew, he had to re-balance his civic and his philosophical lives. Much of his spare time at Gray's Inn or at Gorhambury in his summers away from London he would spend on his next and most ambitious publication, his *Instauratio Magna* (*The Great Instauration*).

Since his brother's death, Bacon needed the assistance of people with access to the European continent. Toby Matthew, who had helped introduce him to King James, performed this role very well. In 1605

Matthew had gone off to Italy, a place always simultaneously dangerous and attractive to Englishmen, and had succumbed to one of the dangers: conversion to Roman Catholicism. Returning to England in 1607, he was clapped into prison. On August 27, accompanied by a keeper, he visited Bacon, a friend who might help him to regain his liberty. Bacon urged Matthew to renounce his new religion, but he refused. After he returned to detention, Bacon wrote to him: "I myself am out of doubt, that you have been miserably abused, when you were first seduced; but that which I take in compassion, others may take in severity.... Good Mr. Matthew, receive yourself back from these courses of perdition" (LL4.10). But Matthew continued in his new faith. In assisting Matthew, a stubborn opponent of the Church of England, the church of his distinguished prelatical father, Bacon was inviting criticism, but he pulled strings for the man, who on February 7, 1608, was released and allowed six weeks to organize withdrawal from the kingdom. In the years that followed Bacon benefited from this relationship with his European agent.

Although his work, both political and philosophical, was advancing, Bacon sat down one morning in the summer of 1608 in his vacation home to do at the age of forty-seven what many men do at this time of life—recognize and tackle a climacteric, a kind of male menopause. This recognition, resulting in a burst of note-taking, lasted almost a week, and because the results of it have come down to us, we get this infrequent, although often obscure and confusing, opportunity to view Bacon's life as he saw it. Dissatisfactions loom larger than accomplishments. A dissatisfied man of forty-seven realizes that the time for doing well is narrowing. In 1608, when men could not expect many more years, it narrowed much more.

5

Prospects and
Possibilities

It is the morning of July 25, 1608. Bacon is at work in his study. We cannot be sure, but it is probably his study at Gorhambury, for summer vacation has begun, and people fortunate enough to have country estates repair to them. We also know that one month later Bacon will write a letter from Gorhambury in which he considers returning to London. The memorandum he is compiling covers many serious subjects. It is the kind of document a man writes for himself, employing all sorts of shortcuts that would puzzle anyone else, but it was preserved nonetheless, probably because it later fell into the hands of a man who perceived some value in it. To a person trying to get close to Bacon several centuries later, it has considerable value. If Bacon wrote other documents of this type, they have not come down to us. He expected that many of his writings would interest the world, but not a series of prompts for himself.

This document occupies fifty-five pages in Spedding's edition of the *Letters and Life*. The style is helter-skelter, the content often abbreviated. The first entry identifies one major theme of Monday's note-taking: "To make a stock of £2000 allwaies in readyness for bargaines and occasions" (LL4.40). The expected income from the position of clerk of the Star Chamber, to which Bacon had been appointed nine days earlier, equaled that sum. The clerk received, entered, and certified the bills, pleadings, records, rules, and decrees of the court.

Shifting to the realm, he considers that many legal and financial details of the Union remained unresolved five years after James's arrival, and its economic prospects also looked unclear. He names influential

Scotsmen with considerable financial resources who, with the assistance of a Parliamentarian who also was an influential part of the king's judiciary, might help solidify the Union. Bacon contemplates the personal economic problems of public officials, who, lacking guaranteed incomes and pensions, had constantly to examine and elevate their own financial status and security. The number of officials holding multiple positions, sometimes incompatible ones, also preoccupied him. His list included his friend Lord Ellesmere, who as Lord Keeper retained his position as Master of the Rolls. Bacon knew that his own father had simultaneously served as Lord Keeper and Attorney of the Wards, but these multiple holdings block the paths of other ambitious men. He notes one person with "Long stay 21 years" (LL4.51), while he finds the Earl of Dunbar "nibbling solemly[;] he distinguisheth but apprehendes not" (LL4.51).

Bacon did not accomplish much early on that day, for he suffered "that lightness and cooling in my sydes which many tymes I doe, but soon after I found a symptome of melancholy.... I tooke 3 pilles of aggregative [a sort of collection of ingredients?] ... then though my medicine was not fully settled I made a light supper without wyne, and fownd myself light and at peace after it" (LL4.54). He went back to work, and his mind turned to several initiatives, including one "to wryte some treatise of advise towching prohibiciouns and jurisdictions of Cowrts" (LL4.54). He also reminded himself "to think of matters against next Parlam for satisfaction of K[ing] and people ... otherwise with respect *ad Poll è gem*," (Spedding, caught in the tide of such entries, recommends *policy* and *people* for the apparently foreign abbreviations.) Bacon is acknowledging an adjustment between the needs to fill the Exchequer for the king and to keep the people content. These entries reflect a head full of considerations and plans which move back and forth between personal and public concerns, often interconnected and thus intermixed in his mind. Before the day ends he jots down many items beginning with phrases like "to speak," "to digest," "to harken," "to acquaint," "to send"—in short, he is making a long list of things to do. The mere fact that he can make such a list suggests the extraordinary pace he maintained.

The manuscript indicates the calendar of the week's work. One page begins with a notation at the head: "Transportat. [presumably something like "moving to"] July 26, 1608," which would have been Tuesday. On that day his thoughts focus on his own and the world's intellectual life. In one phrase, "Q of learned men beyond the seas to be made" (LL4.64), the Q obviously stands for *questions* or *queries* to be directed to men abroad. He refers to aphorisms, those favorite probing devices he favored, to a translation (into Latin) of *The Advancement of Learning* and to some books he must acquire. He senses a lack of scholars to assist him in his reformation of knowledge. His work on providing for the *postnati*—the young men, Scotsmen in particular, born after James's ascension to the English crown—has reminded him of the possibility of an intellectual *postnati*, consisting of promising young men from the universities. The problem is not the lack of young men but the condition of existing schools and universities: institutions like Westminster and Eton, Trinity College at Cambridge where he and Anthony studied, Magdalen College at Oxford. These are mighty, but tradition envelops them. Peopled with admirers of the classics, they are not promoting the advancement of knowledge. As on several other occasions, he considers the need for a different kind of place for study, a college that could encourage inventors (by which he means *discoverers*) by appropriating "allowance for travailing, allowance for experiments" (LL4.66), boons for scholars that would not become common for centuries. These allowances which scholars take for granted today in 1608 existed chiefly in the envisaging mind of Sir Francis Bacon. In later writings he would add to scholarly incentives the notion of rewards for scholarship in the form of an establishment that we would call a Hall of Fame.

From these visions he turns to his conception of history, for one cannot invent something new without knowing—and of course criticizing—something old. Bacon himself revered the classics. A continuing problem was the relationship between becoming a good classicist and possessing the capacity to filter out the inadequacies of the scholars of old. He hopes to obtain a history of marvels, some no doubt true, others of course merely fantasies, but how efficiently can one distinguish between truth and fantasy? To what extent does the time required to become a perceptive classicist justify the effort?

On Wednesday, the third day of this week of short- and long-term planning, he muses on one of the largest and oldest philosophical topics:

motion. Heraclitus had argued that the world is subject to restless change. Parmenides disagreed: there is an abiding basis. The classic example is the river; the water keeps going by, but the river remains. Latin dominates his notes, for a philosophical subject calls for the international language. He speculates on how things move, why and where they move. He inquires into "the severall kyndes or diversities of mocion" (LL4.69). From our own century it is easy to see that his discussion employs language richly, yet very traditionally, and mathematics not at all. A notion like *miles per hour*, simple even for a nonmathematical person today, could exist only vaguely in Bacon's time, for it represented "a thousand paces," a measurement dependent on the varying expanses of a walker's steps. Bacon refers to "the times and moments wherein motions work," but he tells us nothing about speed.

He even combines his English and Latin resources in the same sentence, for instance: "Nodi et globi motuü, and how they concurre and how they succeed and interchaunge in things most frequent" (LL4.69). Nodi usually meant "knot," while globi suggests "ball" or "sphere." So what agents are succeeding and interchanging here—something tied up and something more expanded? A knot is an interesting image applicable in many ways, suggestive but not precise. From our standpoint, precision is what Bacon needs, but the imagery he employs works against precision. Suspicious as he was about words that did not pertain to realities, Bacon did not do much to promote a technical vocabulary. Although scholars differ in their judgments as to what Bacon lacked to function as a scientist rather than merely an interested amateur observer, they cite skill in mathematics very often; Bacon himself called attention to this deficiency. He notes the relationship between heat and motion, the power of motion, the effects of motion. He is, like Heraclitus and Parmenides in past centuries, philosophizing.

As he works along, he moves into Latin almost exclusively, occasionally breaking back into English. Stuck in the midst of Latin passages we find "all ripenings, coction, assation, the gathering perfection of wines, beers, syders, &c. by age and tyme" (LL4.72) as representing one type of motion. Coction has to do with change, in boiling as the result of heat, assation is just a variation of the word for testing or trying out which gives him the word essay, and then he uses the generalized expression of several processes as "gathering perfection." What he lacks here is just as important as mathematics, but it has not yet arrived: chemistry. Whether any contemporary could have found enlightenment in Bacon's work on Wednesday is difficult to say. He feels impelled to pursue, as much as he can, what we call physics, a science not yet born, because he venerates nature, which is at the heart of it. An intense observer of nature who can fashion analogies based on these observations, he lacks a Newton's or an Einstein's mental avenue capable of measuring material forces and describing them denotatively.

Thus on Thursday morning he turns, perhaps with relief, to subjects more clearly within his scope: possible means of renewing the kingdom's sense of greatness; "civilizing" Ireland, for instance, establishing further colonies, perhaps annexing the Low Countries before Spain accomplished the same. He does not get far, however, with these projects. He ponders his own life in connection with the nation's prospects. Perhaps after his long session of the previous day he has gone out and looked his estate over, for he makes quite specific proposals about walks and walls and ponds and streams and timber. He wishes

> the grownd to be inclosed square with a bricke wall, and frute trees plashed upon it; on the owt side of it to sett fayre straite byrches on 2 sides and lyme trees on 2 sides, some x foot distante from the wall, so that the wall may hide most of the shaft of the tree and onely the tufts appear above.
> From ye wall to have a waulk of some 25 foote on a higher level.
> Under that waulke some 4 foote to have a fine litell stream rune upon gravell and fine peppell [pebbles] to be putt into ye bottome, of a yard and an half over, wch shall make the whole residue of the grownd an Iland; the banque to be turfed and kept cut; the banq I mean of the ascent to ye upper waulk: no hedg hear but some fine standerds well kept [LL4.76].

He continues in this description for several lines longer. After some contemplation of his own health, he reviews his financial situation, also in close detail. Concluding that his assets outweigh his expenses, he cheers himself with a list of debts "absolutly cleered." He closes by reminding himself of some legal business at hand: the king is interested in straightening out some warrants on properties of two lords. No doubt he must get about this business soon.

On Friday he returns briefly to his obsession with an official who he still thinks may provide assistance. Robert Cecil, now Lord Salisbury and Lord Treasurer, must deal with the king's debt of more than a million pounds. Bacon cannot do much about the debt, but he can help this man do his duties more effectively; he can, for instance, show him how to be more graceful in his speech. Salisbury could do much for him, if so inclined. Finally Bacon turns to his "services on foot," for he still hopes to equalize and recompile English laws. He still ponders the never-ending task of countering the herders' appropriation of peasants' agricultural plots. He is preparing for the next session of Parliament, which promises—threatens—to be all about money.

For most of a week he has jotted down many extremely varied proposals both personal and public, both possible and unlikely. His musings have had a stream-of-consciousness quality. He will never be able to fulfill many of these plans and prospects, but he has perhaps motivated himself to continue doggedly, and he has reminded himself that at the age of forty-seven he cannot expect many more years of activity. Can he imagine that he will have the eighteen years we know he will be granted?

The following year Bacon wrote several letters to Matthew, now back on the Continent. In one he enclosed "a leaf or two of the Preface [to *The Great Instauration*], carrying some figure of the whole work" (LL4.132–33). His good friend may have been the earliest reader of a portion of a major work that would occupy Bacon for more than another decade. It is impossible to judge how closely this "leaf or two" resembled the version composed in Latin and published in 1620, or in Bacon's English translation of the same. Nor can we judge whether the preface Bacon referred to in 1609 is more like the preface of 1620 or Bacon's *Proemium*. The former begins with this heading: "*That the state of knowledge is not prosperous nor greatly advancing; and that a way must be opened for the human understanding entirely different from any hitherto known, and other helps provided, in order that the mind may exercise over the nature of things the authority which properly belongs to it*" (W8.25).

Or did Matthew read something more like the eventual *Proemium* of this work? Let us assume that he did, for it demonstrates a vital aspect of Francis Bacon that has often been, and indeed continues to be, ignored. In the long, periodic first sentence he proposes the investigation of "that commerce between the mind of man and the nature of things, which is more precious than anything on earth, or at least than anything that is of the earth" (W8.17). Any serious study of Bacon's works will confirm the intensity of this conviction.

Around the end of 1609, Bacon brought out a volume called *De Sapientia Veterum*, which would be known, in its translation, as *The Wisdom of the Ancients*. To a considerable extent this work features Bacon's own thoughts, which he judged would be more palatable to his readers if they represented thoughts certified by the ancients, who in some cases, Bacon points out, may have been anticipating good seventeenth-century wisdom. He retells, for instance, the race between the swift Atalanta and Hippomenes, who could marry her if he could beat her in a race but would lose his life if he could not. For Bacon, Atalanta is not just a swift girl: "Art, which is meant by Atalanta, is in itself, if nothing stand in the way, far swifter than Nature" (W13.143). Atalanta is Art and Hippomenes is Nature. But Hippomenes, beating her by strewing apples, helps Bacon prove Art's subjection to Nature. Sir Arthur Gorges verified Bacon's prediction of suitability for an English-reading audience by providing a translation in 1619.

In 1610, King James's main problem matched that of his solicitor general. Like his predecessor, especially in her late years, James was plunging into debt; unlike her, he was not a good economist. When the Earl of Dorset, his Lord Treasurer, died in 1608, he had replaced him with the ever-present Salisbury. Like all executives dealing with a legislative body determined to maintain control of the budget, James sought to escape the horrors of raising taxes. Salisbury fiddled with his plan for impositions on imports and exports, lessening them on such necessary or popular products as sugar and tobacco and increasing them elsewhere, but the debt still amounted to several hundred thousand pounds. For a 1610 meeting of Parliament, Salisbury began, directly but perhaps not wisely, by presenting the balance sheet—more specifically his cousin Bacon presented the balance sheet. The funeral of the queen (now dead nearly seven years) had mushroomed the debt, as had money owed to the Low Countries, funds for the army in Ireland (they had beaten Tyrone and wanted to be paid for it), and various other projects.

Bacon's job was to obtain funds; Parliament showed more interest in questioning the apparatus that was sustaining—at least in part—the monarch. Did the king have the right to increase impositions, or for that matter, to control them in the first place? Like all legislatures, this House wanted to know what they could get in return. Items such as purveyance and wardships were still unsettled. As the nominal possessor of wardships, James could give them away "at certain reasonable rates" (LL 4.161). As the session dragged on, Bacon spoke on wardships, unconvincingly to members of the Lower House. After a resubmission of the royal request, "He persuaded the House to present these matters of Impositions as grievances to the Commonwealth (which the King had given us leave to do), but not to question his power and prerogative to impose" (LL4.183). Bacon, who had sat among these men for decades and heartily wished to reconcile Parliament with the monarchical side he now represented, found this conflict a particularly testing one.

It was now May, and several months of wrangling had produced no agreement. Other matters of concern had arisen. Henri IV was assassinated in Paris on May 14. Regicide petrified Englishmen, who had breathed a sigh of relief when the aging Queen Elizabeth died, no undesirable claimants to the throne came forth, and a peaceful succession took place—despite the appearance of a new king overbearing in his insistence on power and prerogative. Summer beckoned; Parliament was prorogued until the fall.

That summer brought an end to a life of which nothing has been told for many years for the lack of letters or other materials. Bacon wrote to Sir Michel Hicks: "It is but a wish and not any ways to desire it to your trouble. But I heartily wish I had your company here at my Mother's funeral which I purpose on Thursday next in the forenoon. I dare promise you a good sermon to be made by Mr. Fenton, the preacher of Gray's Inn; for he never maketh other. Feast I make none. But if I mought have your company for two or three days at my house I should pass over the mournful occasion with more comfort.... I commend myself to my Lady, and commend my wife to you both and rest. Yours ever assured/Fr. Bacon" (LL4.217–18).

Bacon's mother, long at Gorhambury, had lived for over eighty years. Anthony had saved her letters in the 1590s. Later there were few letters and for years no necessity for any. She was buried in St. Michael's

Church in St. Albans, near Gorhambury. A stormier person than her two sons, she commanded their respect despite the frequency of her untimely advice on their welfare. Perhaps Bacon had absorbed his own fondness for conveying advice from her. Her powers of mind probably influenced her younger son more than did her highly-developed maternal instincts. Later he chose to be buried near her rather than near his father at St. Paul's.

Back in London, Parliament and the king hoped to achieve a "Great Contract" that would protect the rights of the former and adequately supply the latter, but once negotiations resumed, they went essentially nowhere. Each side distrusted the other, and the middlemen in the debate about purveyance and wardships expected to be the inevitable victims of any substantial reform. Bacon's account of the proceedings before the dissolution of Parliament in November, hardly a stylistic masterpiece, fumbles toward a less than embarrassing expression of the stalemate (featuring four uses of the inconsequential *may*), finally articulated in a metaphor from nature: "The proportion of the king's supply is not now in question: for when that shall be, it may be I shall be of opinion that we should give so now, as we may the better give again. But as things stand for the present, I think the point of honour and reputation is that which his Majesty standeth most upon; that our gift may be least be like those showers that may serve to lay the winds, though they do not water the earth" (LL4.234).

Bacon's part in this budgetary failure was minor, for his task was merely to present Salisbury's argument on the king's behalf. Had his stature been a little higher, he might have been able to inspire James, who used language more clearly when not obsessed about asserting his authority, to a more proficient level of discourse. Early in 1611, Bacon wrote to the king to remind him that should the present attorney general falter—his health was failing—he was ready to assume the position. He also wrote to Salisbury, from whom experience should have told him nothing was to be expected, "Though I find age and decays grow upon me, yet I may have a flash or two of spirit left to do you service" (LL4.246). Indeed, Bacon soon would complete a half-century.

In another letter to the king, he opined on a matter involving a rich man, Thomas Sutton, who had died on December 12 after leaving bequests for a new hospital, the establishment of a grammar school, and a measure of aid to the religious establishment. Since Sutton had left little to individuals who probably expected more, they challenged him. Although not officially involved in the case, Bacon advised the king that if the will were judged deficient, the king might usefully modify it. These modifications never happened, but Bacon's criticism of the will reveals his thoughts on hospitals, ecclesiastical matters, and more importantly, the advancement of learning.

Sutton had wanted to establish a new grammar school, of which Bacon said, "There are already too many." His explanation of this anti-educational judgment was "that which he meant for the teachers of children, your Majesty should make for teachers of men." The state had more scholars than it could employ, and those excessive scholars would become "indigent, idle, and wanton people" (LL4.253). We must remember that Bacon probably meant by *scholars* somewhat educated people, not university professors. Bacon would rather see the money go to real professors. He makes a long and cogent argument, ending with one of the homely images of which he was fond, recommending that "that mass of wealth, that was in the owner little better than a stack or heap of muck, may be spread over your kingdom to many fruitful purposes, your Majesty planting and watering, and God giving the increase" (LL4.254).

His judgment—undoubtedly wrongheaded to twenty-first century readers, especially Americans—would have been widely accepted in Bacon's time and place. Education was for boys judged most educable, a common conviction in many societies. We can argue that Bacon's recommendation for not increasing facilities for primary education might prevent a young boy or two here and there from becoming a scholar that the state might someday need, but Bacon sought an inducement to attract outstanding men into the vital profession of teaching "men."

In 1611, challenges to the authority of the old Court of the Marshalsea resulted in a request for a new court. The challenges pertained to the coverage of the court, which had been established to try certain offenses committed in the monarch's household or nearby, no matter where that household gathered at a given time. The new court would be the Court of the Verge, the verge defined as an area within twelve miles of that household. The offenses to be considered by this court were those concerning "God and his church … the King and his estate" and any concerning "the King's people" (LL4.267). Bacon as solicitor general recommended that the new court should express the legal order and precision for which he characteristically strove but could not seem to get through other legal minds.

The year 1612 brought an important death that subtracted from the administration of King James the Earl of Salisbury, formerly Sir Robert Cecil. He had carried on during James's first nine years, as his father had for many years with Queen Elizabeth. James had called Burghley's small and malformed son his "little beagle," and although the man had done little for Bacon, he had served James well. Bacon attempted several times to advise the king about a successor. In an unfinished and obviously unsent first letter he described himself in Salisbury's day as "having been as a hawk tied to another's fist, that mought sometimes bait and proffer but could never fly" (LL4.279). Whether the metaphor applied specifically to his deceased cousin or more generally to other human obstacles to Bacon's advancement, we cannot be sure.

By printing Bacon's preliminary attempts, as he often did, Spedding gave insight into fits of moodiness that Bacon almost always decided to exclude from the finished copy. One notable and deleterious exception we will notice later. He began again, this time characterizing Salisbury as "a fit man to keep things from growing worse but no very fit man to reduce things to be much better" (LL4.280). Spedding could not establish whether this assessment was ever sent, but in one which the king did receive Bacon emphasized that his majesty should work with the Parliament, especially the House of Commons, of which he continued to be a member: "I will be ready as a chessman to be wherever your Majesty's royal hand shall set me" (LL4.282). For the time being James did not replace Salisbury. Bacon applied also for the position of Master of the Rolls, which would have supplemented his income, without success.

Prince Henry, the heir to the throne, sickened and died on November 6. The Princess Elizabeth, on the verge of a marriage to a German count, had to postpone the event until the following February, baffling the inns of courts' attempt to promote an elaborate ceremony. Eventually

Gray's Inn finally managed to present a masque for the occasion, of which "Bacon was the chief contriver" (LL4.344), despite his occasional disparagement of the theatrical arts.

Bacon published the second edition of his *Essays* in 1612, an important step in his literary career, although less so than the third edition. The first book had consisted of only ten short essays but drew public attention and confirmed Bacon's desire to expand it. Had the second edition been the last, it would certainly have become a famous book like the third. It contained thirty-eight essays, some of which—such as "Of Great Place," "Of the True Greatness of Kings and Estates," and "Of Judicature"—represented a man who had gained much experience in contemplating such topics in the last fifteen years. The individual essays, including the retained ones, were longer. Although the 1612 edition did not carry the final title, *Essays or Counsels, Civil and Moral*, he was clearly on the way to characterizing the collection as a morally instructive work. Baconian scholars have also pointed out that a number of the 1612 essays contribute studies of moral principles mentioned as desirable in Book Two of *The Advancement of Learning*, showing it to be an adjunct to his most important work to date. The 1612 essays rely less often on aphorisms, although he improved some of the remaining ones.

As Bacon noted, calling attention to the example of Seneca's letters to Lucilius, "The word [essay] is late, but the thing is ancient" (LL4.340). "Of Judicature," right from the beginning, illustrates Bacon's conventional judicial bias: "Judges ought to remember that their office is *jus dicere*, and not *jus dare*; to interpret law, and not to make law, or give law" (W12.370). Another characteristic—his love of nature—he demonstrates by including natural objects both literally and metaphorically. Although his essays "Of Gardens" and "Of Plantations" come later, there are many tributes to nature in his mid-career. In "Of Greatness of Kingdoms" he argues for the militant spirit in a great kingdom but ridicules having what we might call too many chiefs and not enough warriors. "Nobilitie & Gentlemen multiplying in too great a proportion maketh the common subject grow to bee a pesant and base swaine driven out of heart, and but the Gentlemans laborer; like as it is in coppices, where if you leave your straddels [young trees] too thick, you shall never have cleane underwood, but shrubbes and bushes" (W12.377).

To look ahead for a moment in the somewhat expanded later version, which also has an expanded title, "Of the True Greatness of Kingdoms and Estates," he reminds the reader a few lines later that King Henry VII, whose biography Bacon had by that time written: "was profound and admirable; in making farms and houses of husbandry of a standard; that is, maintained with such a proportion of land unto them, as may breed a subject to live in convenient plenty and no servile condition; and to keep the plough in the hands of the owners, and not mere hirelings" (W12.180).

Bacon also demonstrates the precision of his references to the small features of nature and the artifacts for dealing with it in "Of Goodness and Goodness in Nature." He begins with a distinction: "*Goodnesse* I call the habite; and *goodnesse of Nature*, the inclination" (W12.318). The habit of goodness, which Bacon believed derived from Christianity, prevails, if nature's goodness has roused it. Goodness, however, can bestow inappropriate gifts: "Neither give thou *Æsops* Cocke a *gem*, who would be better pleased and happier, if he had had a Barly corn" (W12.318). Givers must also be careful not to overtax their resources: "Thou maiest doe as much good with little meanes, as with great. For otherwise in feeding the stremes, thou driest the fountaine" (W12.319).

A moment later Bacon uses a natural image from Plutarch to characterize misanthropes, who "bring men to the bough, and yet have never a tree for the purpose in their gardens, as *Timon* had. Such dispositions are the very errors *of human nature*: and yet they are the fittest timber to make great Politques [politicians] of; like to knee-timber that is good for shippes that are ordained to be tossed, but not for building houses that shall stand firme" (W12.319).

One might suppose the last image to be inaccurate: do not mariners want straight timbers? Not entirely. The *Oxford English Dictionary* tells us that a knee timber is "a piece of timber naturally bent used to secure parts of the ship together, esp. one with an angular bead used to connect the beams and the timbers." In *Timon of Athens,* Act V, Scene I, Shakespeare dramatized Timon's tree:

> I have a tree which grows here in my close
> That mine own use invites me to cut down,
> And shortly must I fell it. Tell my friends,

> Tell Athens, in the sequence of degree
> From high to low throughout, that whoso please
> To stop affliction, let him take his haste.
> Come hither ere my tree hath felt the axe.
> And hang himself.

Timon stomps back into his cave and dies before anyone can respond to his invitation.

Shakespeare's play surely predates Bacon's 1612 *Essays*, but there is no reason to suppose that his Timon influenced Bacon.

Several of the essays introduced in 1612 focus on topics that he had seen displayed time and again in his years under King James. Observe his sharpness in the opening lines of "Of Ambition." "Ambition is like choler, which is an humor that maketh men active, full of alacrity and stirring, if it be not stopped. But if it be stopped, and cannot have his way, it becometh adust [scorched or parched], and thereby maligne and venomous" (W12.349–50). As an ambitious man, he surely recognizes this susceptibility.

The opening lines of "Of Counsel," like so many of his openings, describe the sort of man Bacon, from the days of his friendship with Essex, strove to be: "The greatest trust betweene man and man is the trust of giving counsel. For in other confidences men commit the partes of their life, their lands, their goods, their child, their credit; some particuler affaire. But to such as they make their counsellors, they commit the whole; by how much more are they obliged to all faith, and integrity. The wisest Princes need not thinke it any diminution to their greatnesse, or derotation to their sufficiency, to rely upon counsel" (W12.330).

To take a 1612 essay on a subject that Bacon clearly had pondered deeply, the opening lines of "Of Great Place" reflect the anomalies of the position for which he saw so many men striving. "Men in great place are thrice servants; servants of the Souveraigne, or state; servants of fame; and servants of businesse. So as they have no freedome, neither in their persons, nor in their actions, nor in their times. It is a strange desire, to seeke power and to lose liberty: or to seeke power over others and to lose power over a mans selfe. The rising unto place is laborious, and by paines men come to greater paines; and it is sometimes base; and by indignities men come to dignities: the standing is slippery; and the regresse is either a downfall, or at least an *Ecclipse*; which is a melancholy thing" (W12.324–25).

One 1612 essay that does not pertain to the political world is "Of Friendship." The following passage poses a couple of curiosities: "Live not in continuall smother, but take some friends with whom to communicate. It will unfold thy understanding; it will evaporate thy affections; it will prepare thy businesse" (W12.337). To *evaporate affections* is literally to draw out the affections like vapor from a solid substance. Yet it makes sense; we talk about "drawing people out." What kind of business is meant, and how would friendship *prepare* it? We will come back to this relationship at another point. This aphorism has a neat, rhythmical tripartite force, a characteristic found so often in Bacon, but it begs for the development that in 1612, at least, he was requiring his reader to work out for himself. An aphorism can on occasion be feasted upon, but it is not on the whole a sustaining construction.

Another essay that touches on friendship is "Of Followers and Friends," which, unlike "Of Friendship," appears in all three editions. One tends to wonder about the junction of these two concepts, for the emphasis, up to the conclusion of the essay, is on followers. One statement, which appears near the end of the essay each time, counters his positive attitude toward friendship: "There is little friendship in the world, and least of all between equals." He then adds the qualification, "That that is, is between *Superiour* and *Inferiour*" (W12.366). In this essay Bacon may have been thinking of the possibility of followers *as* friends, although it is odd that he did not have made a small verbal change to solidify the point and not appear to contradict himself.

Bacon sometimes develops relationships between topics by pairing essays. He links several pairs in 1612: "Of Love" and "Of Friendship," "Of Atheism" and "Of Superstition," "Of Beauty" and "Of Deformity," "Of Marriage and Single Life" and "Of Parents and Children." The one about marriage brims with its bald assertion that "hee that hath wife and children, hath given hostages to fortune" (W12.321). Bacon had married only two years before, but his thoughts about families are very impersonal. He could speak more kindly of marriage and family. In *The Wisdom of the Ancients* he describes Orpheus as "averse from woman and from marriage; for the sweets of marriage and the dearness of children commonly draw men away from performing great and lofty services to the commonwealth" (W13.112–13). Duty pulls men away from recognizably sweet and dear family members. Bacon and his wife produced no children, but many a couple would agree with his opening aphorism of the paired essay, "The joys of *Parents* are secret; and so are their griefs and fears. They cannot utter the one; nor they will not utter the other" (W12.99). The essay goes on to express fondness, not hostility, to the family. Personal experience counts for Bacon—but less than observation and resources from his extensive reading, and all of these sources celebrate the family even as the author plausibly insists that they frequently detract from the performance of public duties.

The king's financial problems continued, and Bacon served on an ad hoc committee for "Repair of the King's Estate and Raising of Monies." He wrote the report, which had somehow to balance the royal need he was obliged to express and a Parliament determined to prove that its members did not constitute the namby-pamby body James had dominated in Scotland. Just about every possibility was considered, even a duty on imported starch. A committee wrote one report, Bacon another, not radically different but concocted for the king's eyes only. It would be necessary to call another session of Parliament, which the king expected to advise in his usually heavy-handed way. Royal servant and veteran Tudor respecter of the primacy of the monarch though he was, Bacon had learned that Stuarts differed from Tudors and James from Elizabeth. Bacon wrote (for himself) that "it is fit for the king to call a Parliament, or at least not fit for any man to dissuade it." Then in his customary way he dissected the issue.

There were nine reasons for calling a Parliament and twenty of what he called 'incidents of a Parliament.' Then he wrote to the king, telling him at the outset that it was "a great problem of estate" (LL4.369). James and some of his advisors believed that the Parliament should concern itself with the matter of the needed funds in the traditional manner, but Parliament saw the opportunity to maintain and possibly increase its legislative authority. The seventeenth century, we now know, brought about the shrinking of the English king's "divine" and even civil authority beyond recall. Believing in monarchy as he did, Bacon had to feel less at home in Parliament as his career at Court progressed.

Fortunately for him, however, another death made it possible to strike out on another judicial path. On August 7, 1613, Sir Thomas Fleming, the chief justice of the King's Bench, died. Bacon anticipated that the king might favor the installation of Bacon's old rival, Edward Coke, in Fleming's position and suggested just such a move, which he had determined would enhance his own status.

6

A Greater Place

The king would surely approve Bacon as attorney general—if James approved of Bacon's suggestion that he move Coke from Common Pleas to the King's Bench to replace the deceased Sir Thomas Fleming. Bacon knew that in his present position the independent-minded Coke exercised a bit too much judicial latitude to suit the king, but could be much better controlled on the King's Bench. He also knew that Coke enjoyed his present position, but such a move would constitute a promotion that he could hardly reject. Then Sir Henry Hobart, the present attorney general, could assume Common Pleas, and the way would be open for Bacon. Bacon's suggestion prevailed, and on October 26, 1613, Bacon finally attained a position he had first sought twenty years earlier.

Meanwhile, the king did not recall Parliament, of which Bacon remained a member. Sir Henry Neville, a member of the Lower House with hopes for an appointment, perhaps as secretary of state to replace the as yet unreplaced Salisbury, was offering relatively simple advice for the king. If you want money from Parliament, call it into session and ask for it. In a letter Bacon presented the king with more sophisticated counsel. He suggested that James "proportion your demands and expectation" (LL4.371). The people, he pointed out, would like to hear of something more congenial than taxation. Furthermore, the king should not remind Parliament of his dependency on them, for "there are means found in his Majesty's estate to help himself (which I partly think is true)" (LL4.372). Not appreciating this counsel, James by the end of the year still had not summoned Parliament.

Late in the year the king took aim at the practice which Bacon also opposed: dueling. Speaking before the lords, Bacon pointed out, perhaps with a smile, that since duels were a matter of honor, they had more to protect than anyone and therefore dominated the world of dueling. The king had made a proclamation which he would have the duty of enforcing, so he brought the matter to the Star Chamber in judgment of a man—William Priest, not a lord at all—who had challenged an opponent, and Richard Wright, who had sinned by delivering it. Using one of his animal images to justify this unlordly challenge, Bacon observed "that it was not amiss sometimes to beat the dog before the lion" (LL4.410). James committed both men to Fleet Prison and made both pay fines, but whipping these dogs did not seem to admonish the lions. The popularity of dueling continued into the late eighteenth century. In the long reign of George III, according to the *Encyclopædia Britannica*, 171 duels resulted in ninety-one deaths.

The Parliament intended for 1613 finally took place the following March, still 1613 by the calendar of the time. Indeed, there were many proposals, one "for the breeding and preserving of timber and woods," one for "the beautifying and better government of the city of London, and the suburbs of the same," one "for the better plantation of Virginia and supply thereof," even one condemning that old enemy of medieval Christianity, usury (LL5.16–17). No one knew what might pass, for two-thirds of Commons were newcomers, and the king's new secretary of state, Sir Ralph Winwood, although an able man, had been out of the country for some time and had no experience as a Parliamentarian.

Much more important, Bacon knew, loomed the king's desperation over the emptiness of the Exchequer. He wrote a "memorial" for the king to study: James must let them know "the causes of the calling of this Parliament," he must "declare the manner of the proceeding," and he must "acquaint them with certain of his intentions and resolutions (L5.24). *Causes, manner, intentions*—such weak language irritated James. Parliament must realize, as he did, the significance of his daughter's status as the mate of a German count hounded by enemies. Under such circumstances negotiations should not take the form of a contract by which the legislature would gain certain tangible rights.

Bacon knew that James must not speak like an accountant or a tyrant, but like a magnificent prince such as Elizabeth or King Arthur, as depicted in Spenser's *Faerie Queene*. Approaching his mid-fifties and the veteran of a lifetime around political men, Bacon still urged grandiose concepts like *magnificence*. He perhaps failed to realize that James had no more inclination to follow his advice than had the Earl of Essex. Whether James listened to him or not, Parliament saw Bacon standing closer to the king with more royal responsibilities. No rule against an attorney general remaining in Parliament existed, but someone raised the question, and an investigation established that such a consummation had never existed, and Parliament moved, with Bacon's supporters gaining for him a grandfather clause against their ruling: any *future* attorney general would have to yield his membership.

Sir Henry Neville, a prominent figure, wanted to begin, as James did, with a decision to supply the monarch. His followers earned the name of *undertakers*. Parliament generally wished to begin by withholding any rise in impositions. They called upon the flexibility of the English language to assist them. The House of Lords favored a proposal for a "voluntary oblation" to support the king. Then as now, an oblation constituted what you offered to a deity; the Lower House judged James already too much of a deity. On the subject of language Bacon stood supreme. Such a sum could be called a *gift* or a *present* or at most an *offering*, not an act of benevolence (forbidden by an act of Parliament) or a *contribution*, which would make it seem like a tax. Nor could the king, for his part, enact any *fees*, *collections*, or *communications*.

Such descents into linguistics suggest that the Parliament of 1614 was running out of steam. Early in June, the king, seeing no possibility of any imposition, called it off and supported his financial needs by another old standby: granting monopolies. From this point Bacon served in the Lower House no longer, for the body just dismissed, termed the Addled Parliament, did not meet again before Bacon passed into the peerage.

In January, Bacon penned a lengthy charge against a member of the Irish Parliament, William Talbot, for asserting too baldly his Roman Catholic faith. Bacon sought a more moderate position based on his faith in the monarchy. As a successor of Henry VIII, James prevailed as head of the church and defender of the faith. Talbot proclaimed his submission to James as his temporal ruler, but Bacon regarded the pope, not without cause, as a temporal ruler. Talbot's submission to King James was only conditional. For him James was "a fellow who thinks with his magistrality and goose quill to give laws and manages [managements] to crowns and scepters" (LL5.9). It should be pointed out that *fellow* did not carry any of the condescending intimations that it sometimes does today. A fellow was a colleague, as a fellow usually is today in an academic setting. Nonetheless, Bacon found Talbot's allegiance uppity; for him *magistrality* meant using robust language to persuade. Talbot had to pay a fine (it is not clear that he ever did), and he was ordered back to his position. Bacon's position on faith was essentially live-and-let-live except where religious conviction threatened the temporal rule of a monarch.

Soon another religious conflict developed, more serious because the defendant, Edmund Peacham, was an English minister, though a puritanical one. Already in trouble for having insulted his bishop, Peacham had to endure the searching of his private effects. He had written things such as "King James has promised mercy and judgment, but we find neither. It is the duty of preachers to lay open the infirmities of princes and let them see their evil ways."[1] Should this man be brought to trial? James, perceiving all too many Parliamentarians with puritan sympathies, suggested that Bacon consult with other judges. Among the judges, Coke, Bacon's old rival, disagreed with the procedure. A judge's duty was to judge, not to seek advice from other judges. Many fellow judges disagreed, and the establishment of the possibility of such judicial conferences would impel Coke to consult endlessly with other judges in matters before the King's Bench. After several weeks of investigation Bacon and two other judges went to the Tower of London, Peacham's place of confinement. He came away convinced that Peacham "did but turn himself into divers shapes to save or delay his punishment," as he put it to the king (LL5.126).

Bacon did not participate in Peacham's trial. Arraigned in Somersetshire, his own territory, Peacham defended himself, insisting that he never intended to use any of his treasonable comments in sermons or in print, and he was neither pardoned nor liberated but made to reside "unmolested," as Spedding expressed it, in a jail in Taunton where he died in March of 1616. Although religio-political motives lay behind officialdom in matters like these, judges generally, although not the individualistic Coke, considered that even private attacks on the monarch threatened the whole institution and thus the order that maintained Britain.

An event of 1613, the suspicious death of Sir Thomas Overbury in the Tower, generated the most notorious issue of 1615. Overbury served as secretary of King James's Lord Chamberlain, the Earl of Somerset, who as Robert Carr, a Scotsman to whom James had taken a liking, had advanced quickly to the nobility as Viscount Rochester and then the earldom. Somerset married Frances Howard, formerly the wife of the third Earl of Essex (son of the man Bacon had not been able to save from execution in 1601). Overbury, with an animus against the bride even before the marriage, viewed her as a severe impediment to his great influence over Somerset. Yet Overbury, exemplifying the unhappy duties that servants, even highly-placed ones, often had to endure, was expected to promote the marriage. Lady Frances had married Essex very young and several years later fallen for Somerset, as indeed James had also. Essex's presumed impotence justified the annulment of the lady's first marriage. Overbury possessed some distinction as a poet and could project his emotional conflicts vicariously into literature. Readers of his poem *The Wife*, it appears, had no difficulty identifying the new countess as the disparaged wife of the poem. Somerset himself, no doubt with assistance from his wife, began to view his secretary as a dangerous troublemaker for a master whom he knew so well.

Furthermore, James shared in the dislike of this secretary. Spedding, good Victorian that he was, asked whether we have to assume, as some did, "that James and Somerset were guilty of certain secret unmentionable vices" and "that Somerset and Overbury were guilty of similar secret unmentionable vices" (LL5.345). It cannot be demonstrated that James possessed sufficient motive and facility for using his power mischievously to have contributed to the episode that soon unfolded. Certainly, however, his friendship with Somerset gave him much to worry about. The couple found it easy enough to concoct lies about Overbury and have him confined to the Tower, where in 1613 officialdom reported him to have died of natural causes.

In 1615 evidence arose that Overbury had been poisoned. The unhappy king found himself obliged to call forth his judge of the King's Bench to charge Lord and Lady Somerset as assessories. First the actual poisoner or poisoners had to be prosecuted, so four people—two prison officials, the woman who allegedly administered the poison, and an apothecary—were accused, confessed, and hanged. Their testimony and that of other witnesses, however, pointed to the countess. On May 24 in Westminster Hall she faced judgment. Seats in the courtroom proved difficult to come by; scalpers operated vigorously. Coke presided, and other judges, including Bacon, assisted. Her confession surprised nobody.

Bacon addressed the Lord High Steward and a number of nobles: "I am very glad to hear this unfortunate Lady doth take this course, to confess fully and freely, and thereby to give glory to God and to justice. It is, as I may turn it, the nobleness of an offender to confess" (LL5.297). He went on to observe that her confession prevented him from giving evidence. He made a few comments about the king's sense of justice overcoming "his affections private" and about justice in partially theatrical terms: "The great frame of justice (my Lords) in this present action, hath a Vault, and it hath a Stage; a Vault wherein these works of darkness were contrived; and a Stage, with steps, by which they were brought to light" (LL5.299). After further efforts to distance James wherever possible, Bacon admitted that "where I speak of a stage, I doubt I hold you upon the stage too long" (LL5.304) but soon exited anyway.

Lady Somerset had guessed, or judged, that confession in a noble key might avail her much. Of the case against the earl, Bacon had reported to the king that the evidence was "of a good strong thread" (LL5.231), and his defense did not deal effectively with it. He had enjoyed plenty of opportunity to take part in the crime, but proof seemed insufficient. His peers nevertheless found him guilty as charged. Bacon, who almost certainly did not suspect the king of any part in the murder, had done his job. Both husband and wife went to the Tower.

Legal philosophies as well as personal dislike effected the discord between Coke and Bacon. Coke had a passion for English common law; Bacon, dedicated to the monarchy, favored the king's prerogative in any legal conflict. In 1615 Coke challenged the right of the Court of Chancery—essentially the king's court—to interfere with decisions based on common law, a body of law grounded on a long judicial tradition, not always written but relying on custom and precedent. Coke's study of common law profoundly influenced legal thought in England and also the United States. Lord Chancellor Ellesmere, a strong supporter of the king's prerogative, had with Bacon long formed an imposing duo against Coke.

Two Latin expressions, both ecclesiastical in origin, sum up much of this legal friction. One is *commendum*, the custody of an ecclesiastical benefice in the absence of a regular incumbent. The term also relates to the revenues of the benefice. Readers of English novels of the nineteenth century, particularly those of Anthony Trollope, know that a clergyman could be hired to administer a church nominally held by another clergyman who, let us say, had other things to do. A *commendum* might seem more the concern of a local bishop rather than grounds for a legal tussle between kings and judges, but Henry VIII had made the monarch the English equivalent of the pope. Bacon informed the king of a man named Serjeant Chibborne, who had worked in behalf of two men who claimed that a certain benefice belonged to them. Bacon intimated that the king had the right to grant *commenda*. James ordered Coke to consult with him before proceeding on the case. Coke thought that such a command ought to come from his old rival, the attorney general, a situation which would give Coke the opportunity to argue against a smaller fish than the king himself. Bacon distributed letters conveying the king's wishes to the King's Bench. Coke, who had a dozen other judges on his side, wrote James that "we have advisedly considered of the said letter of Mr. Attorney, and with one consent do hold the same to be contrary to law, and such as we could not yield to the same by our oath" (LL5.360).

The king, confident that the law could not contradict the ruler, called a meeting on June 6, 1616. He came with his own backing of lords and officials, chiefly to lecture the judges who were maintaining that the attorney general's action was delaying justice. Admitting that he had never studied the common law of England, James insisted that he nevertheless understood justice and affirmed that "although your oath be, that you shall not delay justice betwixt any private parties, yet was it not meant that the king should hereby receive harm, before he be forewarned thereof" (LL5.362). Coke, however, continued to insist that justice was being delayed, while the king insisted that justice required the king's intervention whenever he thought it necessary.

The other Latin expression was *praemunire*, which originally had to do with the summoning of a person accused by a foreign court, and from the time of Henry VIII on in England which meant a papal court. As the supreme ecclesiastical authority in England, Henry (and his successors) could not tolerate this sort of foreign intervention in the judicial system. By 1616 *praemunire* had turned into another aspect of the king's struggle with his judges. Early that year two jewel merchants were charged by the King's Bench with forcing customers to pay excessively. The Court of Chancery, at Bacon's instigation, stopped this judgment. How could another English court block a ruling by the King's Bench? Unhappily for Coke, the King's Bench could be overruled, for the Court of Chancery, under the king, was independent of all other courts. The king was being accused of *praemunire*, which now could mean one court overruling another—the king against himself, so to speak—plainly impossible.

On June 20, James spoke in a symbolically important place—Star Chamber, where whether a judgment should be repealed might be taken up, but Henry VIII had made it a court by which other courts could be bypassed. There were no appeals, no jury, no witnesses, and no access by the public. Here authority could exert itself without impediments. Ned Wakeman, a barrister, was there to hear James assert that the dignity of kings signified that "they sit in the throne of God and therefore are in scripture turned Gods."[2]

On the 30th of that unlucky month for Coke, James suspended him from duty and gave him a summer assignment: a review of his "Reports"—the record of his hundreds of judgments—with an eye to determining and reporting on the errors he had committed therein. Coke had disputed with the king, but he could not flatly disobey such a command. About this time Bacon prepared a proposition for reforming the laws of the kingdom. It appears that he did this no earlier than that busy June of 1616 and no later than sometime early the next year. Perhaps it might be discussed here, while Coke, so to speak, is at his task of correction.

Bacon assured the king that he had no quarrel with the legal system.

"Certainly they are wise, they are just, and moderate laws; they give to God, they give to Caesar, they give to the subjects, that which appertaineth." Nor was he interested in "taxing the laws. I speak only by way of perfiting [perfecting] them." He may not have been thinking at all of Coke at the moment, but he makes a statement that crystalizes the difference between these two men of law. "What I shall propound is not to the matter of the laws, but to the manner of their registry" (LL6. 63). Coke devoted his thought to "matter"; Bacon, dedicated to a principle of legal orderliness, wanted, in his larger pursuit of the advancement of learning, to put the law into better order. More than once Bacon suggested this process to the king, who avoided encouraging it. He probably feared that his attorney might, in an inevitably profound analysis of this vast project, swing around to the common law advocacy held by many of his colleagues. Conventional in many ways, Bacon nevertheless projected himself as—and might, the king feared, actually emerge as—a reformer.

Bacon's list of "incertainties" in his letter to the king illustrates what was on his mind:

> But certain it is, that our laws, as they now stand, are subject to great incertainties, and variety of opinion, delays, and evasions whereof ensueth,

1. That the multiplicity and length of suits is great.
2. That the contentious person is armed, and the honest subject wearied and oppressed.
3. That the judge is more absolute; who, in doubtful cases, hath a greater stroke and liberty.
4. That the chancery courts are more filled, the remedy of law being often obscure and doubtful.
5. That the ignorant lawyer shroudeth his ignorance of law in that doubts are so frequent and many,
6. That men's assurances of their lands and estates by patents, deeds, wills, are often subject to question, and hollow, and many the like inconveniences [LL6.64].

How much judicial "stroke and liberty" could a monarch accept? He had seen enough of it from Coke. Still, the cumbersome English legal system needed reform, and if Bacon had been allowed to exercise his talent for orderliness, he might have made considerable improvements which, in James's mind, might disable prerogatives. Many generations later opinions, delays, evasions, and "multiplicity and length of suits" continue to be more or less inevitable features of the law in England and elsewhere. Bacon may have vastly overrated the possibility of a tidier judicial world.

On October 2, Coke appeared to recount his errors in his several decades upon the bench, but their triviality signaled Coke's contempt for the whole procedure and surely convinced James that he had made an impracticable demand. Ellesmere and Bacon indicated that they were ready to carry out necessary orders, if James decided that Coke must be displaced and replaced. Bacon, who insofar as possible had helped manipulate Coke's career, nevertheless insisted that "justice requireth that he be heard and called to his answer" (LL6.81). Bacon and Ellesmere were simply acknowledging that Coke interfered with the operation of the king's government. Bacon drew up seventeen charges against Coke, and the king declared to his Council his resolution to remove him from the bench, "yet gave him this characteristic," as the great letter writer of the time, John Chamberlain, wrote to his friend Dudley Carleton, "that he thought him in no way corrupt, but a good justice … as if he meant to hang him with a silken halter" (LL6.94).

Bacon wrote a dismissal of Coke for the king in November of 1616 and left a blank in a form prescribing a new Lord Justice which he knew would be filled by Judge Montagu, with whom, presumably, both Bacon and James would more easily carry on business. This dismissal, however, was a gross insult to a man who, despite severe faults, possessed a great legal mind. The reports which he sullenly refused to "correct" for his sovereign would be the texts over which future generations of lawyers would pore. Off went Coke storing up venom that would wait for its expression until his opponent was ready to slip from grace. Was Coke's dismissal essential for King James and Bacon? Did Coke's age—sixty-four—provide enough assurance that he could thereafter do his opponents no great harm? Bacon most likely did not foresee that Coke would outlive him by eight years.

George Villiers, twenty-four years old, a native of a not particularly important family in Leicestershire, had replaced Somerset as James's favorite young man. On November 29, 1616, Bacon offered Villiers a characteristically numbered list of points of legal and financial advice.

In a witty conclusion he reminded James's new favorite that the advice did not translate into an immediate nest-egg. "So as you are a strange heteroclite [deviant] in grammar, for you want the present tense; many verbs want the præterperfect tense, and some the future tense, but none want the present tense" (LL6.118). Until the end of his life Bacon would be writing to this opportunistic man.

7

Lord Keeper, Lord Chancellor

For twenty years Lord Ellesmere, who by 1616 had been created Viscount Brackley, had kept the Great Seal, but in March of the following year, ailing at seventy-seven, he asked to be relieved of his position. Bacon, long an ally of the old man, and now in good stead with James's latest favorite, George Villiers (now a viscount), probably felt that the king's right-hand man was delivering his messages to the king. James named Bacon as Brackley's replacement a few days before the venerable man died. Taking his seat in Chancery as the keeper, Bacon proclaimed in his characteristically alliterative way that "the Chancery is to supply the law, and not to subvert the law" (LL6.184). Conscious of that old impediment that all litigants despise, delays in the prosecution of the law, he predicted that his dutifulness would prove not only fair but expeditious and called on vegetative imagery to declare the law's solidity: "Because the law roots so well in my time, I will water it at the root" (LL6.192). His enthusiasm makes it difficult to agree with those who lament—as Bacon himself occasionally did—the fact that he did not attempt to choose the life of a scholar. He may have begun the study of the law as the thing to do, the thing that his father wanted him to do, but it became a passion with him. As for Alice Bacon, who surely found Francis a less than exciting husband, she was receiving what he and society considered a suitable reward. She now ranked just below the baronesses of the realm. Not too far away, most likely, stood the prize that would place her among those ladies.

Bacon, an energetic but never physically hardy man, now suffered from the gout. A man who kept careful track of his ills, he could not

expect to hold the Great Seal as long as had his father or his own immediate predecessor. He could, however, envision rising higher. He received
the seal on March 7 and wasted no time writing to Lord Villiers, whose
blessing had surely helped secure it. While acknowledging assistance,
he supplied Villiers with a little additional moral advice. "It is the life
of an ox or beast always to eat, and never to exercise; but men are born
(and especially christian men), not to cram in their fortunes, but to exercise their virtues." Today, Bacon noted, "Money and turn-serving, and
cunning canvases, and importunity prevail too much…. As for cunning
and corrupt men, you must (I know) sometimes use them; but keep
them at a distance" (LL6.6–7). In another letter he counseled this man
who, thanks to James's fondness for brisk young men, had rocketed
upward in the realm: "If you sleep, or neglect your charge, you are an
undone man, and may fall much faster than you have risen" (LL6.55),
little expecting how much this advice would someday apply to himself.
Did Villiers believe him when he wrote, in another letter, "This matter
of pomp, which is heaven to some men, is hell to me, or purgatory at
least" (LL6.194)? Bacon was describing the ceremony of his own creation
as Lord Keeper that entailed a parade of two hundred horses, a row of
judges, representatives from the inns of court, the queen, and Prince
Charles, the king himself being on an extended trip to Scotland. Pomp
was one sin, if it be a sin, that Bacon enjoyed.

In September of 1617 he affirmed his stand on the law, so different
from that of his legislative rival, Sir Edward Coke, in a speech in the
Exchequer at the installation of an official: "First therefore, above all
you ought to maintain the King's prerogative, and to set down with yourself that the King's prerogative and the law are not two things; but the
King's prerogative is law, and the principal part of the law; the first-born
or *pars prima* [first part] of the law; and therefore in conserving and
maintaining that, you conserve and maintain the law. There is not in
the body of man one law of the head, and another of the body, but all
is one entire law" (LL6.203).

Bacon could not divorce law from monarchical authority, although
men like Sir Edward Coke disagreed strongly with him. Common law
for them stood tall: ancient, unwritten, traditional, imposing. Common
law cases could be brought to Chancery, the court of the Lord Chancel-

lor, but in the opinion of royalist judges like Bacon, no decision reached there could possibly contradict the judgment of the monarch. Both sides had a problem, the supporters of common law in their allegiance to, their appointment by, the monarch; the royalists in their awareness of this great body of cases which, in late medieval times, religious reformers began to prefer to any adverse and undesirable ruling by a pope. From Henry VIII on, the English monarch was, so to speak, the English pope, and rather clearly not an infallible one.

Legally, Coke could not be put away, but Bacon, in maneuvering him to the King's Bench in 1613, where King James could more easily restrict his independent spirit, had defanged him. Writers on Bacon often call him *wily*, but the two men probably tied for the lead in wiliness. Coke had a marriageable daughter, and in 1617 he was cooperating with Lady Compton, the mother of George Villiers (having shot up even further, we must now call him Earl of Buckingham) to arrange a wedding agreeable to both: the new earl's older brother, Sir John, and Coke's daughter Frances. From Coke's point of view the proposed marriage represented an alliance with the increasingly powerful Buckingham, while Lady Compton could not resist a chance of attaining a chunk of the considerable fortune held by Coke and his wife, who continued to be known, from her previous marriage, as Lady Hatton. That couple were feuding, however, and although both could benefit from this sort of connection with the king's special favorite among favorites, she bitterly opposed a match with a man who possessed nothing beyond his connections. And she controlled her stepdaughter, a beautiful girl of fourteen. Furthermore, Frances loathed Sir John Villiers.

Lady Hatton had in mind a better partner for Frances: Henry de Vere, Earl of Oxford, whose father's first wife had been her aunt. Because Henry had sprung from a second wife, he did not present the difficulty of blood relationship. Frances had silly thoughts of marrying someone else for love, but because she did not know Oxford, at least she could not despise him as she did Sir John Villiers. Maybe this nobleman could prove lovable. Beyond the problem of the opposing group—Coke, the Villiers family, and of course the king—Oxford was in Italy; negotiations would require much more than the available time. Lady Hatton devised as a solution the composition of a letter, supposedly from the absent earl (whom she knew would appreciate the handsome dowry she was able and willing to provide), promising to be Frances's husband. This fake letter, which would have astonished Oxford and many other people, attracted this naive young woman. To solidify her plan Lady Hatton composed another letter, one of obligation, supposedly written by Frances, stating that the girl "do gyve myselfe absolutely to Wyffe to Henry Vere, Viscount Balboke, Earl of Oxenford" (retaining in this case the lady's spelling), which Frances and her mother as witness both signed.[1]

In July of 1617, Lady Hatton had withdrawn her daughter to a house called Oatlands in Hertfordshire, north of London, rented by a cousin, Sir Edmund Withipole. Coke was also residing in Hertfordshire with another of his daughters, Anne Sadleir. Coke, eager to get Frances under his own control, obtained a warrant to search the Withipole house. The Privy Council noted that Coke, "with his son and 10 or 11 servants, weaponed, in violent manner repaired to the house where [his] daughter was remaining, and with a piece of timber or form broke open the door, and dragged her along to his coach" (LL6.227). This rowdy behavior from a great person of the law did not alarm the council excessively, for, after all, he was the girl's father, but they indicated that for Lady Hatton's benefit they would look into it.

Her daughter having escaped, she knew that she must exert her own force. Who could be better than the man who had long ago sought her hand and now prevailed as the great judge of Chancery? Accompanied by a male friend, Lady Hatton set out for York House, where Bacon had come into the world and now lived and worked. Spedding reported this episode thus: "At last to my Lord Keeper's they came, but could not have instant access to him for that his people told them he was laid at rest, being not well. Then my La. Hatton desired she might be in the next room where my Lord lay, that she might be the first that [should] speak with him after he was stirring. The door-keeper fulfilled her desire and in the meantime gave her a chair to rest herself in, and then left her alone" (LL6.225).

One might suppose that she would wait until the ailing judge should arise. Lady Hatton sought a quicker response. "But not long after, she rose up and bounced against my Lord Keeper's door, and waked him and affrighted him, that he called his men to him; and they opening the door, she thrust in with them, and desired his Lordship to pardon her boldness, but she was like a cow that had lost her calf, and so justified [herself] and pacified my Lord's anger, and got his warrant and my Lo. Treasurer's warrant and others of the Council to fetch her daughter from the father and bring them both to the Council" (LL6.225).

Having frightened Bacon into compliance, she was ready to do battle with the rest of the realm's legal elite. Coke took refuge in the law he knew so thoroughly and drew up a series of charges against his wife. She had secretly conveyed her daughter away, she had attempted to marry her off without the consent of the girl's father, she had counterfeited a letter alleging that the intended husband had offered his hand, and she had assembled some "desperate fellows" to assist her.

The council no doubt expected some fireworks from this formidable woman. She rose in her own defense, and as her biographer puts it: "Lady Hatton dominated them all. In spite of the brief held for her by the Lord Houghton—a most sound lawyer—she preferred to plead her own cause. And with such emphasis she did it that every breath set twinkling the jewels on her dress. She was as dramatic a tragedy queen and as efficient as any lawyer who ever took silk."[2]

She responded to her husband's charges in sequence with the addition of a clause noting that he too had abducted his daughter. Bacon, doubtless convinced that losing Lady Hatton's dowry long ago might have been a truly fortunate turn of events, could allow the council to make its decision. He did not, however, escape a further involvement. The king was still in Scotland, and Bacon assured himself that neither James nor Buckingham desired this marriage for the daughter of the Lord Justice. Coke's riotous behavior surely offended Bacon, who judged that the king would agree with him—but good psychologist as he normally was, Bacon did not realize that James, upon learning the story, saw no sin in a man's appropriating his own daughter. From Gorhambury on July 25, Bacon wrote the king, reminding him of how well things were going. Judging Villiers no great asset, he intimated as much to James. On the same day he wrote to Buckingham referring to an earlier letter in which "I then shewed my dislike of the matter." Now he dislikes "the carriage of it here" (LL6.235). Buckingham's reply must have chilled

Bacon's heart: "In the business of my brother's that you overtrouble yourself with, I understand from London by some of my friends that you have carried yourself with much scorn and neglect both toward myself and friends" (LL6.237).

Buckingham wanted the match, and what he desired the king desired also. Furthermore, the king, unlike Lord Keeper Bacon, held no grudge against Coke. It had been useful to send him away, but circumstances might justify bringing him back. On September 28, Coke was readmitted to the Council table. On the next day Sir John Villiers and Frances Coke became one—legally, at least. But as Spedding pointed out, "The game had gone altogether against Lady Hatton into the Star Chamber, and to save her daughter from a marriage which she (Lady H.) disliked: but she was threatened with prosecution herself" (LL6.256). Lady Hatton, placed under temporary arrest, could not attend the wedding.

On November 2 this indomitable lady was set free, and one week later "gave a great dinner … which seems to have been the celebration of her reconciliation with everybody—except her husband" (LL6.271). A letter from John Tory to Sir Dudley Carleton dated November 8, 1617, gives further details: "This day was the great feast at Hatton House made to the King and Prince and their followers, lords and ladies, by the most notable lady my Lady Elizabeth Hatton. My Lord Coke only was absent, who in all vulgar opinions was there expected. His Majesty was never merrier nor more satisfied, who had not patience to sit a quarter of an hour without drinking the health of my Lady Elizabeth Hatton, which was pledged first by my Lord Keeper and my Lord Marquis Hamilton, and then by all the lords and ladies with great gravity and respect, and then by all the gallants in the next room" (LL6.271).

Now what playwright could have devised anything similar to this happy gathering? But were the smiles of this savvy group a bit twisted?

A few weeks later, just after New Year's Day, there was a party at which Buckingham became a marquis and Bacon the Lord Chancellor. The post had reached its peak of power in the days of Henry VIII's Lord Chancellor, Cardinal Wolsey, the last Lord Chancellor at the same time a major functionary of a church that claimed universality. No Lord Chancellor could dominate affairs of state as Wolsey had. Bacon had experience serving as a legislator, a judge, and an advisor to the king, though not a spokesman for him. This experience of balancing different and even competing governmental functions prepared him as well as anyone could be prepared for his present duties as judicial head, arm of the king, and—potentially, at least—the foremost member of the House of Lords. He would still have to prosecute people he knew—and might be his friends. He would still have to tell James things he would not want to hear. Life would be more of a balancing act than ever. He received a £600-per-year increase, he could continue working on *The Great Instauration*, and he had improved his chances of accomplishing one of his legal goals, the compilation of the nation's laws.

Spedding's comment on the likelihood of his accomplishment of this goal continues to stand caution to anyone who yearns for this kind of reform: "The law cannot be made simpler, cheaper, speedier, surer, and more generally intelligible, without the help and consent of lawyers; and it is in the interest of the lawyers that the law should be intricate, costly, slow, uncertain, and intelligible to none but themselves. All the work is paid for by others, and the more uncertainty the more work" (LL6.268).

Bacon had re-established his relations with James and Buckingham after his blunder at the time of the marriage of Buckingham's brother, evidenced by his promotion and his newly awarded title of Baron Verulam six months later. The title accurately describes the location of Gorhambury. From about 50 AD for four centuries, the Roman town of Verulamium occupied a site about three miles from Gorhambury. Around the fifth century it became a Saxon town, its later name, St. Albans, honoring a man designated as the first Christian martyr in Britain, who is thought to have died around 304. Alban, a pagan at the time, according to the *Catholic Encyclopedia*, sheltered a priest whose religion and, therefore, life, the officials of the day did not relish. Impressed by the man, Alban turned Christian, and when he refused to rescind his decision, suffered execution.

The name Verulamium did not die. The Roman historian Tacitus had called Verulamium a *municipium* early in the second century AD, which signified that its citizens were Roman citizens and that the town's own magistrates and laws had the authority to administer it. They were entitled to set and collect their own taxes. Bacon would not have known, but might have appreciated knowing, that the town possessed a basilica which also functioned as a town hall, religious center, and law court; it also had a theater. These buildings had sunken out of sight by the time his father acquired the property. Bacon saw some of the walls, which enclosed 203 acres and had made Verulamium the third largest of the walled towns in Roman Britain.

Archaeology did not exist in Bacon's time. For him history signified not a record of human culture but a record of what authors had said about the world they observed. It was important to study the Roman writers, especially a man interested in natural history like Pliny the Elder, but none of Bacon's contemporaries would have thought about digging up the things of his world, even if only a few feet below them in Roman Britain. Yet a few men attempted to discover specific aspects of the past.

In appropriating the specifically Roman Catholic wealth in his kingdom, Henry VIII instructed John Leland to gather rare and costly books from monastic libraries. Examining the monastery than had risen near the site where Sir Nicholas Bacon chose to build his summer home, Leland learned that the "noble street which is commonly called Watelynstrete was discovered in 1531 within the ancient city of Verulamium, when sand was being sought for repairing the public roads…. I found the pipes of an aqueduct, made of baked tiles."[3] We can be sure that Leland did not ponder details of the construction of the pipes or tiles as modern students invariably do. He could see Watling Street as essentially contemporary, for it stretched all the way to Canterbury; he probably did not picture Chaucer's mounted pilgrims trekking over it, but we can.

Another Tudor writer, William Camden, observed that "nothing now remains but ruins of walls, chequered pavements and Roman coins now and then digg'd up there."[4] A wall, however, was a wall, not for him or for Bacon an avenue to the construction habits of its builders. Perhaps Bacon's servants, who knew that their master wedded much of his soul to Latin words, brought any coins they found to him. Or when he was supervising the laying of his paths, he may well have stooped and found a coin or two himself. The imagery would have intrigued him but not its date or its place in the archaeological calendar of ancient coins.

Antiquarianism, another approach to the past, also had a few earlier practitioners. Probably the greatest was John Stow, maker of *A Survey of London, Written in the Year 1598.* A self-taught man, Stow deserves credit for contriving the kind of guided literary tour popular in our time. Of York House he managed to learn that near one of his stops, Durham House, there stood "another great house, sometime belonging to the bishop of Norwich, and was his London lodging, which now pertaineth to the Archbishop of York by this occasion." After noting its use by Cardinal Wolsey, Stow distinguished it from York Place, which became Whitehall, and brought it up to date as the workplace of "the lord chancellors or lord keepers of the great seal of England."[5] It would probably have done no good to drag Stow to St. Albans; a Londoner by birth and vocation, he might not have found its past entrancing. Lovers of the past usually turned out to be men seeking information necessary to acquire or maintain property that dated back to medieval times, before Henry VIII rearranged the economy and upset primogeniture.

Baron Verulam, a great user of Roman texts, in some sense recognized himself as tangibly connected with a wedge of the Roman and Saxon past. This title gave him a new identity—one for which peers gladly yielded their old identity. He would be *Verulam* (and, as we will see, later, *St. Alban*) rather than Bacon, and readers would connect his literary works with the new and grander identity, but not in a way satisfactory to Spedding, his great editor, who, noting that Bacon's political downfall came soon after he became a peer, lamented the fact that the new identity did not catch on, that people began to speak erroneously of *Lord Bacon.* They *could* refer properly to *Lord Coke,* because Coke, though not a peer, deserved the designation as a chief judge. With Bacon enrolled as a true peer, he could shed *Bacon* for all formal purposes. But people reasoned, "As a man, he must be Bacon; as a Peer, he must be Lord: and two together make 'Lord Bacon.' And so, I fear, it must remain," Spedding conceded (LL6.317). Many of Bacon's readers, however, at least through the nineteenth century, aware that he retained his place in the echelon even in his period of punishment, customarily referred to him by his title.

Nothing of this tradition remains. The current way of referring to

Bacon would have appalled Spedding much more, for biographers, scholars, and the world at large generally call him *Francis Bacon*, seldom recognizing even his knighthood. It seems likely that this social snub—which the present author too finds it necessary to adopt—derives in his case from posterity's frequent habit of further traducing a fallen personage. Throughout his last five years Bacon barely endured his social ruination. On the other hand the world acknowledges, for instance, Villiers's grandest title, Duke of Buckingham.

The city of St. Albans acquired the Verulamium site from the Earl of Verulam in 1929, some of it for a public park and some for preservation. Archaeologists discovered what Bacon could not have known: even before Roman times the site harbored a Celtic settlement. The name, then, is not precisely Roman, for about two thousand years ago it was Verlamion. Sir Nicholas Bacon could not have guessed what archaeologists discovered: that a pre–Roman man of distinction, name unknown, had built his own stately home a short distance from Verulamium. The Celtic dwellers in Verlamion, researchers suppose, were chiefly farmers. Coins, pottery, and even a linchpin intended to secure a carriage wheel or chariot wheel to its axle have been found.

Bacon would have felt more at home with the Roman remains. The theater existed from 140 to 390 AD. One had to wonder whether the plays by Plautus and Terence from which boys like Francis Bacon learned their Latin entertained audiences at Verulamium. *The Comedy of Errors*, which Bacon did see at Gray's Inn, he would have recognized as a variation of a theme of Plautus's *Menaechmi*. At Gorhambury he may have been closer to Rome than he knew. Researchers found here a Roman empire town with basilica, forum, shops, public baths, temples, and theater. They have called one villa site *Gorhambury*.

Bacon's new duties, one might suppose, would require him to give up York House, but the old building, his father's workplace for years and home to him in his early years, meant much to him. He applied, through Buckingham, to Tobias Matthew, Archbishop of York and father of Bacon's close friend Toby Matthew, for a twenty-one-year absolute lease. Matthew had no use for it and was willing to lease it to him for life. Bacon pointed out that he had spent more on its upkeep than "all the tenants that have been in it since my remembrance, answerable to that particular circumstance which is peculiar to myself, that I was born there, and am like to end my days there" (LL6.271).

For the period surrounding this accession to the nobility we have an account of his financial status and a list of his servants. Bacon has often—and justly—been accused of spending beyond his means. For the period from June 24 to September 29, 1618, however, if we believe the record at hand, he took in more than he spent—£4160/12/10 as opposed to £3711/4/2. The former total includes sums from his legal work and positions. Some of its details baffle us today. We will probably never know the story of £100 from "Mr. Hatcher for the business of the Pedlers," for instance (L6.327–36).

The payments include such matters as, under "Gifts and Rewards," five shillings "to my La. Hatton's man that brought Lp. Garden seeds," a reminder that the lady who had "affrighted" him at the door of his bedroom remembered him kindly; five shillings "to the Washwoman, for sending after the Crane that flew into the Thames" (one would really like to know more of this story); 2 pounds 4 shillings "to the King's trumpeters"; but 3 pounds 6 "to the Prince's trumpeters" (why should he get more trumpeters?); and five shillings six "to Mr. Gibsons maid of St. Albans that brought your Lp. Six Turkies" (all on LL6.328). A number of gifts went to poor people such as Goodman Fossey and goodwife Smith, he getting one pound and she one pound two (LL6.329). "The weeders in the garden" (LL6.330) received only 2 shillings, which does not seem decent payment from a man who loved gardens, but perhaps they did not weed well (LL6.330); "the Musicians at Windsor" received 2 pounds 4 (LL6.331).

The list of Bacon's servants in this period may presumably be used to make the case for Bacon's extravagance. There are about sixty-six names, although a few obscure details in the manuscript may distort that figure a little (LL6.336–38). The list starts very much as might be expected from a great man: two chaplains, a sergeant-at-arms, a steward, a seal-bearer, and two secretaries. There are six "gentleman ushers of the chamber" and no fewer than twenty-six "gentleman waiters," but perhaps some of these waiters may not have been full-timers, for on occasion a lord would be called upon to feed many people. The servants are all male. This probably does not mean that Lady Bacon suffered through life without attendants, who probably populated another list of servants that may not be extant. Such a list, of course, might have put him into debt for this period. Some of his servants probably were encamped at Gorhambury, some probably at York House, for several years the base of his official life, some no doubt at Gray's Inn, where he always maintained chambers, while some of course would have traveled with him.

One name appears twice, and must be specified, to satisfy those who, like John Aubrey in his celebrated *Brief Lives*, assert that Bacon was a pederast.[6] Another seventeenth-century writer, Sir Simonds D'Ewes, names "one Godrick a very effeminate faced youth to be his catamite."[7] Godrick's name appears twice in the list of servants, once as one of the gentlemen of the chamber and again as a gentleman waiter (his name spelled differently each time), so D'Ewes's allegation seems plausible. Furthermore, in the will Bacon prepared seven years later Goodrick (Godrick) was given £40—which suggests that Bacon exhibited more consistent loyalty to favorites than did his king (LL7.542).

Another fact about Henry Godrick (or Goodrick) goes unmentioned. In a letter to Secretary of State Conway on April 2, 1623, Bacon, who has some important papers to send, writes, "These papers are not so well written as they should, because I am not master of pens as I have been; but if his M[ajesty] grant my suit, I shall be again more than ever. This gentleman, the bearer hereof, Mr. Goodrick, hath lived in Spain and hath the language; if (as time serveth) you will be pleased to put a packet into his hands, he is fit for the trust, fit for the journey" (LL7.414).

His business was rather complicated. At the time, the Spanish ambassador, Gondomar, a friend of Bacon, had volunteered to intercede with the king for him. Also at this time Prince Charles and Buckingham were in Spain trying to promote a marriage between the prince and the Spanish infanta, as she was called. What concerns us here is that Bacon names Goodrick as a trustworthy man whose knowledge of Spanish will prove helpful. Whatever Bacon's other relationship to this man, he certainly meant more to Bacon than D'Ewes's (and presumably Aubrey's, although he does not name him) bedroom companion. Attitudes in our time have changed; for all we know, Bacon may have loved Goodrick.

A great many students of both Bacon and Sir Walter Raleigh would have liked to be on one of the Gray's Inn walks one day not long after Bacon's appointment as Lord Keeper, for the period also corresponded to an eventful period in the life of a man who had emerged in 1616 from a long prison sentence. The king allowed Raleigh freedom for another trip to "the south part of America" where he would perhaps obtain "some commodities and merchandise" for England (LL6.244). Before he left the two men met in this favorite place of Bacon's, and for the sake of this conference Bacon kept an earl waiting (W13.392). Was Bacon warning Raleigh, as he had warned Essex, against excesses in his duties abroad? Spedding speculates that Bacon may have been one of the men who counseled Raleigh about his upcoming voyage to Guiana out of fear that Raleigh was acting the part of a pirate. Raleigh is recorded as having responded jauntily to one such charge: "Did you ever hear of any that was counted a pirate for taking millions? ... If I can catch the (Spanish) fleet, I can give this man ten thousand and that man ten thousand, and 800 thousand to the King, and yet keep enough for myself and all my company" (LL6.347).

King James instructed Raleigh not to provoke Spain. Raleigh sailed off, lost his son in his assault upon Guiana, and provoked Spain, of course, with the result that the Spanish ambassador, Bacon's friend Gondomar, complained mightily enough to propel a group of judges, Bacon among them, to prosecute him. Having spent most of King James's reign imprisoned, Raleigh had been declared "civilly dead" and therefore not liable to be charged with anymore crimes—but he could still be tried for his initial crime of plotting against James back in 1603. Consequently Bacon, surely with no more enthusiasm than he had felt for participating in Essex's condemnation, became one of a half dozen judges who decided to behead him. But an important judge, especially in a small society, must sometimes rule against friends and neighbors.

Although Bacon did not publish anything of importance at this busy time of his life, he no doubt worked on *The New Organon*, which would reach print in 1620. It might be well to include here one of the few poems that can be confidently credited to him. It is based on a short poem in the *Greek Anthology*. Like Raleigh, a sometime poet who did not "publish" but circulated his work in manuscript, Bacon wrote poetry at least occasionally. Its date is unknown; indeed he could have done it at almost any time in his life, despite the fact that its lugubrious tone might encourage people to see it as a late and despairing work. Many poets of the Renaissance could gear up for a poem of this sort as a literary exercise.

> The world's a bubble, and the life of man
> less than a span;
> In his conception wretched, from the womb
> so to the tomb:
> Curst from the cradle, and brought up to years
> with cares and fears.
> Who then to frail mortality shall trust,
> But limns the water, or but writes in dust.
> Yet since with sorrow here we live opprest,
> what life is best?
> Courts are but only superficial schools
> to dandle fools.
> The rural parts are turned into a den
> of savage men.
> And where's the city from all vice so free,
> But may be term'd the worst of all the three?
> Domestic cares afflict the husband's bed,
> or pains his head,
> Those that live single take it for a curse,
> or do things worse.
> Some would have children; those that have them moan,
> or wish them gone.
> What is it then to have or have no wife,
> But single thraldom, or a double strife.
> Our own affections still at home to please
> is a disease:
> To cross the seas to any foreign soil
> perils and toil.
> Wars with their noise affright us: when they cease,
> we are worse in peace.
> What then remains, but that we still should cry
> Not to be born, or being born to die [W14.117].

He may have said to himself, perhaps pointed out to a few friends, that he could do this sort of thing more often if he wished, that he might turn out others as competent as this one—but he had other things to do.

8

Still Ascending

The spring of 1619 brought many references to the health of the king—and to that of his Lord Chancellor. On April 24 John Chamberlain wrote: "The Lord Chancellor's slackness (caused by the delicateness of his constitution) hath raised a rumour as if he were like enough to have a Lord Keeper for a coadjutor, or rather to have the place executed by commission when his health will not suffer him to follow it. But to disperse such mists, he is gone this day to Theobald's to see and congratulate his Majesty's happy recovery" (LL7.10).

Toby Matthew two years later alluded to this period as one of Bacon's "great sickness." A paucity of letters from Bacon during this spring may also suggest a period of ill health. On May 9, however, Bacon wrote briefly to Buckingham expressing satisfaction that the king was recovering and that "I hope to see him this summer at Gorhambury. There is sweet air as any is" (LL7.13).

He wrote to Buckingham more often than to the king, and one senses the deference he now exhibits to a man he once regularly advised. Take for example this message to Buckingham on July 19: "I find every day more and more occasions whereby you bind me to you, so this morning the King of himself did tell me some testimony that your Lordship gave of me to his Majesty even now when you went from of him, of so great affection and commendation.... I must do contrary to that that painters do, for they desire to make the picture to the life, and I must endeavor to make the life to the picture, it hath pleased you to make so honourable a description of me. I can be but your's, and desire to better myself, that I may be of more worth to such an owner" (LL7.37).

He is *bound*, he is must *make the life to the picture*, he is *owned*. Frustration breaks through the compliments. He uses the word *picture* as people today use *image*. Could he not leave the picture or image to others and simply concentrate on doing his job—or did his job rest squarely on the perception of this young nobleman originally from nowhere, that is, Leicestershire?

If Bacon was growing personally more deferential, and if he worried some of his colleagues in his insistence on the importance of the king's prerogatives, he continued to campaign for an organized and accessible system of justice. Near the end of 1619 or perhaps in the following January, Bacon was making this recommendation to the king: "The Star Chamber in the institution thereof hath two uses; the one as a supreme Court of Judicature; the other as an open Council" (LL7.70). Observing that the king has used it twice in its former function, Bacon suggested that he might use it in the second way to establish the limits of the various courts. Today the Star Chamber is best remembered as the agency of such archbishops as Wolsey and Cranmer under Henry VIII and Laud under Charles I to punish enemies and prosecute dissenters. The fact that it was closed to the public reminds us of the danger of secret justice, not only irremediable but surreptitious—capable of remaining unknown to outsiders. Star Chamber permitted no juries; anyone, whether or not aware of Henry VIII's despotic use of it, could see that it might be an agency of despotism.

To a legal mind in Bacon's time this court seemed appropriate to accomplish necessary things such as deciding issues in cases where no existing law seemed to apply. Bacon knew that Henry VIII's father, whose life he wrote, used Star Chamber to check the power of the landed gentry. As an avenue of redress, its secrecy could offer protection to a precariously situated person seeking to overturn an injustice. Given Bacon's longstanding desire to reform the judicial process, he hoped that the king would establish several commissions under Star Chamber to concentrate cases pertaining to manufacturing, the provision of grain, and other matters. As with his other efforts along this line, he received little or no cooperation. James, whose opinion of legal procedures was that he already faced too many of them, nevertheless perceived that the Star Chamber provided a wonderful place to set forth his own opinions.

On June 29, 1620, as part of the installation of James Whitelock as chief justice of Chester, Bacon spoke on the duties of judges. He advised

Whitelock "to suppress the power of such gentlemen in the country that seek to oppress and suppress their poor neighbors, for it is no great ill thing in a judge ... that in cases before them the poor have advantage against the rich. If it be so it is an error on the best side" (LL7.104). Bacon continued to speak in defense of the poor as well as dispense benefits to them. The poor, he knew, lacked what Englishmen called, and to an extent still call, *quality*, the capacity for, or the possibility of, social status, but they deserved to be treated fairly under the law. Bacon often demonstrated such solicitude in instructing new judges.

In another matter of judicial discretion, he faced a stiffer problem. In that same month of June a man he had long known and worked with was accused of imposing unwarranted clauses into a new charter for the City of London. The nature of these clauses need not bother us, but the king depended on Attorney General Sir Henry Yelverton to establish this charter correctly. On October 27 the judges, meeting in the Star Chamber, would consider the case against Yelverton. Bacon's relationship with the man extended far back; he wrote for his own reference the facts and opinions that he must consider before bringing the matter before his compatriots. The following is not a public document, but the private reflections of a man facing one of the severities of the judicial life.

> Sorry for the person, being a gentleman that I lived with in Gray's Inn; served with when I was attorney; joined with since in many services; and one that ever gave me more attributes in public than I deserved; and besides a man of very good parts, which with me is friendship at first sight; much more joined with so antient acquaintance.
>
> But, as a Judge, I hold the offense very great, and that without pressing measure; upon which I will only make a few observations, and so leave it.
>
> 1. First I observe the danger and consequences of the offence: for if it be suffered that the learned counsel shall practice the art of multiplication upon their warrants, the crown will be destroyed in small time. The great seal, the privy seal, signet, are solemn things, but they follow the King's hand. It is the bill drawn by the learned counsel and the docket, that leads the King's hand.
> 2. Next I note the nature of the defence. At first that it was an error in judgment; for this surely if the offence were small though clear, or great but doubtful, I should hardly sentence it. For it is hard to draw a straight line by steadiness of hand, but it could not be the swerving of the hand. And herein I note the wisdom of the law of

125

England, which termeth the highest contempts and excesses of authority, *Misprisions;* which (if you take the sound and derivation of the words); is but *mistaken:* but if you take the use and exception of the word, it is high and heinous contempts and usurpations of authority; whereof the reason I take to be, and the name excellently imposed, for that main mistaking, it is ever joined with contempt; for he that reveres will not easily mistake; but he that slights, and thinks more of the greatness of his place than of the duty of his place, will soon commit misprisions [LL7.133–34].

Yelverton, suspended from his duties since June, had acknowledged and continued to acknowledge his error but denied any corrupt element in his actions. He requested, however, that the king examine the judicial motion before the legal proceeding continued—a request that Bacon, among a minority of the judges, was not inclined to honor, as it put the king "in a strait." As a man experienced in the law, he had to consider deeply the status of a leader who might be influenced by such foreknowledge but who ultimately had to make a decision that could not be countermanded. The majority of judges prevailed, and James read the opinion—but he avoided the "strait" by sending the document back to the judges with no judgment but an indication he was "somewhat satisfied" with Yelverton's submission, but not entirely, because someone might conclude that the king had begged for the submission—which he had not. He would not "interpose between hearing and judgment" (LL7.136).

Left free to recommend Yelverton's punishment, Coke proposed a fine of £6000; the other judges would accept £4000. Bacon agreed with the lesser fine but insisted "for his place I declare him unfit for it, and so leave it to his Majesty to dispose of it" (LL7.139). It was a painfully long judicial session. Writing to Buckingham, Bacon alleged that he had "almost killed myself with sitting almost eight hours," a situation that people of a equivalent age today can easily recognize, "but I was resolved to sit through it" (LL7.140).

Another form of misprision faced the Crown. The patent system granted to individuals monopolies of certain products or services. To hold a patent, a man had to pay for it or be an especial friend of the monarch, who dispensed them and profited from them, as needed, especially at times when Parliament managed to delay his requested subsidies. By James's time patents protected the monopolies of many common products. On November 21, 1620, five judges, including Bacon and Coke, meeting at York House, produced a document on the matter for the king. Anticipating the prospect of future Parliamentary criticism of the patent situation, the judges determined that some patents were illegal, some lawful but poorly executed, and some both unlawful *and* poorly executed. They wanted to forestall the unlawful patents and re-establish the lawful ones that profited but did not dishonor the Crown. Bacon joined in this judgment despite the fact that he had previously refereed transactions involving the reward or maintenance of patents.

In the meantime James was wrestling with foreign policy, complicated by royal marriages. In 1613 he had married his daughter Elizabeth to the young elector of the Palatinate, a district corresponding to part of today's southwestern Germany. Frederick, the elector, also claimed to be king of Bohemia, but in November of 1620 his forces were driven out of Bohemia by a Catholic league including forces from Spain. Frederick and his family fled. What did these activities mean to James?

Because he hoped to marry his son Charles to the Spanish Infanta, James, despite having less zest for war than many of his royal contemporaries, was trying to appease Spain, much to the chagrin of most Englishmen, especially those of Bacon's age, who recalled the great struggle against the Spanish Armada. The Council, twelve men, Bacon being one, had been attempting to subscribe money from wealthier Englishmen for Frederick (Parliament having not yet been called), but the funds had not been pouring in. Frederick, territorially out of Bohemia, saw his rule in the Palatinate also threatened. James did not like the irritating complications that his marriage counseling had brought on. When Parliament convened, James would insist, with some justification, that his family problem also presented a problem for his kingdom. For the needs of his offspring, who would undoubtedly contribute to subsequent European history (although James could hardly have guessed that Charles—with no assistance from this particular Infanta—would precipitate a bloody breakdown or that the Hanover line would descend from his daughter), he desperately needed funds, impossible without the compliance of a Parliament that appeared more interested in asserting itself than in supporting its sovereign.

As 1620 wound down, the Council planned for the summons of Parliament. Bacon had often told James that his agenda must blend smoothly with Parliament's agenda. James attempted (in a proclamation that Bacon wrote for him) to draw a line between "convenient freedom of speech" and what in James's mind constituted "more licentious passage of lavish discourse and bold censure in matters of state than hath been heretofore, or is fit to be suffered." Parliamentarians must "contain themselves within that modest and reverend regard of matters above their reach or calling that to good and dutiful subjects appertaineth" (LL7.156). Such overreaching, he told his subjects on Christmas Eve, he would not tolerate. Legislators presumably fumed through the holiday season.

On January 22, Bacon turned sixty; five days later he was elevated to the status of Viscount St. Alban. Ben Jonson, whose verses helped many eminent men and women celebrate, contributed a poem of ten comforting couplets, beginning:

> Hail, happy genius of this ancient pile!
> How comes it all things so about thee smile?
> The fire, the wine, the men! And in the midst,
> Thou stand'st as if some Mystery thou did'st!
> Pardon, I read it in thy face, the day
> For whose return, and amany, all these pray:
> And so do I.[1]

What is the "Mystery"? To Bacon it may only have been that it took so many decades to bring about. The fire, wine, and guests in the "pile," York House, where Sir Nicholas Bacon had long served Queen Elizabeth and where Francis Bacon had been born, were being tended by a squadron of Bacon's servants. He thanked his king numerically: "This is now the eighth time, that your Majesty has raised me" (LL7.168). James had made him member of the Learned Counsel, solicitor, attorney general, privy councilor, lord keeper, lord chancellor, Baron Verulam, and now Viscount St. Alban. James even granted Bacon, in a carefully edged way, one of the wishes that in his own scheme of things seemed extraneous: a survey of all statutes and a scheme for bringing them together in one neat legislative amalgamation. A committee must supervise it, however, including Sir Edward Coke, Bacon's old opponent but a recognized storehouse of legal lore. He could and did work with Coke, for some judicial proceedings required committee action. The art of trimming up the law did not appeal unflaggingly to the legal gentlemen of Bacon's day—and, one suspects, seldom does to people with intricately legalistic minds. Thus the project glimmered and died.

Both of Bacon's lordly designations accentuated Gorhambury, a component of Bacon's life since its construction in the 1560s, and his estate since Anthony's death. He probably began making changes immediately that would help him declare himself as master, but before his rise under King James he had lacked resources for extensive remodeling. By the time he composed his week-long memorandum in July of 1608, when he was solicitor general and clerk of the Star Chamber and more prosperous, he could do more. Under the heading of "Debts separate," there is a considerable figure marked "Gorhambury": £7304 (LL4.85). In his financial records for June through September of 1618 there are no such dispositions, but there are many entries, usually of £200 or £400 to his steward, many of which could have been meant for projects he had ordered at the estate (LL6.333–335). According to Aubrey, Bacon spent money on both the original house built by his father and a new house that he built nearby. The new house cost "nine or ten thousand," Aubrey wrote.[2] From Bacon's existing financial records, one cannot verify Aubrey's figures.

It does not seem likely that Bacon built this house primarily because of the inadequacy or neglect of the older house. Rather one should consider why wealthy people built houses at the time and what these houses meant to them. The basic source of wealth was land, and a great landowner had to have a great estate. By the sixteenth century, however, men who earned their living in town or in court also needed a terrestrial establishment to mark their achievement. Sir Nicholas Bacon's service of Queen Elizabeth made him wealthy enough to construct his house in the country. While he was building Gorhambury his somewhat wealthier colleagues were erecting houses also. Lord Burghley built Theobalds in Hertfordshire. Sir John Thynne, who was only a steward—but a steward to the brother of Jane Seymour when she was queen of Henry VIII—could erect Longleat, a symmetrical neoclassical house with two courts instead of the one-court estates that dominated Tudor architecture. These were traditional buildings for the most part, and neither was finished before Gorhambury. A scholar writing on garden history argues that Sir Nicholas had Theobalds and the Earl of Suffolk's Audley End, both with double courtyards and open galleries, in mind as models for his new mansion.[3]

Styles change, however, as well as circumstances, and a later generation of great men expected their summer homes to be in the forefront of fashion. The risk of constructing a building that would be outmoded before being finished posed a problem four hundred years ago, for then construction could drag out over many years. Sir Nicholas's building, which probably entranced the young Francis Bacon, most likely looked outmoded to him a couple of decades later. It would survive and, as the quotation below suggests, blend into the landscape of a new building with a name that called attention to antiquity: Verulam. Future developments sometimes justified great men's hopes of raising buildings that would perpetuate them; sometimes they did not. We can visualize it only through the account of a one-time seventeenth-century visitor, John Aubrey:

> I am sorry I measured not the front and breadth; but I little suspected it would be pulled down for the sake of the materials. There were good chimney pieces; the rooms very lofty, and all were very well wainscoted. There were two bathing-rooms or stuffs, whether his Lordship retired afternoons as he saw cause. All the tunnels of the chimneys were carried into the middle of the house; and round about them were seats. The top of the house was very well leaded: from the leads was a lovely prospect to the ponds, which were opposite to the east side of the house, and were on the other side of the stately walk of trees that leads to Gorhambury-house; and also over that long walk of trees, whose tops afford a most pleasant variegated verdure, resembling the works in Irish-stich. In the middle of this house was a delicate staircase of wood, which was curiously carved, and on the posts of every interstice was some pretty figure, as of a grave divine with his books a spectacles, a mendicant friar, etc., not one thing twice. On the doors of the upper story on the outside (which were painted dark umber) were the figures of the gods of the gentiles, viz. on the south door, 2d story, was Apollo; on another Jupiter with his thunderbolt, etc., bigger than the life, and done by an excellent hand; the heightenings were of hatchings of gold, which when the sun shone on them made a most glorious show.
>
> The upper part of the uppermost door on the east side had inserted into it a large looking-glass, with which the stranger was very gratefully

deceived, for (after he had been entertained a pretty while, with the prospects of the ponds, walks, and country, which this door faced) when you were about to return into the room, one would have sworn *primo intuitu* [at first look], that he had beheld another prospect through the house: for, as soon as the stranger was landed on the balcony, the concierge that showed the house would shut the door to put this fallacy on him with the looking-glass. This was his Lordship's summer-house: for he says (in his essay) one should have seats for summer and winter as well as clothes.[4]

By the time Aubrey composed his brief life of Bacon a few decades after the latter's death, Verulam, no longer commanding the respect that would preserve it, was sold, around 1665 or 1666 to two carpenters for a mere four hundred pounds. That fate, one guesses, would have brought tears to Bacon's eyes. "This magnanimous Lord Chancellor had a great mind to have made it a city again, and he had designed it, to be built with great uniformity: but Fortune denied it him."[5] The historical aspect of Verulam will be discussed later.

At this heightened time in Bacon's social life, his publisher was distributing a work formulated over many years, his *Instauratio Magna*, written in Latin to be available to scholars everywhere, and eventually to be put into English as *The Great Instauration*. "I am persuaded," he wrote, "the work will gain upon men's minds in ages" (LL7.120). It has gained—and it has lost—but it remains a monument of its time.

Bacon's frontispiece to *The Great Instauration* is highly significant. It depicts two ships. Although it would be possible to speculate on the significance of a ship that is far off, we will ignore it as irrelevant. In the foreground the second ship is about to pass between two pillars set close together on two stretches of land. These are the Pillars of Hercules, and represent one of the twelve labors that the mythical Hercules had to perform. Supposedly he had split apart a mountain into Gibraltar, on one side, and Mt. Abyla in Morocco on the other. A Latin quotation at the base of the picture represents a passage in the Book of Daniel 12:4: "Many shall run to and fro, and knowledge shall be increased." What is the connection between the myth and the Old Testament passage? Hercules broke the original mountain beyond which man was not to enter to gain the apples in the Garden of Hesperides, but traditionally the mountain represented the western limit of the habitable world, as exemplified, for instance, in Dante's *Inferno*, Canto 28:

The frontispiece to *Instauratio Magna (The Great Instauration)* by Francis Bacon, 1620 (courtesy Folger Shakespeare Library).

> I (Ulysses) and my companions were old and tardy, when
>   we came to that narrow pass, where Hercules
>   assigned his landmarks
> To hinder man from venturing further.[6]

By designating the ship as a seeker of knowledge, Bacon was certifying *The Great Instauration* as a Herculean breaker of the supposed limits of knowledge. His use of the Book of Daniel appropriately supplied a connection between the myth from the ancient world and Western Christianity, for he viewed no impasse or struggle between that tradition and the advancement of learning.

He dedicated the book to King James hoping "that your Majesty will be aiding to me, in setting men on work for the collecting of a natural and experimental history" (LL7.130). His investigation of nature necessitated the production of many histories of natural forces such as wind, water, light, magnetism, and the like. The task, as he saw it, loomed large and variegated. Although Bacon still desired to pursue "all knowledge," he recognized that he would need many associates. He also realized that the work fell far short of completion, the aura of definitiveness, for which he had striven. It was meant to include six books, but only one, the *Novum Organum* (in English *The New Organon*), stood complete. The larger work would require the assistance of many scholars before the world would have a massive collection of "natural and experimental history." James, with his own troubles without and within, would not, as Bacon hoped, help uncover these assistants.

In his "Proemium" to the unfinished whole, here quoted in its later English version, Bacon alleges his intent to determine "whether that commerce between the mind of man and the nature of things, which is more precious than anything on earth, or at least than anything that is of the earth, might by any means be restored to its perfect and original condition, or if that may not be, yet reduced to a better condition than that in which it now is" (W8.17).

Like many of the essays, Book I of *The New Organon*, especially its opening section, is based on the aphorism. The early aphorisms shoot out briefly and pointedly as in Bacon's 1597 essays, but at Aphorism 39 of the 130 in *The New Organon*, where he introduces the most famous part of the work, his classification of the four Idols of the Mind, they become longer and more argumentative. Today, reading these aphorisms is still an invigorating—if not wholly convincing—experience. He stresses the importance of inductive reasoning as a mode not sufficiently tried and makes statements about nature with which we, if not some of our predecessors, can endorse, as for instance the beginning of Aphorism 10: "The subtlety of nature is greater many times over than the subtlety of the senses and understanding." He reiterates this statement in Axiom 24, except that instead of "senses and understanding" he has "argument." Bacon calls *Idols* the opposite of *Ideas*. If they have been introduced to you, undergo the delight of coming again to the Idols of the Tribe, the Cave, the Market-place, and the Theater.[7]

The Idols of the Tribe emanate from the "false assertion that the sense of man is the measure of things," for "human understanding is a false mirror." The Idols of the Cave are individual, for everyone "has a cave or den of his own." Bacon may well have invented *den* as the now enormously popular name for a secluded place of one's own, for the only human dens cited in the *Oxford English Dictionary* are those of robbers. His image, however, is optical as well as bestial, for this den "refracts and discolours the light of nature." He may have appropriated this image from Plato's cave in Book 7 of the *Republic*, although for Bacon nature is the thing to be seen, not a distraction from the world of the soul.

In addition to the idols we suffer from human nature and those that emanate from our peculiar nature and our various habitudes of reading, conversation, and education, we are subject to the Idols of the Market-place, a set which, as "the intercourse and association of men," might seem little different from those of the cave (for this is true of conversation and education also), except that here Bacon is thinking particularly of our mode of discourse, which is too often an "ill and unfit choice of words." When he illustrates this point, he is also leading us toward his last class of Idols, for these words that derail our thought are "either names of things which do not exist ... or they are names of things which exist, but yet confused and ill-defined, and hastily and irregularly derived from realities." Words like *Fortune, the Prime Mover, Planetary Orbits, Element of Fire*, he places among the nonexistent; words which name "substances" are distortions: "the notion of *chalk* and *mud* is good, of *earth* is bad," as is *humid*. We are used to much more sophisticated classifications of general and abstract language today, but Bacon is working quickly here, interested in clearing a linguistic path through what can easily become impenetrable layers of abstractions. It might be interesting to imagine what names a twenty-first-century Bacon would disparage. He would like *net* but probably not *social network, baseball* but not the great phenomenon America makes of it, *national pastime*.

The Idols of the Theater migrated into men's minds from the various dogmas of philosophies, and also from wrong laws of demonstration. It is easy to see that such Idols owe a good deal to some of his examples of the Market-place Idols. These philosophies need language to carry on their nefarious trades; inevitably they make it up or dig into a pile of already-distorted words. Indeed, Bacon finds the Market-place Idols "the most troublesome of all." This section of *The New Organon* is one of several places where Bacon draws negatively on the theater. The Idols come from "the play-books of philosophical systems." It even leads to an illusion to the make-believe of poetry: "And in the plays of the philosophical theatre you may observe the same thing which is found in the theatre of the poets, that stories invented for the stage are more compact and elegant, and more as one would wish them to be, than true stories out of history." Bacon often disparages the theater as we disparage the movies, but find that we cannot do without their "compact and elegant" untruths. For Bacon has discerned that we are far short of absorbing and understanding what he calls history (what we must call a conflation of philosophy and science).

Baconians, pro and con, are likely to agree that he is better at pinpointing errors of old than at charting specifically the new path that he insists is necessary. The art which he calls *the interpretation of nature* is invigorating but fragmentary. In his sketchy outline of Part VI, *The New Philosophy and the Active Science*, he confesses that its development is not merely yet unwritten but "above my strength and beyond my hopes" (W8.52–53). He makes, however, what I take to be his most profound assertion: "For man is but the servant and interpreter of nature. What he does and what he knows is only what he has observed of nature's order in fact or in thought; beyond this he knows nothing and can do nothing (W8.53).

How much credit is Bacon allowed for his inductive investigation of nature beyond his hearty endorsement of it? In Aphorism 105 he describes his process: "The induction which proceeds by simple enumeration is childish; its conclusions are precarious and exposed to peril from a contradictory instance; and it generally decides on too small a number of facts, and on those only which are at hand. But the induction which is to be available for the discovery and demonstration of sciences and arts, must analyse nature by proper rejections and exclusions; and then, after a sufficient number of negatives, comes to a conclusion on the affirmative instances" (W8.138–39).

This explanation, using terminology somewhat different from that of the scientific world of today, nevertheless seems to reflect a clear understanding of the process.

Uncommon things, he says, cannot be understood apart from common ones: "I … am of necessity compelled to admit the commonest things into my history. Nay, in my judgment philosophy has been hindered by nothing more than this—that things of familiar and frequent occurrence do not arrest and detain the thoughts of men, but are received in passing without any inquiry into their causes" (W8.151).

Then there are the great things, much noticed but little understood. He offers a trio of discoveries "unknown to the ancients, and of which the origin, though recent, is obscure and inglorious; namely, printing, gunpowder, and the magnet. For these three have changed the whole face and state of things throughout the world" (W8.162). It would have been difficult to make a better short list of "great things." An equivalent today might be the computer, nuclear energy, and DNA, perhaps—or could a modern Bacon have made a better list that might only become clear to others later?

How helpful is his assertion "*Nor can nature be commanded except by being obeyed*"? In recent decades we have witnessed the repercussions of nature—we might even call them *retaliations*—upon being "commanded," and we agree with Bacon about the necessity of obeying. How far did Bacon's insistence on obedience extend? In a short treatise appended to *The New Organon*, which he called "A Preparative towards a Natural and Experimental History," he divides nature into three categories. Nature can be "free," as it usually operates; it can be modified by "the violence of impediments"; and it can be modified by man. The first two categories we can consider as one, for a situation that he might consider an impediment such as an earthquake or a great flood we more likely see as one aspect of nature. We can agree with him that "in things artificial nature takes orders from man, and works under his authority: without man, such things would have been made. But by the help and ministry of man a new face of bodies, another use or theatre of things, comes into view" (W8.357). *Ministry*, by the way, meant any useful service and was not confined to religious use as it tends to be today. I might call attention to one other word in this statement. *Theatre*, which Bacon often uses negatively as signifying the opposite of "real" things, is here a figurative word signifying a place where something happens. Only in Bacon's maturity did it begin to be used this way, with no negative connotation.

Bacon at this point refers to nature working under man's authority, nature working as it would not do otherwise. What limits on this authority would Bacon have considered appropriate to maintain obedience to nature? To what extent could he have imagined humans' capacity for damaging nature? Do we have warrant for supposing that he would have cautioned the world against extending human "authority" over nature disrespectfully? I am pushing this matter into the area of speculation, but Bacon's observations about the particular aspects of nature are keen. If we consider his interest in gardening, he wanted to *arrange* the elements of nature, of course. He wanted broad paths, elevations, ponds, and such in his garden. He wanted covered sections where people could rest comfortably on warm days. If he had guests who fished, he would want fish in his ponds. All such things are well within the limits any good horticulturalist today might honor.

Within a few lines of a work already cited several times, *The History of the Winds*, he makes specific observations about crows, ducks, herons, ravens, owls, dolphins, swine, and spiders (W9.456–57). In some notes of Bacon's apparently intended for his correspondence with the Duke of Buckingham, he wrote, "I love birds"; in the same notes he writes, very literally, it seems: "Weeding time is not yet come" (LL7.444). Did this important judge do any of his own weeding? The very fact that he writes such things implies not just a tendency to make pronouncements about earth but a true devotion to the things of earth. In *Sylva Sylvarum*, in Volume 4 of Bacon's *Works*, edited by Robert Leslie Ellis and Douglas Denon Heath as well as Spedding, one can find hundreds of references, many of them very specific, to trees. In my judgment, Bacon would have been appalled by a reckless interpretation of humans' *authority* over them.

Scholars have pointed out that in enumerating 130 subjects of nature-in-itself or nature modified by humans, Bacon was not simply listing things for further study. His investigations were tied to a theory of natural history based on an assumption that the principles of nature were far simpler than we know them to be.[8] One of the men most influenced by him, Robert Boyle, set forth as early as 1661, in *The Sceptical Chemist*, a theory of chemistry that would have greatly sharpened Bacon's analysis of nature. One can sense in Bacon's late pleas for help in carrying out his work a growing awareness that his scheme would require a great network of assistants. He insists on the necessity of others completing what he regards as a philosophical jumping-off place. "I will proceed with my plan of preparing men's minds; of which preparation to give hope is no unimportant part" (W8.129).

Aphorism 113 of *The New Organon* boasts of his accomplishment but cites his limitations. "I think that men may take some hope from my own example. And this I say not by way of boasting, but because it is useful to say it. If there be any that despond, let them look at me, that being of all men of my time the most busied in affairs of state, and a man of health not very strong (whereby much time is lost), and in this course altogether a pioneer, following in no man's track, nor sharing those counsels with any one, have nevertheless by resolutely entering the true road and submitting my mind to Things, advanced these matters, as I suppose, some little way" (W8.144–45).

For Bacon *Things* deserve its capital letter. Bacon thought that workers in the field of advancing knowledge so far "have been either men of experiment or men of dogmas. The men of experiment are like the ant; they only collect and use; the reasoners are like spiders, who make cobwebs out of their own substance. But the bee takes a middle course; it gathers its material from the flowers of the garden and of the field, but transforms and digests it by a power of its own" (W8.131). For

Bacon experimentation is not mechanical but philosophical; he is not a maker of gadgets. His favorite experiments are *experimenta lucifera*, experiments of light rather than *experimenta fructifera*, experiments of fruit. He wanted his work to continue, and continue it did, specifically in the activity of the Royal Society of London and generally in the interrogation of nature ever since.

Among the recipients of the *Novum Organum* in its early Latinate form was Bacon's old rival, Sir Edward Coke. At times the men worked successfully together, and probably Bacon hoped that Coke, despite their differences, would acknowledge his achievement. Catherine Drinker Bowen, who wrote biographies of both men, described Coke's reaction. On its title page the recipient wrote a couplet:

> It deserveth not to be read in Schools
> But to be freighted in the ship of fools.

Coke's audience would have known of Sebastian Brant's 1494 allegorical narrative *Das Narrenschiff* (*The Ship of Fools*), depicting a ship both laden with fools and driven by one to a place of fools, Narragonia. In Latin, Coke added the following: "You propose to reconstruct the teaching of wise men of old. Reconstruct first our laws and justice."[9] Of course Coke was himself an interpreter of the law rather than of nature, and of course Bacon had sought opportunities to reconstruct British law. Had he done so, however, Coke, more consistent than Bacon in his affirmation of English common law, would have found much to challenge. If Coke's rebuke got back to Bacon, he probably shook it off. He had no reason to be less than intensely proud of *The Novum Organum*, which would circulate in its Latin form among the educated men of the European world.

9

A Broken Reed

It was January 1620 by the calendar of Bacon's time, 1621 by the calendar in use today, and as Lord Chancellor of Britain, author of an important philosophical work now circulating in Europe, and possessor of the title of Viscount St. Alban, he had to feel extremely confident. We will, in the habit of our time, continue to call him Francis Bacon. Long, laborious (and some would say obsequious) efforts had enabled the attainment of these political, intellectual, and social consummations. From the tone of his letters to the king and, increasingly, to Marquis Buckingham, it is clear that Bacon practiced attentively the art of obsequiousness. We judge it, of course, as one of his less admirable traits, but it accompanied a zealous performance of his duties. Bacon acknowledged himself, however, as an old and not especially healthy man. A man of sixty could not in the seventeenth century consider himself at the peak of middle age, as men can do today. He maintained hopes for a still productive future (LL7.169).

Six days before that birthday on the 22nd, Parliament would meet. He had plenty to do. When the session was postponed until the 30th, he probably appreciated the additional time to prepare for it. Most importantly, he had to make King James understand—not merely understand but recognize—that because of the disparity between his priorities and those of the House of Commons, strategic and diplomatic planning must fortify his speech and that of his Lord Chancellor.

Having two young hostages to fortune, Elizabeth in the Palatinate and Charles, just reaching his majority and surely requiring a suitable mate before ascending to the throne, James realized that the son-in-law he already had, Frederick V, had surely become victim of a situation now known as the Thirty Years' War (1618–1648). After the Protestant factions of Bohemia had championed him against their Catholic King Ferdinand, Austrian and Bavarian forces had, the preceding November, routed Frederick's Bohemians in the Battle of the White Mountain. Routed after only a year as king of Bohemia, Frederick now faced the invasion of his Palatinate domain. He sought his father-in-law's help, and James understood the difficulties of any extensive participation in these uproars in the middle of the European continent. James would rather play off the Protestant-Catholic struggle by marrying Charles off to a Spanish princess, but his Parliament loved Spain very little. James saw himself as a possible negotiator, but what would he do if negotiations failed? Someone in the Court (it may or may not have been Bacon) prepared a paper assessing the contrasting possibilities of a conquering army, a diverting army, or an army of assistance. Parliament had little taste for any of those armies, especially for the very expensive one considered capable of conquering.

Before the body came together Bacon celebrated his new rank. In a lavish ceremony Bacon took the name of an early saint, St. Alban being early enough to retain Anglican plaudits. With robes and coronet carried by lords of the realm, Bacon rose a step in the peerage. In a letter to the king, Bacon noted that this rise was the eighth for which he thanked James. He responded in a burst of musical imagery: "So this is the eighth rise or reach, a diapason in music, even a good number and accord for a close." Originally, Spedding noted, Bacon closed with the following: "Which is a joyful heart, a studious thought, an incessant endeavour, and the best of my time, which I hope shall conclude with your favour and service in your remembrance." Bacon marked out this sentence in his draft and substituted: "And lastly, your Majesty shall have the best of my time, which I assure myself shall conclude in your favour, and survive in your remembrance" (LL7.169). He was willing to give up what was for him an extremely typical round of phrases and rely on "the best of my time."

On February 2 a speaker named Serjeant Richardson opened Parliamentary proceedings according to tradition by pleading his incompetence; then Bacon, now for the first time in forty years ineligible for Parliament, assured Richardson of the king's favor. Richardson's next traditional speech praised the monarch and recited the benefits owing to him, necessitating Bacon's royalist account of those benefits. The king had enlarged the kingdom by bringing Scotland into it, he continually worked at bringing to Ireland "plantation and reduction to civility," he had planted Virginia across the Atlantic (now including New England, for less than three months ago a group of English persons, unfortunately dissenting ones, had struggled ashore at a cape on the American coast). Furthermore, James had verified his role as Defender of the Faith, he had preserved the peace in the realm, he had done all and well.

Ceremonies concluded, work began—the establishment of committees. One considered the Palatinate, determined in due time that any proficient force would require £500,000 annually, and recommended appropriation of part of the first year's fund. Parliament did its best to convey the impression that, after all, diplomacy might work more cheaply than an invasion. Or attention could focus on internal improvements. Perhaps Edward Coke and other men of law would carry out an old item from Bacon's wish list: drawing together the myriad laws of the land into "one plain and perfect law." Another would look into tightening restrictions against "Jesuits, seminary priests and popish recusants." These suggestions indicate a distinct preference for supposedly practicable reforms within the realm rather than warfare on the continent.

Parliament ultimately decided to energize the Committee for Grievances, the main grievance being monopolies, especially ones that perhaps harbored illegalities or had inept administrators. Because the men who administered these monopolies worked to effect the king's pleas and profit, the committee efficiently directed responsibilities for such failures to them rather than James. Sir Edward Sackville argued that the misdeeds of some referees had in effect abused the king and the commonwealth. Sir Lionel Cranfield insisted on the review of the patent for Inns, previously awarded to Sir Giles Momperson. Bacon could hardly have generated any great enthusiasm for this turn of events.

Since Cranfield, by this effort, was emerging as Bacon's most implacable enemy, surpassing even Coke, whose clashes with Bacon we have already seen, it is appropriate to examine their relationship. One of the apothegms attributed to Bacon provides a hint. Some of these sayings, however, come from a commonplace book of Bacon's earliest champion, his former physician, Dr. Rawley. Presumably Rawley based such commonplace entries on Bacon's notes, but whether the following passage comes ultimately from Bacon or not, it must be considered here. "A flattering courtier undertook to make a comparison betwixt my Lord St. Alban and Treasurer Cranfield. Said he, My Lord St. Alban had a pretty turning wit, and could speak well: but he wanted that profound judgment and solidity of a statesman that my Lord of Middlesex hath. Said a courtier that stood by: Sir I wonder you will disparage your judgment so much as to offer to make any parallel between these two. I'll tell you what: when these two men shall be recorded in our chronicles to after ages, men will wonder how my Lord St. Alban could fall; and they will wonder how my Lord of Middlesex could rise" (W13.407–08).

Several things from this passage need emphasis. Cranfield, soon to become Earl of Middlesex (we will continue to call him Cranfield), charged Bacon with criminality, and as Lord Treasurer he would control matters pertaining to the public aspect of Bacon's invariably precarious financial situation. Bacon would have laughed at the proposition that Cranfield excelled him in statesmanship, viewing him as a rich merchant without the saving graces of a prominent family, collegiate and legal education, and oratorical gifts.

Buckingham's employment of Cranfield as an advisor owed much to his financial expertise. A scholar who has studied the Bacon-Cranfield connections claimed that "the two men were by far the ablest of the royal minorities."[1] The two men had worked together, as Bacon had worked with Coke. Cranfield possessed sincere reforming instincts and wanted to proceed boldly against referees suspected of ineptness or malice in the maintenance of monopolies, and Bacon refereed two of the monopolies that seemed to require particular investigation, one having to do with inns and one with gold and silver thread. Did Cranfield's mission against Bacon as referee owe more to his crusade against vice in the administration or to his resentment of a man who may have denigrated him within reach of attentive ears? As surely as Bacon's propensity for making friends, he knew how to make enemies. Furthermore, to be a judge in a small nation with a small knot of highly competitive officials in the seventeenth century made contention inevitable. For whatever reason, at this point Cranfield, assisted by Coke and others who disliked Bacon, led the charge against the newly created viscount.

To look ahead for a moment, during the first two and one half years Bacon, after his fall from power, depended on Lord Treasurer Cranfield (from September 1622, Lord Treasurer Middlesex) for the distribution of his pension. In a 1622 letter to Buckingham, apparently after a series of delays by the Lord Treasurer, Bacon pleads: "My Lord, let it be your own deed; and to use the prayers of the Litany, Good Lord deliver me from this servile dependence; for I had rather beg and starve than be fed at that door" (L7.397). Spedding's note claims that "than beg and be fed" had been written first. Nevertheless, Bacon did have to do some begging from his opponent.

The final irony is that in 1624, Cranford's tightfistedness as Lord Treasurer had infuriated many men, roused Buckingham and Prince Charles (the latter offended not only by the man's stinginess but by an additional tendency to speak disrespectfully to royalty) to lead a move to impeach the Lord Treasurer. Although Cranfield, unlike Bacon, resisted the charges vigorously, the House of Lords found him guilty, and he "was given a sentence that was almost exactly the same as the one that had been imposed on Bacon."[2] To return to the charges against Bacon early in 1621: Momperson, the holder of the inns patent, had consulted with several men, Bacon among them, in connection with his monopoly. Spedding concluded that Bacon had been cautious in reviewing this patent (LL6.98–99).

Bacon had also approved the transfer of the patent for gold and silver thread to the king (LL6.339). He had to face the fact that Coke would judge these operations and recommend befitting punishments. Writing to Buckingham on March 7, Bacon stated that "tomorrow's conference is like to pass in a calm, as to the referees," but he added, "I do but listen, and I have doubt only of Sir Edward Coke, who I wish had more round *caveat* given him from the king" (LL7.192). Bacon seemed confident, perhaps anticipating the investigators' reluctance to accuse referees—men of high judicial standing and royal favor. Nevertheless, the committee named him among the referees whose work the group found questionable but acted no further against the other referees. For Spedding, this result demonstrated that the committee had made him "the real object of attack" (LL7.197). In other words, the war on monopolies was softening Bacon for a more pointed assault.

Bacon wrote to his good friend Toby Matthew a letter whose date is not known, but it fits into this period when forces were gathering against him while he continued to express confidence. "I would not have my friends (though I know it to be out of love) too apprehensive either of me or for me," he assured Matthew, "For I thank God my ways are sound and good, and I hope God will bless me in them" (LL7.201).

On March 15, once a fatal day for Julius Caesar, the Lower House delivered a Declaration of Grievances to the Lords recommending penal statutes for the three monopolies, on two of which Bacon had worked. In his capacity as Lord Chancellor, Bacon had the duty of outlining the judicial process: three patents (including the two with which he had been involved) required the assessment of charges against the guilty, proofs, and punishment. The Upper House recommended that the Lords' grievance committees meet with those from Commons. Bacon at this point knew that on the previous day a different and more serious allegation had erupted to wrench attention away from his possible blunders as a referee. A man named Christopher Aubrey had presented to Commons a petition charging Bacon with having received from Aubrey, more than two years previously, £100 while a case involving Aubrey and a man named Sir William Bruncker pended. Bacon had eventually ruled against Aubrey, but he had received the money (LL7.257).

On the day before the Ides of March, Bacon wrote to Buckingham: "Your Lordship spoke of purgatory. I am now in it, but my mind is in a calm, for my fortune is not my felicity. I know I have clean hands and a clean heart, and I hope a clean house for friends or servants.... But the King and your Lordship will, I hope, put an end to these miseries one way or other. And in troth that which I fear most is lest continual attendance and business, together with these cares, and want of time to do my weak body right this spring by diet and physic, will cast me down, and then it will be thought feigning or fainting. But I hope in God I shall hold out. God prosper you" (LL7.213).

Traditionally, the prospect of purgatory generated a sigh of relief. His guilt purged, a sinner might expect salvation. Bacon, however, was not confessing guilt, only recognizing that a reputation for cleanness might not protect a man from the dirt that might be cast at him. Of his hands and heart he could be sure; too many people worked in the "house" of an official as busy as Bacon to ensure that all underlings were behaving properly. Bacon, the king's underling, hoped that his record of service would forestall any tendency to blame him for the occasional slips that all good men make.

How often has one man's case inspired others? A second man, Edward Egerton, also dug into the past and alleged another payoff when Bacon was Lord Keeper, presumably in 1617. Neither of these men apparently hesitated to admit that they had offered such gifts to Bacon. Soon other charges were dropping on the Lord Chancellor. On March 19, he wrote to the Lords, who, like the United States Senate today, received for their judgment impeachments coming from the other body. He insisted that he could not appear before them because of "sickness both of my heart and of my back, though joined with that comfort of mind, that persuadeth me that I am not far from heaven, whereof I feel the first fruits. And because, whether I live or die, I would be glad to preserve my honor and fame, as far as I am worthy" (LL7.215). The self-confidence that he had expressed now was crumbling. Bacon reminded the lords of the immensity of the task of investigating complaints against a man whose decrees and orders in a year he estimated at two thousand, and who customarily could accept gifts as long they could be demonstrated untied to the judicial knot.

Buckingham, visiting Bacon twice and indeed finding him ill, though somewhat better on the second occasion, brought the letter to the assembled lords. At this time Bacon did not know the number of charges against him, for indicting season had sprung open on the Lord Chancellor, and more were streaming in. Some came from the recently dismissed registrar of Bacon's Court of Chancery, John Churchill. Did the fact that Bacon had apparently not been able to supervise Churchill weigh more heavily with the peers than the fact that the man had lost his job because of his own corruption?

Although judges clearly should not accept gifts such as those administered by Aubrey and Egerton, Spedding points out that "the difference between a gratuity which a Chancellor might and one which might not lawfully accept, was in those days a very nice one—not only in common opinion but in law.... If his judgment is not affected by the gratuity, he is a just judge notwithstanding" (LL7.217). Just, perhaps, but imprudent in the extreme. In his essay "Of Suspicion," which did not appear until the 1625 edition, Bacon considered suspicions "defects, not in the heart, but in the brain." A good person might harbor suspicions, but he should "frankly … communicate them with the party that he suspects" (W12.190–91), presumably before charging him publicly. Bacon's assertion that "base" men do not do so comes as close as he ever does to criticizing his accusers (W12.190–91).

On March 25, Bacon wrote again to Buckingham with an enclosure for the king: "I fly unto your Majesty with the wings of a dove, which once within these seven days I thought would have carried me a higher flight" (LL7.225). It is not clear what in the past week might have energized his flight, and as the letter goes on it reveals a shockingly troubled mind. "I have been no haughty or intolerable or hateful man, in my conversation or carriage. I have inherited no hatred from my father, but am a good patriot born" (LL7.226). None of this could do him any good, and why he brought up his father, whom he honored, is difficult to see. This man, who never revealed himself in his letters, was confessing thus to his royal employer. He hopes to be found innocent, but "I may be frail, and partake of the abuse of the times." (LL7.226). Bacon was at this point weak both physically and mentally; his normal clarity of his mind had vanished.

The king spoke to the Lords the next day, leaving judgment to them and announcing that he would "strike dead" the patents complained of: inns, ale houses, and gold and silver thread (LL7.227). From May 27 to April 17 the two houses adjourned for their Easter recess. Lying ill at York House, Bacon, convinced that he was dying, made a ridiculously simple will. It begins: "I bequeath my soul to God above, by the oblation of my Saviour. My body to be buried obscurely" (LL7.228). This is not the will of a man with many servants, estates, and responsibilities but of a man in the pit of depression, a man desiring to inform the world that he wishes to be obscure. His compositions would go to his brother-in-law, Sir John Constable, who would declare whether they were "fit to be published." His wife was to receive merely a box of rings. Various lands, leases, and chattels would be in the hands of his executors to pay his debts, but Gorhambury and Verulam, the house he had built himself, would, after his wife's decease, go to "the Prince's Highness." At the time of this will he still did not know the specifications of the charges against him. Some months before his death several years later he would compose a more sophisticated will.

Bacon finally composed a memorandum which reflects a man with rationality restored. In rehearsing what he would communicate to the king, he distinguished three situations in which someone might make "gifts and rewards" to a judge. The first, *pendent lite*, that is when a case involves a "bargain, contract, or promise of reward" when the judge knows that a judgment is actually pending. Bacon would not do such a thing. The second is "a neglect in the Judge to inform himself whether the cause be fully at an end or no, what time he receives the gift; but takes it upon the credit of the party, that all is done; or otherwise omits to enquire." This sort of neglect strikes the reader today, and surely had to strike investigators then, as a serious deficiency. The third situation, when the judge receives a gift made after the judgment is given, Bacon considers "no offense" (LL7.238).

On April 20, Bacon wrote the king. After calling himself "infinitely bounden to your Majesty," he goes on: "I see your Majesty imitateth him that would not break the broken reed, nor quench the smoking flax; and as you Majesty imitateth Christ, so I hope assuredly my Lords of the Upper House will imitate you." Of the charges against him, "I shall without fig-leaves or disguise excuse what I can excuse, extenuate which I can extenuate, and ingenuously confess what I can neither clear nor extenuate" (LL7.240). Realizing that he must make some sort of offering to the king, he wrote again the next day with a promise wittily put: "I will … present your Majesty with a bribe," which would consist of "a good history of England and a better digest of your laws" (LL7.241–42). To the second of these projects, several times promised, he never addressed himself, probably fearing how much time they would subtract from his continuing process of advancing learning, but he was making some progress in the former, which would turn into a biography of Henry VII.

A committee of four lords, fairly selected, it appears, were asked to judge Bacon, but they decided to pass judgment off to the Archbishop of Canterbury, who had to be concerned because one of his bishops had also involved himself in the corruption at hand. Bacon's former clients, in either a fever of confession or an opportunity for retaliation, had driven the list of charges to twenty-eight. Would Bacon offer a defense? He was allowed a paltry five days to prepare it. Analytical as always, he went through the list. To some he confessed guilt, even confessing a severe level of guilt for the first time, thereby contradicting his earlier claims of cleanness. Although he insisted that in none of these instances did the gift affect his judgment, he recognized his untenable position. He summed up the case: "There is a great deal of corruption and neglect; for which I am heartily and penitently sorry, and submit myself to the judgment, grace, and mercy of the court" (LL7.261).

A twelve-man group consisting of three committees accepted his confession. He knew that the Lords collectively lacked the judicial capacity of the men of law among whom he moved, but he recognized the committee members as honest men—if not immune to any possible royal fear or favor. They asked Bacon whether his responses to the charges, some of which may have astonished them, were in his own hand, and whether he stood by them. He responded eloquently, repeating one of the images he had used writing to the king. "My Lords, it is my act, my hand, my heart. I beseech your Lordships, be merciful to a broken reed" (L7.262).

The Lords judged him severely. He was fined £40,000, he would receive imprisonment during the king's pleasure, he was never again to be employed in State or Parliament, and he was not to come within the verge of the Court. His time in the Tower differed greatly from that of another man who proposed, and actually wrote, a history (not just of England but, in his distinctive way, of the world), Sir Walter Raleigh, the "king's pleasure" lasting only a few days instead of Raleigh's thirteen years. On the other hand, Bacon's verge—twelve miles—would not have bothered Raleigh, who had designs on many places in the world quite remote from the monarch's precincts, whereas Bacon had spent most of his life within that verge. After the brief imprisonment, Sir John Vaughan received Bacon at his home in Fullham outside James's verge.

Early in June Bacon wrote briefly to the king and to two other men who had helped him. After thanking the king for his "liberty," he closed briefly: "But your Majesty that did shed tears in the beginning of my trouble, will I hope shed the dew of your grace and goodness upon me in the end. Let me live to serve you, else life is but the shadow of death to Your Majesty's most devoted servant, Fr. St. Alban" (L7.281). For many years before the House of Commons began to assert itself as a body with higher ambitions than occasional supplier of the king's financial needs, Bacon remained devoted to the monarchy as the indispensable instrument of governance.

Along with the obligation to thank these men stood the possibility of continuing to be of use in the realm. He thanked Buckingham also: "Now my body is out, my mind nevertheless will be still in prison, till I maybe on my feet to do his Majesty and your Lordship faithful service" (LL7.281). He wrote to Toby Matthew in an undated letter, begging for a visit. He wrote the longest letter of gratitude to the man who had done the most, Prince Charles: "When I call to mind, how infinitely I am bound to your Highness, that stretched forth your arm to save me from a sentence; that took hold of me to keep me from being plunged deep in a sentence; that hath kept me alive in your gracious memory and mentions since the sentence, pitying me as (I hope) I deserve, and valuing me far above that I can deserve, I find my words almost as barren as my fortunes, to express unto your Highness the thankfulness I owe" (L7.287).

Bacon went on to praise the prince as "judicious, accomplished, and graceful in all your doings" and much more. Charles, eventually the only king his British subjects felt obliged to execute, in 1621, when just reaching his majority, received much praise of this type. Bacon's reply to the king, perhaps only a few days later, after James had asked for Bacon's opinions on reforming the courts of justice—a task, if sincerely rather than consolingly offered, that Bacon recognized as unworkable—contains a sentence that Charles, unfortunately, had even more trouble accepting than had his father. Filled with sweetness and light, it also demonstrates how unfortunate Charles was to lack his own Francis Bacon to counsel him during his reign—how regrettable for him and the kingdom. Bacon elegantly declined the king's offer. No, he could not predict the future of Great Britain's governance, but Charles needed the simile, again musical. "That it doth well in church-music when the greatest part of the hymn is sung by one voice, and then the quire at times falls in sweetly and solemnly, and that the same harmony sorteth well in monarchy between the King and his Parliament" (LL7.290). With that personal pronoun before *Parliament*, however, Bacon proved that he was not up to a new order of disbursers turned true legislators. Historians generally agree that Charles's incapacity to perform as lead vocalist for Parliament did as much as any other shortcoming to bring about his downfall.

Bacon's downfall is much more famous than the work he did. Daniel R. Coquillette, a historian of English law, has determined that Bacon performed creditably as a judge.[3] As of June 1817 he had cleared a backlog of cases and by dealing with as many as 1,700 cases per year, did not allow it to rebuild. He replaced judges involved personally in cases on which they worked. He defended widows and took action against husbands and fathers who mistreated women. Even after his impeachment few of his orders and decrees were reversed, one example being his judgment that granted protection to bankrupted individuals, very unpopular with creditors.

Although he supervised subordinate judges carefully in matters of improper influence, even his defenders find him careless in his own practice. He did accept gifts from people whose cases he decided, although he insisted that no gifts affected his decisions, and existing records support him, showing that in fact he judged against these gift-givers, who were clearly trying to overcome damaging evidence against them. In Bacon's time in England and elsewhere, practices which today are considered corrupt were not only acceptable but often necessary, for Court officers did not receive salaries and had to depend on the bestowal of handsome New Year's gifts. The system in place in the period of Bacon's judicial career required reform, and men like Coke and Cranfield did indeed work for it. If denied funds by Parliamentary inaction or delay, the king himself had to depend on income from such devices as patents, which of course constituted, or could lead to, monopolies. For his loyalty to the king in this matter Bacon attracted the enmity of Parliamentary reformers led by Coke and Cranfield, who had other grudges against him. In the system for investigating misconduct, the House of Commons was the accuser and the Lords served as judges, the rights of the accused to defend themselves being meager and ill-defined.

Bacon's loyalty to the King and Buckingham, who had his own

record of corruption, went unreciprocated. It is true that Bacon's fine was never collected and his imprisonment was short, but he remained excluded from his public career, in most respects an outstanding one. The realm could have used his experience and industriousness in his late years. By the time Charles, better disposed towards Bacon, replaced his father as monarch, however, the former Lord Chancellor had entered his last year of life. Always determined to employ his leisure constructively, he deployed his energies to his intellectual work.

Of his last years in Gorhambury, Spedding, an honest biographer and in the long run perhaps Bacon's greatest champion, considered his life "for the most part depressing and melancholy." Bacon, however, turned from "broken reed" to thinking reed, as Blaise Pascal would memorably put it later in the century: *un Roseau pensant.* He hoped that the king would value his work in the historical vein, both in our sense of the term and in his application of it to the study of nature. In his application of *history* to science, which seems so odd to us today, we must remember the generality of its meaning in Bacon's time and long afterward. A history was a story, true or imagined; a true story could take up any subject. Eighteenth-century novelists like Richardson and Fielding would routinely call their works histories.

Bacon's main work of history (in our use of the term) turned into a biography of King Henry VII with a prominent theme. As a man who had unified Britain by bringing together England and Scotland, James, Bacon hoped, would appreciate a narrative and a character—a Lancastrian who married Elizabeth of York—and thus consummated the union of the red and white roses who had strained and struggled over so many decades before that marriage. Absence from the verge restricted his research. He borrowed materials from Sir Robert Cotton, whose library, supplemented later by his offspring, became the basis of the British Library, but Bacon could not visit him. Bacon, however, with his advantage of being an experienced political insider over substantial parts of the reigns of two monarchs, understood and could explain the pressures upon the first Tudor monarch.

Bacon begins his work with a distinction of history from poetry and philosophy most memorably presented in his time by Sir Philip Sidney in his *Apology for Poetry*: "The books which are written," Bacon noted, "do in their kinds represent the faculties of the mind of man. Poesy his imagination, Philosophy his reason, and History his memory. Of which three faculties least exception is commonly taken to memory; because imagination is oftentimes idle, and reason litigious" (W11.33). Of litigiousness Bacon knew as much as anybody. Sidney had found the poet the most noble of the practitioners of these three realms, for he judged "what may be and should be," but for Bacon, "History possesseth the mind of the conceits which are nearest allied unto action, and imprinteth them so." Sidney's poet is interested in action-as-it-should-be, Bacon's historian in what had happened, in the "acts, instruments, and negotiations of state themselves" (W11.36).

"History, being captive to the truth of a foolish world," wrote Sidney, "is many times a terror from well-doing, and an encouragement to unbridled wickedness." Furthermore, Sidney's historian built his constructs with "mouse-eaten records" and "the notable foundation of hearsay." Bacon would have agreed on the quantity of foolishness and wickedness but possessed a view of history much closer to that prevailing four centuries later, which sees such facts as history gleans as monumentally important and knowledge of the foolishness and wickedness instructive. The advance of learning required the application of humanity's collective memory: "Now if you look into the general natures of the times (which I have undertaken) throughout Europe, whereof the times of this nation must needs participate, you shall find more knowledge in the world than was in the ages before, whereby the wits of men (which are the shops wherein all actions are forged) are more furnished and improved" (W11.35–36).

Except for his life of Henry VII, Bacon's histories are fragmentary. He had written about Queen Elizabeth, and he made short stabs at a life of Henry VIII and an account of Great Britain in general, but his life of Henry VII is his main achievement. "I was towards you but as a bucket, and a cistern to draw forth and conserve," he wrote King James, "whereas yourself was the fountain" (LL7.382). James expressed more interest in the present problems of his kingdom and his children's prospects on the continent. To James's daughter, whom Bacon styled "Queen of Bohemia," he sent a copy of the book, telling her that he had "Leisure without Honour" but desired to have "Leisure without Loitering" (LL7.365).

The life of Henry VII received praise in Bacon's own time. On March 30, 1622, John Chamberlain wrote: "The late Lord Chancellor hath set out the life or reign of Henry the Seventh. It is pity he should have any other employment. I have not read much of it, but if the rest of our history were answerable to it, I think we should not need to envy any other nation in that kind."[4]

Modern writers have also praised this work. Paul Murray Kendall, biographer of Yorkist figures, calls it "a distinguished work."[5] One of the most distinguished modern Bacon scholars, Perez Zagorin, judges Bacon's biography of the first Tudor king superior to any biographical effort from an English writer up to his time.[6] If Zagorin is correct, his failure to continue in the historical vein constituted a loss for the advancement of that particular form of knowledge, but he continued to contribute to other genres.

In September of 1621 Bacon was hoping for a pardon, and Buckingham was hoping to acquire York House from Bacon. Living at Gorhambury and excluded from York, Bacon had not yet received his pardon, presumably written but not yet sealed, because Buckingham, used to getting his way, had not been given the house he claimed he wanted for a friend. Actually the friend was Lionel Cranfield, but Buckingham probably wanted control of this establishment for himself. Bacon could hardly have relished Cranfield in York House, but neither could he afford to offend Buckingham, this most powerful of James's friends, by clinging to a property which stood on land he was barred from entering.

The Duke of Lennox also contacted Bacon about York House on January 29, 1622, and Bacon's answer explained his attachment clearly: "York-house is the house where my father died, and where I first breathed, and there will I yield my last breath, if it so please God, and the King will give me leave; though I be now in the house [the last three words an illegible phrase and thus interpreted by Spedding] (as the old proverb is) like a bear in a monk's hood. At least no money nor value should make me part with it. Besides, as I never denied it to my Lord Marquis [Buckingham], so yet the difficulty I made was so like a denial, as I owe unto my great love and respect to his Lordship a denial to all my other friends" (LL.327).

Perhaps he was hoping that Buckingham, realizing how deeply he felt about the place of his birth and his father's main activity, would withdraw his designs on York House. To Matthew he wrote that he wished "to demonstrate my affection to his Lordship [Buckingham], so I hope it will be acceptable to him" (LL7.226). Advised to accede to Buckingham's request by his friend, Sir Edward Sackville, and perhaps also by other friends, Bacon abandoned his determination to draw his last breath there. After conferring with Buckingham, Sackville promised Bacon that "if York-house were gone, the town were yours." One must conclude that Bacon loved the town even more than his father's house where he was born. He surrendered to Buckingham, which meant surrendering it, at least for a time, to Cranfield, to whom he wrote, "I hope to wait upon your Lordship, and to gather some violets in your garden and will then impart unto you, if I have thought of any thing of that nature for my good" (LL7.347).

Must we take this offer as the humility of a conquered man, or is it a piece of wicked irony? Is he not implying that his "good" (other than the pension that Cranford is obliged to dispense to him) can hardly come at the hands of the Lord Treasurer? He is not disparaging the attractions of the garden, however, which a serious Englishman, then or now, might be expected to value. Perhaps he himself had planted the violets and considered them essentially his own.

10

Seeking an Otium

Bacon wrote "I seek an *otium*" in some preliminary notes to the letter he had sent to the king's daughter Elizabeth discussing his "leisure." While in Bacon's time *leisure* could signify free time to do whatever one wished, as it does today, he was employing a narrower meaning. As the *Oxford English Dictionary* puts it, *leisure* could signify "an opportunity afforded by freedom from other occupations." In writing these notes, which he captioned "Memorials of Access," he accomplished something rare for him—something never found in his published essays: an essay detailing personal experiences.

He wanted to use this unprecedented leisure to accomplish writing both postponed and unanticipated. A writer needed a generous patron, a Maecenas, and a Renaissance monarch, if persuadable, would constitute the most likely prospect. Bacon had already dedicated *The Advancement of Learning* and *The Great Instauration* to James. Now he would serve him *calamo* if not *consilio*, "as a reed" rather than "as a counselor." A *calamus* was not just a marsh herb swaying in the wind but a writing reed. A portion of what I am calling a personal essay follows. The references to Tasso and to Belisarius would, he expected, remind the king that his writer is a beggar, potentially if not actually. I have retained the division into short paragraphs, which tend to lend emphasis to the style of the composition.

> What the King bestows upon me will be further seen than upon Paul's steeple.
>
> My story is proud, I may thank your Majesty; for I heard him note of Tasso, that he could know which poem he made when he was in good condition, and which when he was a beggar. I thought he could make no such observation upon me.

My Lord hath done many things to shew his greatness, this of mine is one of them that shews his goodness.

I am like ground fresh. If I be left to myself I will graze and bear natural philosophy: but if the King will plough me up again, and sow me with anything, I hope to give him some yield.

Kings do raise and pull down and restore; but the greatest work is restoring.

For my part I seek an otium, and, if it may be, a fat otium.

I am said to have a feather in my head. I pray God some have not mills in their head, that grind not well.

I am too old, and the seas are too long, for me to double the Cape of Good Hope.

Ashes are good for somewhat, for lees, for salts. But I hope I am rather embers than dead ashes, having the heat of good affections under the ashes of my fortunes.

Your Majesty hath power. I have faith. Therefore a miracle may be soon wrought.

I would live to study, and not study to live, yet I am prepared for *date obsolum Belisario;* ["To give an obolus to Belisarius": an obulus was a Greek coin, and Belisarius, a Byzantine general, was traditionally believed to have been turned into a blind beggar] and I that have borne a bag can bear a wallet [LL7.351].

Here are natural things that Bacon loves: plough, feather, seas, embers. Readers of Bacon's essays will also note the characteristic rhythm, imagery, and aphorisms. In these remarks and in another letter to the king, which he did not send, he expressed similar thoughts. He had no intention to publish anything like this declaration in the third and final edition of his *Essays*, we may be sure, but had he ever developed the intention to write personal essays, or even lyric poems, for that matter, he possessed the capacity. He finally sent a more specific letter—one of complaint. The king had authorized a pension of £1300 which Bacon had not been receiving, as well as a farm which he had assigned to his wife's friends "in trust for her maintenance" (LL7.387). The lease for the latter, Bacon learned, had been seized, for creditors knew that his debt had been accumulating. He was not blaming the king, of course, for details of this sort were left to the Lord Treasurer, Bacon's scourge, Cranfield. Cranfield, however, recommended payment to Buckingham, but the latter, and the king as well, thought that these sums might better be applied to Bacon's debts.[1] A warrant that James finally issued late that year indicates that he would do no more than ask those concerned "to treat with such creditors of his as he shall desire to make some reasonable and favourable composition for him and his sureties" (LL7.394).

Meanwhile, Bacon still offered the monarch his services. As he had attempted before, he suggested an overhaul of the tangle of English laws. "It is true that they are as mixt as our language, compounded of British, Roman, Saxon, Danish, Norman customs: and surely as our language is thereby so much the richer, so our laws are likewise by that mixture the more complete ... but surely they ask much amendment for the form" (LL7.362–63).

Bacon always sought richness and form. The proposed task, for which Bacon would need assistance, did not interest James. Had James agreed, it is possible that such works as the final expansion of the essays and his *New Atlantis* might never have been issued. In January, James had returned his advance copy of Bacon's life of Henry VII, the man whose role in uniting the families of York and Lancaster Bacon thought paralleled James's in bringing England and Scotland together. He did not rave about it, but Bacon confidently had it printed for general consumption in 1622.

A letter Bacon wrote to a young Italian scholar in June of 1622 affirms that *The Great Instauration*, unfinished as it was and unfinished as Bacon by this time knew it must remain, continued to rank as his favorite work. A letter from Father Redemptus Baranzano, which has not survived, occasioned it. Baranzano had read and commented on the prospective second part of this work, *The New Organon*. Bacon replied in Latin, offering the priest one interesting piece of advice, here offered in the editor's translation: "Do not be troubled about the Metaphysics. When true Physics have been discovered, there will be no Metaphysics. Beyond the true Physics is divinity only" (LL7.377). Bacon clearly did not anticipate a future conflict between divinity and physics. At this point he still intended to offer the king a choice: "The recompiling of the laws, the disposing of wards and generally education of youth, limiting the jurisdiction of courts and prescribing rules for every of them, reglement [regulation] of trade, [or] if contemplative, going on with the story of H[enry] the 8th (LL7.351–52).

He did none of these things. The major effort of his last years had not changed since he wrote to his uncle, Lord Burghley, three decades earlier that he had "taken all knowledge to be my province." The objective remained the same; the best way to pursue it at the advanced age of sixty-one vexed him. The unfinished portions of *The Great Instauration* posed problems. He decided to ignore, for the time being, the imperfections in its most nearly completed part, Book II of *The New Organon*. Of the last three parts he had done little, if anything. These parts, he decided, must wait upon the natural histories, deliverable, he hoped, at the rate of one per month.

Historiography, as we understand it, appealed less to Bacon than what he called natural history. He published a list of one hundred thirty subjects for historical inquiry, which, even at the projected rate of one per month would require over a decade. The list contains celestial topics such as the sky, comets, meteors and "Lightnings [*sic*], Thunderbolts, Thunders, and Coruscations," more earthbound elements of nature, and many human activities involving nature. Of natural forces, winds fascinated him, so much that he elevated *Historia Ventorum* (*The History of the Winds*) from sixth place behind the celestial ones to the leadoff position. This work is not his masterpiece, and it receives almost no attention from biographers, but it investigates a topic of constant general interest today. One scholar argues that it "really constituted the beginning of meteorology as a science."[2] The work also says a great deal about Bacon. From his one-paragraph introduction to this work, the reader senses why he began his proposed series of natural histories with this topic:

> To men the winds are as wings. For by them men are borne and fly, not indeed through the air but over the sea; a vast gate of commerce is opened, and the whole world is rendered accessible. To the earth, which is the seat and habitation of men, they serve for brooms, sweeping and cleansing both it and the air itself. Yet they damage the character of the sea, which would otherwise be calm and harmless; and in other respects they are productive of mischief. Without any human agency they cause strong and violent motion; whence they are as hired servants to drive ships and turn mills, and may, if human industry fail not, be employed for many other purposes. The nature of the winds is generally ranked among the things mysterious and concealed; and no wonder, when the power and nature of the air, which the winds attend and serve (as represented by the poets in the relation of Aeolus to Juno), is entirely unknown. They are not primary

creatures, nor among the works of the six days; as neither are the other meteors actually; but produced according to the order of creation [W9.381].

Here some readers grow suspicious. They see Bacon's keen interest in mastering nature: the winds are "a vast gate of commerce," they are "hired servants to drive ships and turn mills" and perform for humans in other ways yet undiscovered. It seems to be an invitation to devastate the environment. In an age when nature submitted to humans in few of the ways familiar to us, however, Bacon (although acknowledging that one aspect of nature can damage another), did not, and could not, imagine most of the harms, so familiar to us, that humans can inflict on nature. We make vast distinctions between beneficent and baleful appropriations of nature—distinctions that we have been refining only in recent decades and will be subject to more refining as the present century advances. In Bacon's eyes nature conveyed bounteous gifts that humans had hardly begun to explore.

Among the wind's gifts he first mentions flight—not literal flight but the marvelous passage of a ship across the seas. He did not need to go off in ships as Donne and Raleigh did and as he had done briefly only as a teenager between England and France when he assisted the ambassador in Paris. Bacon seems to have scrutinized the ways of ships and shipmen carefully, and as a London resident, of course, he observed much docking and embarking on the Thames, at the edge of which York House stood. Boys who grew up near the sea often dreamed of sailing upon it. Bacon's spirit enjoyed adventure far more than his body. He did not have to attempt any foray upon the "whole world" beyond rejoicing that some of the men he knew could find it "accessible." The "vast gate of commerce" could bring him literary and scientific texts from around the world.

In writing *The History of the Winds*, Bacon gathered commentaries old and new together with his own observations. This procedure is common today, more strikingly among travel writers, nature writers, historians and popularizers of science, and scientists writing for the casual reader rather than in works for professionals. To take a few of very many examples, before Sebastian Smith wrote *Southern Winds: Escaping to the Heart of the Mediterranean* (2004), he sailed on the Mediterranean as

Bacon did only literarily, but he also, like Bacon, made effective use of Homer and Pliny. When Henry Hobhouse wrote *Seeds of Change: Five Plants that Transformed Mankind* (1985), he cited Plato and Tacitus, as no doubt Bacon would have done if he had investigated Topic 34, about seeds, roots, plants and such. Had he gotten around to Topic 18, "History of the Greater Motions and Perturbations in Earth and Sea," he would doubtless have cited Pindar, Ovid, Pliny, and Plutarch, as does Alwyn Scarth in *Vulcan's Fury: Man Against the Volcano* (1999). In other words, Bacon's accomplished and projected natural histories have more parallels with books written in our time than with those written, or for that matter attempted, in the seventeenth century. Writers today of course have the advantage of four centuries of sources unavailable to Bacon, but their research still takes them back to writers he cherished.

His method in this work as in his others involved asking a series of questions, such as: are there general winds, annual ones, periodical ones? Do sea and land winds differ? In our final chapter we will raise this matter of Bacon's questions about the winds one more time. For now we note how Bacon's metaphorical side comes into play. "Bellows are with men as the bags of Aeolus, whence a man may draw wind, according to the proportion of man" (W9.459). A hand-fan and the bellows of a smith are used to make a wind. And in these "imitation winds" that humans make, the action of a bellows, perhaps, may be used for the cooling of rooms in hot weather "by drawing the air in at one part, and discharging it at another." He often speaks provisionally in discussing man's use of winds. He closes his essay on the winds, nearly eighty pages long in the Spedding edition, with a *desideratum* which says much about his relationship to experimental science: "Methods of performing many amusing and wonderful experiments. Such questions I have no time to consider" (W9.496).

Presumably he had no time to do so, despite the humor and wonder of such an activity, because he has one hundred twenty-nine other topics primed for his attention. He is surveying the ground. His interest in varied topics of natural history appears in a collection—more of a commonplace book than anything else—which his chaplain, Dr. Rawley, published in 1627, the year following his death. *Sylva Sylvarum* is not an important work, and Bacon may not have intended to publish it. Here is one example: "The clarifying of water is an experiment tending to health; besides the pleasure of the eye, when water is crystalline. It is effected by casting in and placing pebbles at the head of a current, that the water may strain through" (W4.162–63).

Bacon reports what has been done and suggests further work, which he usually declined to perform himself. *Sylva Sylvarum* demonstrates that Bacon saw experiments not as parts of a systematic investigation of a topic, as they would be today, but as isolated problems available for further research. If Bacon, for this or other reasons, did not excel at experiments, how often he must have set other people, wondering how such-and-such might be done, to practical applications of his basically philosophical suggestions. Not all philosophers can inspire budding scientists, but philosophers brimming with ideas about practical applications of scientific principle, such as members of the Royal Society of London, established less than two decades after his death, broadened the scientific view. Well over half of his one hundred thirty topics, one scholar has noticed, "pertained to man and the crafts."[3] These include such topics as cooking, baking, basket-making, dyeing, and gardening—the last of which, with help from Pliny and Virgil, no doubt, he was well-qualified to take up. On the other hand, perhaps we rejoice that he did not get around to Topic 46, the "History of Excrements; Spittle, Urine, Sweats, Stools, Hair of the Head, Hairs of the Body, Whitlows [inflammations of the fingers or toes], Nails, and the like."

At this point one asks, "Why histories?" A history to Bacon supplies a collection of incidents from which, with the application of the inductive approach that Bacon often recommends, experimental science can proceed. It must be noted that the topics are not chosen at random. He excludes certain categories, including antiquities, citation, disputes, "everything in short which is philological" (W8.359). Likewise, no "ornaments of speech." No species, no "curious variety." No superstitious stories. On the other hand, ordinary things, even if well-known, need to be investigated, as do "things mean, illiberal, filthy (for 'to the pure all things are pure,'" as well as "things trifling and childish (and no wonder, for we are to become again as little children)" (W8.365). They are important for what they contribute to experimental philosophy.

A few other histories followed. With so many topics on which he could form questions and then discussions—even assuming an inability to provide adequate answers—Bacon had enough material to last him for more years than he might expect to live, but he did not proceed. Any explanation for this failure to go on can only derive from the evidence at hand. Bacon several times expresses the need of a great deal of help to investigate all these matters, and he obviously perceived the lack of volunteers. Few people would have been able to inquire into these topics in the way Bacon had demonstrated in his *History of the Winds* and the ones that followed, *History of Life and Death*, *History of Dense and Rare*, and some other works not called histories but intended in certain cases for use in Part III of *The Great Instauration*. We can only speculate on why these assistants did not quickly emerge. They may have cringed at the laboriousness of the task, they may have doubted that Bacon's method would work, or they may have been busy about matters that seemed more important to them.

But Bacon had other aspects of this major work to develop. For the first part he wanted an expansion of *The Advancement of Learning* within a Latin translation, for it existed only in its English version. He intended his great work for the world, so he worked on *De Dignitate et Augmentis Scientiarum* (*Of the Dignity and Advancement of Learning*), often referred to as the *De Augmentis*. In a long letter to Bishop Lancelot Andrews he confirms his desire to put the whole work into "the general language." How surprised he would have been that the day would come when, even for most educated English-speaking people, English, not Latin, would become the general language. He claimed to have "received from many parts beyond the seas, testimonies touching that work" (LL7.373). He revealed that he "had been thinking of three men of ruined fortune—Demosthenes, Cicero, and Seneca," and observed "how they did bear their fortunes and principally how they did employ their time, being banished and disabled for public business (LL7.372). Two of them had not done well, but Seneca "spent his time in writing books of excellent argument and use for all ages." Mainly the *De Augmentis*, published in 1623, expands the earlier work in English and, because of its rich details, appeals primarily to close students of his process of investigating nature.

The *Advancement* contained two parts; *De Augmentis* had no fewer than nine. Its final words, in the English version, make several points that reflect his convictions, his hopes, his confidence, his profound sense of accomplishment—but also for his admirers, the poignancy of this massive effort.

> For although not a few things, and those among the most important, still remain to be completed in my Organum, yet my design is rather to advance the universal work of instauration in many things, than to perfect it in a few; ever earnestly desiring, with such a passion as we believe God alone inspires, that this which has been hitherto unattempted may not now be attempted in vain. It has occurred to me likewise, that there are doubtless many wits scattered over Europe, capacious, open, lofty, subtle, solid and constant. What if one of them were to enter into the plan of my Organum and try to use it? He yet knows not what to do, nor how to prepare and address himself to the work of philosophy. If indeed it were a thing that could be accomplished by the reading of philosophical books, or discussion, or mediation, he might be equal to the work, whoever he be, and discharge it well; but if I refer him to natural history and the experiments of arts (as in fact I do), it is out of his line, he has not leisure for it, he cannot afford the expense. Yet I would not ask any one to give up what he has until he can exchange it for something better. But when a true and copious history of nature and the arts shall have been once collected and digested, and when it shall have been set forth and unfolded before men's eyes, then there will be good hope that those great wits I spoke of before, such as flourished in the old philosophers, and are even still often to be found—wits so vigorous that out of a mere plank or shell (that is out of scanty and trifling experience) they could frame certain barks of philosophy, of admirable construction as far as the work is concerned—after they have obtained proper material and provision will raise much more solid structures; and that too though they prefer to walk on in the old path, and not by the way of my Organum, which in my estimation if not the only is at least the best course. It comes therefore to this; that my Organum, even if it were completed, would not without the Natural History much advance the Instauration of the Sciences, whereas the Natural History, without the Organum would advance it not a little. And therefore, I have thought it better and wiser by all means and above all things to apply myself to this work. May God, the Founder, Preserver, and Renewer of the universe, in His love and compassion to men, protect and rule this work both in its ascent to His glory and in its descent to the good of man, through his only Son, God with us [W9.372–73].

Bacon has discovered the loneliness of his position: he has made a powerful attack on the old learning but has found that the assistants he needs to promote an Organum that he can still maintain as properly his—although still deficient after all these years—can only offer excuses. This proficient maker of metaphors even finds it prudent to explain the principle metaphor of the passage: the *plank or shell* out of which a philosopher can form a *bark*. Finally, he asks God not just to bless but to "protect and rule this work," a request which most of his contemporaries would have understood. Bacon could not have agreed with a premise cannily but almost inadvertently raised by one intensely religious man whom Bacon certainly had met and may have known better than the available record can certify:

> And new philosophy calls all in doubt,
> The element of fire is quite put out,
> The sun is lost, and the earth, and no man's wit
> Can well direct him where to look for it.
> And freely men confess that this world's spent,
> When in the planets and the firmament
> They seek so many new; they see that this
> Is crumbled out again to his atomies.
> 'Tis all in pieces, all coherence gone;
> All just supply, and all relation.

Yes, Bacon too disowned such things as the "element of fire," but merely in a linguistic manner as a vague concept. He saw the language suffering, but for him the earth only suffers when humans do not use its resources prudently. When John Donne wrote the above lines in "An Anatomy of the World: The First Anniversary," *The Great Instauration* had not been published, but the basic thinking behind it Bacon had accomplished. Today it is hardly surprising that Baconian philosophy can be deemed to have undermined the "coherence" in which Bacon continued to believe.

Apart from significant but minor works in these last years stand two major ones: his *New Atlantis* (1624) and the third edition of the *Essays* (1625). We can consider the former as an outcome, a development in fact, of his natural histories. If we examine the more than one hundred topics that Bacon enumerated but did not investigate, we will find many of them among the projects on which the members of his imaginary college of study, research, and fabrication in *The New Atlantis*, Salomon's House, were working. Bacon could not work out all the details of this aspect of the pursuit of knowledge nor inspire, at the time, enlistees in the project, but he could offer a vision of an institution and depict such enlistees in action. There is some evidence, the Royal Society of London no doubt the best example, that Salomon's House did inspire men to carry on his work.

The New Atlantis is Bacon's only attempt at fiction, but its opening suggests that he might well have practiced this form successfully had he been so inclined. Given his motive of providing his readers with a vision of a series of purposeful activities rather than a question-and-answer approach, he probably had no incentive to tap his readers' passion for literary travel and adventure, but *The New Atlantis* has engaged its audiences. He adopts as a guise a group of travelers, a Spanish-speaking equivalent of the historic (and English-speaking) travelers whose stories his contemporary, Richard Hakluyt, strikingly presented in *The Principal Navigations, Voyages, Traffics and Discoveries of the English Nation*. Because this traveler did not have to begin, as so many of Hakluyt's narrators did, with elaborate praise of patrons, he embarked immediately on the business at hand.

> We sailed from Peru, (where we had continued by the space of one whole year), for China and Japan, by the South Sea, taking with us victuals for twelve months, and had good winds from the east, though soft and weak, for five months' space and more. But then the wind came about, and settled in the west for many days, so as we could make little or no way, and were sometimes in purpose to turn back. But then again there arose strong and great winds from the south, with a point east, which carried us up (for all that we could do) towards the north: by which time our victuals failed us, though we had made good spare of them [W5.359].

The narrative continues in similarly plain and inviting language. Having come from Peru, the narrator was undoubtedly meant to be Spanish in origin, presumably emanating from England's great—and for many decades more successful—rival on the Atlantic. Although no great traveler, Bacon, as in *The History of the Winds*, reflects a passion for the details of a substantial voyage, especially those fascinating winds.

> But then again there arose strong and great winds from the south, with a point east; which carried us up (for all that we could do) towards the north: by which time our victuals failed us, though we had made good spare of them. So that finding ourselves in the midst of the great wilder-

ness of waters in the world, without victual, we gave ourselves for lost men, and prepared for death. Yet we did lift up our hearts and voices to God above, who *showeth his wonders in the deep;* beseeching him of his mercy, that as in the beginning he discovered the face of the deep, and brought forth dry land, so he would now discover land to us, that we might not perish [W5.359–60].

The New Atlantis is the second piece of Utopian fiction by an English writer. Plato's *Republic* is the first such work in the Western literary tradition, but Sir Thomas More's *Utopia* gives the genre its name. More, one of Bacon's predecessors as Lord Chancellor, embeds his narrative in an account of a journey to Belgium paralleling a diplomatic visit that King Henry VIII had imposed on More. The More character in *Utopia* is a modification of its author. On the journey he meets a man, supposedly Portuguese in origin (Portugal of course being along with Spain an incessant roamer of the Atlantic Ocean), named Raphael Hythloday, who tells the tale of his experience in the island of Utopia, which means, literally, "nowhere." More's work is more elaborate and ambiguous than Bacon's, but the latter's work also adopts a foreign narrator who tells of his experiences on a distant island. Utopia is a communistic society, some of whose features appeal to "More" when he hears Hythloday's account, but certainly not all of them. Bacon in no way associates himself with his travelers.

As Bacon's narrative continues, a boat driven by eight men approaches the Spanish ship, and they present a scroll written in several languages and offering a cautious acceptance. The travelers scribble a response, including the fact that some of them are sick and that in return for assistance they can provide some merchandise—including as a reward, some "pistolets," which the leader rejects. Three hours later a "reverend man" comes to them and asks them, in Spanish, "Are ye Christians?" Their reply being positive, the travelers are taken to "the Strangers' House," which contains a first-rate infirmary. For the second of three times an offer of pistolets is smilingly refused because for a man in New Atlantis to accept a reward for doing his duty, they are told, is to be "twice paid." The repetitions of this offer and refusal are suggestive. Is this inclination to dispatch weapons to a peaceful people to be regarded as a Spanish depravity? Or, since Europeans have already compiled a record of bestowing weapons (rather than, say, Strangers' Houses) on the strangers they encounter, is it a criticism of Europeans? Or does this offer simply reveal a lack of imagination in those trying to conceive of a proper reward?

The governor, who is also a Christian priest, comes to them to begin instructing them on "Salomon's House; which house or college (my good brethren) is the very eye of this kingdom," an eye which at this point Bacon decides to reserve for a while. One traveler wonders why his friends have never heard of this island. The governor politely explains that a large island, the Old Atlantis, introduced by Plato in the *Timaeus*, represented a colossal opponent that was allegedly held off by the Athenians and then swallowed by the sea. This Great Atlantis the governor knows to have been an early version of America, a place known to the travelers, recently from Peru. The present America is a much younger land. Atlantis had traded with this America, but such commerce, the travelers are told, had ceased. For there had appeared, "about nineteen hundred years ago," a king named Solomona, who had, like the Biblical Solomon, "a large heart." This man, "inscrutable for good," devoted himself to making his people happy." His foreign policy proved isolationist, but his suspicion of strangers developed into a cautious policy of aiding them when distressed. By his preeminent reform, however, he established Salomon's House, "for the finding out of the true nature of all things" (W5.383). He changed policy to the pursuit of intellectual investigation. Bensalem, as the island was called, would seek knowledge and transport worthwhile merchandise rather than arms, thereby spreading light throughout the world.

Before being allowed to visit this scene of Baconian ambition, two of the travelers are invited to a ceremony called Feast of the Family, headed by a father called the Tirsan. Many critics have noted that this is a myth of male generative power, the mother being upheld, so the speak, but withdrawn from the scene. Boys are the order of the day for the Tirsan, who "is served only by his own children, such as are male ... and the women only stand about him, leaning against the wall" (W5.389). The narrator's interest caught, he wishes to know more about marriage. Did they "keep marriage well?" Were they "tied to one wife?" To answer such questions Bacon introduces a Jewish merchant named

Joabin, who, free of the theological affinities of both Jews and Christians, praises the rectitude of the Bensalem family, in contrast to the European version: "But when men have at hand a remedy more agreeable to their corrupt will, marriage is almost expulsed. And therefore there are with you seen infinite men who marry not, but chuse rather a libertine and impure single life, than to be yoked in marriage; and many that do marry, marry late, when the prime and strength of their years is past. And when they do marry, what is marriage to them but a very bargain; wherein is sought alliance, or portion, or reputation, with some desire (almost indifferent) of issue; and not the faithful nuptial union of man and wife, that was first instituted" (W5.392–93).

This description covers marriage exactly as Bacon himself had practiced it—and written of famously, where men are yoked to a family viewed as impediments to great enterprises, whether virtuous or mischievous. He knows what marriage signifies to the well-bred European and exactly what it had been to Bacon: marrying a woman not much over one-third his own age with whom he had had no children, but providing him with a necessary "portion," although the Bensalemites do not evaluate the position of wives, who in the case of a well-bred man like Bacon in England might expect a considerable set of social rewards. Joabin's final task is to invite the travelers to Salomon's House where its Father, a rather popish figure, explains its purpose: "First, I will set forth unto you the end of our foundation. Secondly, the reparations and instruments we have for our works. Thirdly, the several employments and functions whereto our fellows are assigned. And fourthly, the ordinances and rites which we observe.... The End of our Foundation is the knowledge of Causes, and secret motions of things, and the enlarging of the bounds of Human Empire, to the effecting of all things possible" (W5.398).

The house is of course much more than a house. It has a Lower Region of caves "for all coagulations, indurations, refrigerations, and conservations of bodies," among other things. The reader will note the repetition of one of these processes in what soon follows: "We have high towers ... and these places we call the Upper Region; accounting the air between the high places and the lows, as Middle Region. We use these towers, according to their several heights and situations, for insulation, refrigeration, conservation, and for the view of divers meteors, as winds, rain, hail, and some of the fiery meteors also" (W5.399).

We note here the prominence in Bacon's mind of refrigeration, an idea still much in his mind at the end of his life. There are wells, fountains, streams, wind tunnels, and many buildings serving as scientific laboratories. Many pertain to the Bensalemite obsession with health, a subject preoccupying Bacon frequently in these late years. The natives pursue many arts, including some very practical ones. The two we cite below exemplify some developments—telescopes and microscopes, for instance, which were actually beginning in Bacon's time—and some which perspicaciously anticipate some of our favorite devices today.

We have also perspective-houses, where we make demonstration of all lights and radiations; and of all colors, and out of things uncolored and transparent, we can represent unto you all several colors, not in rainbows, as it is in gems and prisms, but of themselves single. We represent also all multiplications of light, which we carry to great distance, and make so sharp as to discern small points and lines, also all colorations of light: all delusions and deceits of the sight, in figures, magnitudes, motions, colors: all demonstrations of shadows. We also have divers means, yet unknown to you, of producing of light originally from divers bodies. We procure means of seeing objects afar off; as the heaven and remote places; and represent things near as afar off, and things afar off as near; making feigned distances. We have also helps for the sight, far above spectacles and glasses in use. We have also glasses and means to see small and minute bodies perfectly and distinctly [W5.405–06].

Men had been making predictions for a long time. Bacon distinctively embeds his predictions, however, in a workshop which, while much more visionary than practicable—not resembling what we would expect to see in a workshop conducted by someone like Thomas Edison, for instance—reflects great foresight. Although Bacon does not know how to bring about such feats, he has the capacity to envision a world that would require many generations of scientists, engineers, and technicians to bring about. He goes on:

We have also sound-houses, where we practice and demonstrate all sounds, and their generation. We have harmonies which you have not, of quarter-sounds, and less slides of sounds. Divers instruments of music likewise to you unknown, some sweeter than any you have; together with bells and rings that are dainty and sweet. We represent small sounds as great and deep, likewise great sounds extenuate and sharp; we make divers tremblings and warblings of sound, which in their original are entire. We represent and imitate all articulate sounds and letters, and the voices and notes of beasts and birds. We have certain helps which set to the ear do further the hearing greatly. We have also divers strange and artificial echoes, reflecting the voice many times, and as it were tossing it: and some that give back the voice louder than it came; some shriller, and some deeper; yea, some rendering the voice differing in the letters or articulate sound from that they receive. We have also means to convey sounds in trunks and pipes, in strange lines and distances [W5.406–07].

The conquest of the works of nature that Bacon had been urging for decades goes on relentlessly in the Bensalem workshops. The Father does not emphasize achievements but the settings and equipment which will lead to the achievements. His style is monotonous—Bacon's anticipation, one might say, of the style of the typical tour director. Unlike most tour directors, he could have—and perhaps should have—done much better. Almost without exception he commences his account of each project with "we have." Bacon's speaker, and for the most part Bacon himself, who, unlike More's traveler, can be associated with the Bensalemites rather than with the travelers, thought that many of these marvelous achievements could, and would, occur.

Beyond the provision of things useful for human life, Salomon's House employs three men who "raise the former discoveries by experiments into greater observations, axioms, and aphorisms. These we call Interpreters of Nature" (W5.411). Statues of the principal inventors abound, including two people known to the travelers: a great explorer and a man bearing the same surname as the author of the book: "your Columbus, that discovered the West Indies: your monk that was the inventor of ordnance and gunpowder: the inventor of music: the inventor of letters: the inventor of printing: the inventor of observations of astronomy: the inventor of works in metal: the inventor of glass: the inventor of silk of the worm: the inventor of wine: the inventor of corn and bread: the inventor of sugars and all these by more certain tradition than you have. Then have we inventors of our own, of excellent works.... For upon every invention of value, we erect a statue to the inventor, and give him a liberal and honourable reward" (W5.412).

They publish their work, and the Father grants the travelers leave to publish what they have learned here "for the good of other nations." Such largesses Bacon had consistently stressed as vital to those who worked for the common good. Surely all scholars and inventors can only praise Bacon for such recommendations, which did not become common until long after his time. His Hall of Fame, unlike many today, also entailed rewards for the famous.

Bacon's chaplain and earliest editor, William Rawley, called the *New Atlantis* an unfinished work. Some scholars have suggested that Bacon did not intend to finish the work, others that in fact he did finish it. Certainly the giving of rewards to scholars was such an important point to him that he might have decided to end the work at that point. A reader of any story, on the other hand, wants it to conclude more satisfactorily; an author's conviction about rewarding achievement clearly does not do the trick. Bacon might have had his narrator take the record of his experience back to Spain, the equivalent of England. We will never know for sure how he intended to end the fable. Bacon would have loved to see many aspects of Bensalem in England and might well have ended his fable by saying so.

11

They Come Home

Having published *The History of the Winds* late in 1622, Bacon brought out the next longest of his natural histories, *The History of Life and Death*, the following January. Again he asks some questions provocative to us but apparently not to his contemporaries—including himself, for he did not proceed much further with this sort of project. He had not given up on *The Great Instauration*, but except for a few minimal efforts, he abandoned the investigation of the rest of the one hundred thirty topics he had assembled.

In February, Buckingham and Prince Charles went off to Spain to promote a marriage with the Princess Infanta. Before they left, Bacon was still assuring Buckingham that he could have Gorhambury, but either he must have been suspecting that the man was not interested or that he was worrying that only by retaining this property for possible sale could he relieve his considerable debts. He had been staying recently with the Countess of Bedford at Twickenham, also a refuge for him earlier, but now he returned to living at Gray's Inn; his wife must have been in Twickenham or back at Gorhambury. The two men's mission to Spain, though extended, did not prosper, because King Philip IV had no specific motive for an association with England at this time. Bacon, who knew the Spanish ambassador Gondomar well, probably could have told the travelers as much. In an undated letter to Buckingham probably written early in their stay abroad, he hints at the possibility that the project might falter.

Bacon was searching for a suitable place to use as a study. Learning that the Provost of Eton was failing, he wrote to the secretary of state, Sir Edward Conway, about the possibility of an appointment to that post, but the king, who had promised the position to another, led Conway to reply thus: "That he could not value you so little, or conceive you would have humbled your desires and your worth so low" as to grant a former Lord Chancellor such a position (LL7.409). In his response Bacon referred to the possibility of his selling Gorhambury and finding "a retreat to a place of study so near London" (LL7.410). But this man, dedicated to the novel idea of rewarding scholars, received no such rewards himself. He offered to send to Conway as a gift for the king a paper he had been writing on usury. It wound up among the Conway papers and turns out to be essentially the essay that appeared in the final version of his essays.

At the same time—late in March—he had to field a request from Gondomar, the Spanish ambassador, that he use his supposed influence with King James to assist in arranging the marriage negotiations, which he favored more than did his monarch. Bacon ticked off four reasons why he could not answer this request and managed to decline politely— in Latin, of course, the following being Spedding's translation: "I have neither given myself up to sloth nor meddled unreasonably with business, but live in such pursuits and handled such matters as may neither misbecome the former honors which I have borne and will perhaps leave to posterity no ungrateful memory of my name" (LL7.412). Aware how little influence he had to exert, Bacon remembered all too well his infelicitous intrusion into the marriage plans of the Villiers family.

In May he wrote Buckingham, still in Madrid, to compliment him on becoming "the first English Duke that hath been created since I was born" (LL7.426). He had sent his friend Matthew to maintain—or improve—his standing with the newly created duke and to assist in his attempt for a full pardon. After Prince Charles and Buckingham returned from months abroad, the proposed marriage, which James's subjects liked no better than did King Philip, had been put on permanent hold. A full pardon could facilitate Bacon's return to public life, although he must have realized that it would take time away from his philosophical studies. If a former Lord Chancellor would have accepted an administrative post in a school, he would hardly have rejected, say, a seat in the House of Lords or an advisory post with the king. Students of Bacon's life have wondered about this duality in a man so dedicated to learning. Why would a scholar, well into his sixties, care to return to a public life?

Without a place like Eton, he still had his familiar chambers for study in Gray's Inn—but public life remained an intoxicating possibility.

Such unwise desires have infected other experienced men. Consider John Quincy Adams, like Bacon a true intellectual, and like Bacon a man determined, against fierce opposition, to reach a supreme position, yet willing to accept later the humbler position of Congressional representative when he might concentrate on writing more books. (It is also interesting that both men gained their first experience of public life by launching their careers as youthful secretaries to foreign ambassadors.) Had either lacked a politically important father who smoothed the way to significant political positions, the scholarly life might have seemed the ultimate possibility. Both had practiced the public life too long and had grown too accustomed to its rewards, as well as its buffets, to yield it willingly. Neither could tolerate the conception, much less the execution, of a quiet retirement. Both recognized and desired the possibility that scholarly achievements could endure well beyond the time of eagle-eyed critics ready to judge them failures as public figures. Neither was required—but each required himself, even in his sixties—to scrabble at multiple careers if possible.

Bacon sent copies of *De Augmentis*, his Latin translation of an expanded *The Advancement of Learning*, to the king, Prince Charles, and Buckingham (who admitted that he was not very capable of reading the "general language"), but no preferments and very little recognition came from these men. He wrote extensive notes for a conference with Buckingham, containing all sorts of political advice and even advice on bowling: "You bowl well, if you do not horse your bowl an hand too much," that is, if the bowler does not raise the ball more than the measure of one hand. "You know the fine bowler is knee almost to ground in the delivery of the cast" (LL7.445). A small bowler thus has the advantage of ease in laying the ball down smoothly. This expert advice came from a man not notable for athletic activities. Was it meant in some metaphorical manner to apply to politics? This conference may never have taken place, but Bacon sent Buckingham a long letter, probably in October, continuing to counsel the king through his duke, prefacing it with what he expected would be taken as sufficient humility: "My bow beareth not so high as to aim at an advice touching any of the great affairs now on foot, and so to pass it to his Majesty through your hands … though I think also his Majesty would take it but well" (LL7.447). Rebuffed by inattention at Court, Bacon wrote to two earls, Southampton and Oxford, for assistance in dissolving the judgment that forbade him a seat in the House of Lords, but they too declined to take up cudgels for him.

Spedding gives considerable attention to "Bacon's last contribution to the political business of his day" (LL7.505). It was a paper that occupied thirty-five pages in the last volume of *Letters and Life*. It may have been intended to be read in Parliament—but not by Bacon, who could not appear there. The document finally landed in Rawley's Baconian miscellany. It illustrates Bacon's logical and skillful argument based on military history—including ancient sources, of course, but also many pertaining to English history. Despite changes in military strategy, the history of conflicts remained—and still remains—one of the key sources of preparation for a military career. What conditions justified a war? Bacon saw them as "a just quarrel, sufficient forces and provisions, and a prudent choice of the designs." Three motives justified the quarrel: "The recovery of the Palatinate. A just fear of the subversion of our civil estate. A just fear of the subversion of our Church and religion" (LL7.470). He supported all three motives with detail. The speech, had it been made, would have addressed the king, whose military ambition extended only to supplying a military mission to the Palatinate in behalf of his daughter and her beleaguered husband and thus would have targeted the venerable Holy Roman Empire rather than Spain as such.

Bacon was on safer ground with the other two motives. The Spanish, he pointed out, "have now twice sought to impatronize themselves of the kingdom of England" (LL7.479), referring thereby to the rule of Queen Mary and to "88" (functioning like the American "9/11" today), signifying the defeat of the attack of the Spanish Armada on the English coast. Spain had also "intermeddled" with Anglican religion in Queen Mary's time and in other maneuvers, lately even in the treaty that might have brought another Roman Catholic, the Spanish infanta, to England as the wife of the future King Charles, although he had to soft-pedal this example. Despite the cogency of his argument, his mastery of history, and his forensic skill, his paper would have had little chance of overcoming Parliament's reluctance to provide an estimated £700,000 annually to fund even the Palatinate operation. As it turned out, the king, as Spedding saw it, "was obliged to content himself with supplying a contingent to a miscellaneous army under Count Mansfeldt [Frederick's top general], and strengthening and encouraging his continental allies with men and money" (LL7.506–07).

To ask whether Bacon really favored a war whose unlikelihood he certainly recognized is to raise a merely speculative question. For him and for his contemporaries war expressed patriotic spirit and often served as an effective deterrent to public displeasure of problems closer to home. Bacon did not see war as a horror, of course. In his essay "Of the True Greatness of Kingdoms and Estates" he wrote: "No body can be healthful without exercise, neither natural body nor politic; and certainly to a kingdom or estate, a just and honorable war is the true exercise. A civil war indeed is like the heat of a fever; but a foreign war is like the heat of exercise, and serveth to keep the body in health; for in a slothful peace, both courages will effeminate and manners corrupt" (W12.185).

Thanks to a certain persistence of the manly spirit over the centuries, we remain familiar with this argument for militancy. Perhaps a man like Bacon, militant only in a verbal way, would think differently about war in the twenty-first century. Apart from his own work, which the king's inattention to his offers left him free to pursue, Bacon spent time confronting two issues: the debt that was accumulating and his honor. Spedding put the matter well: "He had forfeited the good opinion of his fellow-countrymen, and he extremely desired to recover it, and to have the recovery marked by some public act of absolution. He knew the nature and the depth of his own offence and the state of his own mind. He knew that he had not been a corrupt judge in the sense of one who could be induced by the offer of a reward to decide a cast unjustly; but he had countenanced a practice which he could not deny to be dangerous, not only to the reputation for integrity, but to the integrity itself, of the judicial office" (LL7.512).

To overcome the debt he wrote to King James in the summer of 1624 for the payment of three months' pension, and in a separate letter he beseeched the monarch: "I desire not from your Majesty means, nor place, nor employment, but only, after so long a time of expiation, a complete and total remission of the sentence of the Upper House, to the end that blot of ignominy may be removed from me, and from my memory with posterity; that I die not a condemned man, but may be to your Majesty, as I am to God, *nova creatura*" [a new creature] (LL7.518–19).

The king's response was mixed. In response to the second request, James bade Attorney General Coventry to prepare a bill of pardon. Presumably Coventry did as he was ordered, but no such bill has been found in the records. Bacon acknowledged receipt of the advanced pension in November. By the following January, however, Bacon was still staving off creditors.

On March 27, 1625, King James, who had raised Bacon to a great height but eventually disappointed him in a number of his ways, died. That summer the plague revisited England, and Bacon abandoned Gray's Inn for Gorhambury, where illness afflicted him, but on October 29 he wrote a short letter to Roger Palmer which begins, "I thank God, by means of the sweet air of the country, I have obtained some degree of health" (LL7.534). As always, it is the air, that potent physical thing, that he credited. How interested he would have been in the results of modern study of pollution! Also that fall he answered a letter from the late king's daughter, including his essay upon war with Spain. He wanted her to know how stoutly he had upheld the policy of assistance for her and her husband, but she knew that many of the forces that James had authorized never reached the Palatinate.

In 1625, Bacon brought out the third and finest edition of his essays. With the king recently deceased, he dedicated the book to Buckingham with the comment that "they come home to men's business and bosoms" (W12.77). The new title, *The Essays or Counsels Civil and Moral*, demonstrates that he now considered his advisory self fully as important as his essaying or striving self. Was he still "trying out" ideas, or was he setting forth ideas that had reached maturity? By his own theory, to the extent that they remained aphoristic they were probational and thus required the collaboration of his readers in the essayistic process; to the extent that they had been converted into counsel, they were *magistral*, Bacon's own word to describe the work of the master, something to be accepted and believed rather than examined critically (W6.289). Bacon, we must admit, was having it both ways; in this final version the essays exuded both probational and magistral significance. In a letter to Bishop Andrews he had called them "the recreations of my other studies" (LL7.374). While that description may seem to downgrade them, he likely had in mind their *re-creation*, their *creating* anew, in a different form, ideas previously communicated in *The Great Instauration*, which now included the Latin expansion of *The Advancement of Learning*. The same could be said of *New Atlantis*, probably written before the new edition of the essays but left unpublished at his death.

The 1625 sequence begins with a puzzle. The first essay, "Of Truth," presumably recently written and given the initial spot held by "Of Studies" in 1597 and "Of Religion" in 1612, begins with one of Bacon's memorable sentences: "What is Truth? said jesting Pilate; and would not stay for an answer" (W12.81). Let us suppose that you are Bacon, and that you have just written that sentence. What would you do next? Possibly you would remind your reader that you are quoting John 18:38 and provide some background or interpretation, or perhaps you would proceed in some logical fashion to on to develop the point. What did Bacon write? "Certainly there be that delight in giddiness, and count it a bondage to fix a belief; affecting free-will in thinking, as well as in acting. And though the sects of philosophers of that kind be gone, yet there remain certain discoursing wits which are of the same veins, although there be not so much blood in them as was in those of the ancients."

If there be a logic to this passage, it is obscure. *Giddiness* in Bacon's time could mean "dizziness" or "madness" or perhaps "thoughtlessness." He uses it in the first sense in the penultimate sentence of his last essay, "Of Vicissitude of Things": "But it is not good to look too long upon these turning wheels of vicissitude, lest we become giddy" (W12.280). Perhaps *thoughtlessness* describes Pilate. He governed Judea and knew he must exert his authority but clearly did not want to be involved in a contest between Jesus, a political prisoner, and the men who had brought him forward. He decided to let the Jews dispose of him as they would; he washed his hands of the matter. Even if he thought that their *fixed belief* was a *bondage*, how did that affect him or truth? We might suppose that Pilate was simply being cynical in the way of a man who had heard too much conflicting advice in his time. Not until the next sentence can we gauge where Bacon is going: "But it is not only the difficulty and labour which men take in finding out of truth; nor again that when it is found it imposeth upon men's thoughts; that doth bring lies in favor; but a natural though corrupt love of the lie itself." Pilate hated the truth and did not want to wait around to hear it.

The essay then proceeds logically enough. He concludes by quoting Montaigne—not a usual practice with him—and then paraphrasing him: "For a lie faces God, and shrinks from man" (W12.83–84).[1] This essay furnishes a thought-provoking beginning to the book, but as he put it in Book II of *The Advancement of Learning*, one must present knowledge in a form that may be "best examined" rather than "best believed" (W6.289).

Some essays obviously reflect settled views that he surely hoped would, upon perusal, have to be accepted. In "Of Plantations," one of a number of occasions where Bacon upholds the rights of the people against an authority they cannot challenge, he writes, "I like a plantation in a pure soil, that is, where people are not displanted to the end to plant in others" (W12.194). Like other educated Europeans, he pondered plantations abroad. "Let men make that profit of being in the wilderness, as they have God always, and his service, before their eyes." In *The Advancement of Learning* he became the first English writer to apply the concept of *planting* to religion, referring to "those instruments which it pleased God to use for the plantation of the faith" (W6.142). In the same era New England colonists were planting crops *and* faith in the wilderness they were bringing under control.

Another essay demonstrates the process by which a short, aphoristic work—one stressing vigorous examination by the reader—becomes in its final version a longer and much more advisory work. It also fulfills, as well as demonstrates, its theme, illustrating the profound change by which his essays became not merely invitations for the reader to inquire further, but counsels for the reader, as the new title of his book indicates. The revision began with Bacon's longstanding and very close friend Toby Matthew. Bacon wrote to him, probably in 1622:

> Good Mr. Matthew,
>
> It is not for nothing that I have deferred my essay *De Amicitia*, whereby it hath expected the proof of your great friendship towards me. Whatever the event (wherein I depend upon God, who ordaineth

the effect, the instrument all) yet your incessant thinking of me, without loss of a moment of time, or a hint of occasion, or a circumstance of endeavour, or a stroke of a pulse, in demonstration of love and affection to me, doth infinitely tie me to you....

Your most affectionate and assured friend [LL7.344–45]

In the 1612 "Of Friendship," he claimed that "It will unfold thy understanding; it will evaporate thy affections; it will prepare thy business" (W12.337). He left readers to ponder what he meant by *evaporate* and how friendship performed this last function. *Evaporate* is clearly metaphorical, for to *evaporate affections* is literally to draw out the affections like vapor from a solid substance. The revision throws some light on this assertion about the unfolding or discharge of affections. First, however, he imitates a common procedure of the first great essayist. Montaigne, like writers of his time generally, used illustrations from the classics, but he called upon a friend, Etienne de La Boétie, as his first example.[2] Neither Matthew nor any of Bacon's other friends finds his way into the essay; Bacon's examples are kings, for he knew how important friendships were to Queen Elizabeth and King James, isolated as they were by their glory. Getting down to the "fruits" of friendship, he submits one unmentioned in the earlier essay, the "communicating of a man's self to his friend" which has two effects: "for it redoubleth joys, and cutteth griefs in halfs" (W12.170). Friendship "maketh indeed a fair day in the affections, from storm and tempests, but it maketh daylight in the understanding, out of darkness and confusion of thoughts." One of the great fruits of friendship is understanding, especially in the possibility of receiving counsel from the friend, which he divides into two parts, "one concerning manners, the other concerning business" (W12.171). The first part signifies the counsel of a friend, which keeps men from serious errors—something that Bacon would have had to admit does not always work, as in the case of his advice to Essex—but certainly a worthy and possible effect. Bacon does not develop friendship's capacity for assisting in business here; for a development of the idea we must turn to "Of Counsel," which begins: "The greatest trust between man and man is the trust of giving counsel" (W12.146). Today we want a counselor we can trust, of course, but for us a counselor is usually a paid professional. For Bacon a counselor had to be a friend—

except perhaps in the case of a king's counselor. Bacon often gave King James his counsel, but the great difference in rank prevented friendship.

A counselor who "setteth business straight" had to be a single counselor, for "scattered counsels," even well-intentioned, "will rather distract and mislead, than settle and direct" (W12.173). Bacon no doubt would explain his lack of success with a man like Essex by the fact that the latter received too much of this "scattered counsel" from less skilled advisors. Bacon associated the counsel of a friend with the need for assistance in negotiating. In Bacon's time a negotiator was a trader or businessman, and Bacon had written "Of Negotiating" much earlier for his brief first collection of essays in 1597. "We may see in those aphorisms which have place amongst divine writings, composed by Salomon the king, of whom the Scriptures testify that his heart was as the sands of the sea, encompassing the world and all worldly matters; we see, I say, not a few profound and excellent cautions, we precepts, positions, extending to much variety of occasions" (W6.352).

He then exemplifies this with a range of quotations from Proverbs and Ecclesiastes, such as, "He that covereth a transgression seeketh love, but he that repeateth a matter separateth very friends" (Proverbs 17.9), and "If the spirit of the ruler rise up against thee, leave not thy place; for yielding pacifieth great offences" (Ecclesiastes 10.4), for as been noted in Chapter 4, Bacon ranked King Solomon among the experts on business as well as friendship. Bacon had discussed business in one of his first ten essays, "Of Negotiating," where he advises employing "men of a plainer sort" rather than the "cunning sort who may be out "to grace [i.e., ingratiate] themselves."

He goes on: "Use also such persons as affect the business wherein they are employed; for that quickeneth much; and such as are fit for the matter; as bold men for expostulations, fair-spoken men for persuasion, crafty [i.e., astute] men for inquiry and observation, froward [perverse and contrary] and absurd men for business that doth not well bear out itself. Use such as have been lucky, and prevailed before in things wherein you have employed them; for that breeds confidence, and they will strive to maintain their prescription" (W12.246).

Finally, in "Of Friendship" Bacon rings a change on the platitude that a friend is like "another self," for "a friend is far more than himself," he can do what his companion cannot do, even continuing his companion's efforts after his death. He closes with one of the age's favorite metaphors: "I have given the rule, where a man cannot fitly play his own part; if he have not a friend, he may quit the stage" (W12.174).

In an essay that appears in all three editions of the collection, "Of Followers and Friends," Bacon focuses more on followers whose various motives range between "honourable" and "dangerous." He draws a conclusion at odds with his comments in the more famous essay: "There is little friendship in the world, and least of all between equals." He then adds the qualification, "That that is, is between superior and inferior" (W12.249). Having made friends with men both higher and lower than himself in the social rank, Bacon also kept a wary eye on the men who purported to be seeking friendship.

Bacon sometimes develops relationships between topics by pairing essays. He had linked several pairs in 1612: "Of Love" and "Of Friendships," "Of Atheism" and "Of Superstition," "Of Beauty" and "Of Deformity," "Of Marriage and Single Life" and "Of Parents and Children." The last of course asserts that "He that hath wife and children hath given hostages to fortune, for they are impediments to great enterprises, either of virtue or mischief." The point about mischief balances an assertion that seems harshly anti-familial. Something can be said, no doubt, for an institution that decreases possibilities for mischief. Bacon had married only two years before, but his thoughts about families are notoriously impersonal. He and his wife produced no children, but many a couple would agree with his opening aphorism of the paired essay: "The joys of parents are secret; and so are their griefs and fears. They cannot utter the one; nor they will not utter the other." Like many of his famous utterances, this one is based on observation and reading, as his contemporaries would have recognized.

Two paired essays which appear for the first time in 1625 illustrate advisory essays that are "civil" rather than "moral." Before considering "Of Gardens" and "Of Building," however, mention must be made of the garden he maintained at Gray's Inn. He sometimes addresses these civil essays to a specialized audience, in these cases to the few very wealthy people who alone could afford them. Even before he owned Gorhambury, we have noted, Bacon contributed substantially to the garden of

Gray's Inn. It was a place for legal professionals and for young men learning to join their ranks, but an inn of court was not merely an urban building or an assemblage thereof.

More than Trinity College, Gray's Inn served as a true campus. Bacon studied there, instructed there, and at many times lived there. A nineteenth-century member noted, "There is good reason for believing that the gardens of Gray's Inn were laid out in the year 1597, under the direction of Bacon. In that year, it was ordered, 'that the sum of £7:15s.4d. due to Mr. Bacon for planting of trees in the walks, be paid next term.' In the following year, another order was made for a further 'supply of more young elm trees in the places of such as are decayed and that a new rail and quickset hedge be set upon the upper long walks at the good discretion of Mr. Bacon and Mr. Wilbraham.'"[3]

"On the north-west side of the garden there is still preserved a 'catalpa tree' which, tradition says, was planted by Bacon. It is one of the oldest in England, and may well have been brought from its native soil by Raleigh."[4] This passage suggests another meeting between Bacon and Raleigh, which, along with the meeting referred to in Chapter 7, signifies the likelihood of friendship between these two great and distinctively different men.

Besides lawyers and acquaintances of Bacon, many others have strolled the walks of Gray's Inn. Here is Charles Lamb, in his essay "On Some of the Old Actors":

> I think it is now better than five-and-twenty years ago, that walking in the gardens of Gray's Inn—they were then far fitter than they are now—the accursed Verulam Buildings had not encroached upon all the east side of them, cutting out delicate green crankles, and shouldering away one of two of the stately alcoves of the terrace—the survivor stands gaping and relationless as if it remembered its brother—they are still the best gardens of any of the Inns of Court, my beloved Temple not forgotten—have the gravest character; their aspect being altogether reverend and law-breathing—Bacon has left the impress of his foot upon their gravel walks.[5]

Buildings dedicated to Bacon, then, destroyed some of the glories that he helped engender. Lamb's reference to the Temple, by the way, reflects not membership but the fact that he lived there in his childhood.

In considering the paired "Of Gardens" and "Of Building," we can observe that his civil essays are sometimes directed to a specialized audience, in these cases to the few very wealthy people who alone could develop such things. The building Bacon erected at Gorhambury, as described by Aubrey, was, like the one his father built, relatively conventional. The "palace" he recommends in "Of Building" would have a central tower between a banqueting side and a household side. It would also contain an infirmary (the first use of this word, according to the *Oxford English Dictionary*), in case "the prince or any special person should be sick" (W12.233).

With gardens Bacon was in his element. "Of Gardens" begins: "God Almighty first planted a Garden. And indeed it is the purest of human pleasures" (W12.235). Bacon then proceeds to demonstrate that "there ought to be gardens for all months in the year; in which severally things of beauty may be seen in season." His garden year begins in November.

> For December, and January, and the latter part of November, you must take such things as are green all winter: holly; ivy; bays; juniper; cypress-trees; yew; pine-apple trees [by which he means pines]; fir-trees; rosemary; lavender; periwinkle, the white, the purple, and the blue; germander, flags; orange-trees; lemon-trees; and myrtles, if they be stooved [that is, heated by a stove]; and sweet marjoram, warm set. There followeth for the latter part of January and February, the mezereon-tree [the dwarf bay tree], which then blossoms; crocus vernus [one commentator says that the yellow crocus had not yet been introduced to England, and that Bacon's reference may be to the yellow and white spring saffron], both the yellow and the gray; primroses; anemones; the early tulippa; hyacinthus orientalis, chamaïris; fritellaria (W12.235–36).

His non-princely readers would no doubt have to depend on a conservative selection of items to plant from such a list. Bacon continues with similar recommendations for each month. Other features of this ideal garden are similarly specific. He likes wide paths ("enough for four to walk abreast"—some of these, however, should be covered), fountains, hedges, and aviaries. The latter should be grassed, with "living plants and bushes ... that the birds may have more scope, and natural nesting," one of many Baconian references to the welfare of birds (W12.241). The prince might also want to add "statues, and such things, for state and magnificence" (W12.245). Ordinary readers of the day could gape at the possibilities, as fans of magazines and television programs today gape at lovely displays of properties far beyond their price range.

Clearly, some essays speak more directly to great persons who have available resources, but any thoughtful person can benefit from such an essay as "Of True Greatness of Kingdoms and Estates," an essay expanded to nearly four times its original length in the 1612 edition. Discussing the importance of both military preparedness and success in agriculture as the basis for a great country, he insists that "the infantry, which is the nerve of an army," and ploughmen, especially if they are "owners, and not mere hirelings," are the basis of agriculture (W12.179–80). In expanding these ideas in the last edition, he loses the compactness of a point made thus in the 1612 edition: "For it is the plough that yieldeth the best soldier" (W12.377). Passages such as these advise the man aspiring to greatness but support the morale of all ploughmen; moreover, all citizens, not just recruits, should meditate on greatness.

In the expanded essays and in other late works such as the *De Augmentis*, Bacon weaves more supportive figurative language. Brian Vickers, one of the great Baconian scholars, determined that Bacon's five main image groups are the voyage, natural growth, water, building, and light.[6] In an age of voyaging, the non-voyaging but vicariously expeditionary Bacon characteristically associates the voyage with the pursuit of knowledge: "We will therefore make a coasting voyage along the shores of the arts and sciences received," he comments, rather cautiously, in his plan of *The Great Instauration* (W8.39).

Images of the land abound, of course. In a treatise purporting to teach others how to write natural history, he observes that "what we are now about is only a granary and storehouse of matters" (W8.360). In his essay "Of Custom and Education": "A man's nature runs either in herbs or weeds; therefore let him seasonably water the one and destroy the other" (W12.213). He blends the images of land and water in the essay that reflects his sense of professional responsibilities, "Of Judicature." First published when he had yet to rise above the post of solicitor general, it remains essentially the same in 1625 after the realm had deprived him of all judicial duty. The land images are literal, for of course a judge is often dealing with the land and its marks, but he moves to a metaphor of water. "Above all things, integrity is their portion and proper virtue. *Cursed* (saith the law) *is he that removeth the landmark.* The mislayer of a mere-stone [a boundary marker showing ownership] is to blame. But it is the unjust judge that is the capital remover of landmarks, when he defineth amiss of lands and property. One foul sentence does more hurt than many foul examples. For these do but corrupt the stream, the other corrupteth the fountain" (W12.265–66).

Building and *light* come together in a passage from *De Augmentis*: "For the great building of the world in our age has been wonderfully opened and thorough-lighted." *Light* often signifies knowledge, of course. Two passages from *The Advancement of Learning* express his conviction that "knowledge, or rather rudiment of knowledge, concerning God ... may be obtained by the light of nature and the contemplation of his creatures," but "no light of nature extends to declare the will and worship of God," a concession that probably emerges from the Puritan background of his family (W8.477). In "Of Building," Bacon combines building, light, and this writer's nomination as another favorite image, the wind: "You shall see many fine seats set upon a knap of ground, environed with higher hills round about it, whereby the heat of the sun is pent in, and the wind gathereth as in troughs" (W12.229). A blend of water and wind informs the essay "Of Sedition and Troubles," beginning stormily: "Shepherds of people had need know the calendars of tempests in state; which are commonly greatest when things grow to equality." It goes on like an old extended epic simile: "And as there are certain hollow blasts of wind and secret swellings of seas before a tempest, so are there in states" (W12.123).

With the essays in their final form and *New Atlantis* either finished or not, available for publication, Bacon had completed as much extended writing as his health allowed, but a letter that he wrote to a Venetian priest, Father Fulgentio, expresses his plan to do much more with *The Great Instauration*. He was writing not from Gray's Inn, for the plague had broken out more viciously than at any time since the Black Death of the fourteenth century, but from Gorhambury. The opening sentence of this letter, probably written in October of 1625, reveals one of the hindrances he was facing. "I confess that I owe you a letter, but I had too good an excuse: for I was suffering from a very severe illness, from which I have not yet recovered" (LL7.532). He was not sick from the plague, which during August had killed 16,405 Londoners. In September the number had dropped to less than 10,000, and by October the deaths were negligible.[7] A good Latinist, Bacon nevertheless still needed assistance in getting other works translated into the universal language. He acknowledged that he had not yet put the finishing touches on the second part of *The New Organon* (the second of the six parts of *The Great Instauration*) but expected to go on with all but one of the remaining parts. Part V would be "Precursors of the Second Philosophy." Of the sixth part, the Second Philosophy itself, he confessed, as he had several years earlier, that he had "given up all hope; but it may be that the ages and posterity will make it flourish" (LL7.532–33). Bacon spent so much of his time on expansions and translations that one wonders whether he had come to dread the task of fabricating this new philosophy that he had once expected would alter the world's methodology for advancing knowledge. He had relished flinging insults at some of his forerunners. He thought much about his legacy; would posterity fling insults at him?

On October 29 "by means of the sweet air of the country" (LL7.534), he felt better, but he made a new will. "For my burial, I desire it may be in St. Michael's church near St. Alban's: there was my mother buried, and it is the parish church of my mansion house of Gorhambury, and it is the only Christian church within the walls of old Verulam" (LL7.539). He turns to his most important property, his works, and gives his executors careful instruction for their placement. He meant to dispose of sums ranging from twenty to fifty pounds to a considerable number of groups of the poor. At this point it may be pointed out that most, if not all, of these gifts were not received, for his executors had to deal with his still-extensive debts. He planned much more significant legacies to his wife than had Shakespeare, whose widow received only his second-best bed. There were gifts to friends and to a number of his servants, both men and women.

Bacon intended a number of items for his wife. Although she did not receive them, the principal reason, which we will see, was not his debt. He assured her that those things given to her in a previous will, now revoked, would remain hers, "be it either my lands in Hertfordshire, or the farm of the seal, or the gift of goods in accomplishment of my covenants of marriage; and I giver her also the ordinary stuff at Gorhambury, as wainscot tables, stools, bedding, and the like." After excepting a few things which were personal to him, he continued: "I give also to my wife my four coach geldings, and my best caroache, and her own coach mares and caroache: I give also and grant to my wife the one-half of the rent which was reserved upon Read's lease for he life…. I have made her of competent abilities to maintain the estate of a viscountess, and given sufficient tokens of my love and liberality towards her; for I do reckon (and that with the least), that Gorhambury and my lands in Hertfordshire will be worth unto her seven hundred pounds *per annum*, besides woodfells, and the leases of the houses … besides the wealth she hath in jewels, plate, or otherwise" (LL7.541).

He continues with gifts for friends, including forty pounds to Henry Goodricke (Godrick), as a friend and not as a servant, although Goodricke had been the servant whom he once recommended as a speaker of Spanish and who—according to D'Ewes, a later seventeenth-century commentator—was his lover. He assigns his executors the task of selling his chambers at Gray's Inn to provide proceeds for relief to poor scholars in Cambridge and Oxford. Then he names a number of his servants past and present and adds five pounds "to every mean servant that attends me, and is not already named" (LL7.543).

After a few more features and before signing his will on December 19, he makes a sudden and startling change: "Whatsoever I have given, granted, confirmed, or appointed to my wife in the former part of this my will, I do now, for just and great causes, utterly revoke and make void, and leave her to her right only" (LL7.545). Commentators eager to buttress his unfair reputation have cited this passage without giving any account of the provisions he had previously made for her. Although up to this point he has not spoken negatively of his wife, she did not factor importantly in his life. She surely did not accompany him to Gray's Inn, where he spent many months in his final years. He must have considered that he had done well for the former Alice Barnhart, who, unlike most Englishwomen in their mid-thirties, might have expected the opportunity to remain a dowager viscountess for a long time to come. Bacon had suddenly discovered that she must vanish from his will for "just and great causes." One cannot doubt that he had discovered unfaithfulness. A few weeks after his death she married Sir John Underhill, a gentleman usher in Bacon's household.

12

An Experiment or Two

The next story about Bacon is the last one of his life. An important version comes from Aubrey, a man not even alive at the time, but told to him, he asserts, by Thomas Hobbes, one of the great intellectuals of the seventeenth century, who as a young man had done secretarial work for Bacon. Some writers have been disinclined to believe the story because Bacon had reported himself ill a few months earlier when he wrote his will—but he had frequent spells of illness, he often worked when ill, and he made a number of comebacks. A man did not live to sixty-five in his time without a good share of physical hardiness. Very likely the story of Bacon's death is true. For part of the story we have Bacon's own account. Here is Aubrey's version:

> Mr. Hobbes told me that the cause of his Lordship's death was trying an experiment; viz. as he was taking the air in a coach with Dr. Witherborne (a Scotchman, physician to the king) towards Highgate, snow lay on the ground, and it came into my Lord's thoughts, why flesh might not be preserved in snow, as in salt. They were resolved they would try the Experiment presently. They slighted out of the coach and went into a poor woman's house at the bottom of Highgate Hill, and bought a hen, and made the woman exenterate it [i.e., remove the contents thereof], and then stuffed the body with snow, and my Lord did help to do it himself. The snow so chilled him that he immediately fell so extremely ill, that he could not return to his lodging (I suppose then at Gray's Inn) but went to the Earl of Arundel's house at Highgate, where they put him into a good bed warmed with a pan but it was a damp bed that had not been lain-in in about a year before, which gave him such a cold that in 2 or 3 days as I remember Mr. Hobbes told me, he died of suffocation.[1]

Some commentators doubt that Bacon, who often reported the experiments of others and who preferred to leave them to others while he worked on the general outline of *The Great Instauration*, would at this stage of his life be out in the field, so to speak, experimenting. But Bacon did do experiments, and the book called *Sylva Sylvarum* refers to a number of them, many originally done by others, while Bacon, in recommending that readers try them, provides details suggesting that he performed them himself. It is hardly possible, however, to determine how many of them are original with him.

Here is Bacon's version. You will notice that he has no idea that his death is approaching. Later his illness worsened, or another weakness of which we know nothing soon emerged. The source of the letter is a book published in 1660 containing his letters to his friend Toby Matthew and cited several times in this biography. The *etc.* therein indicates that unfortunately, the editor of the book shortened the letter, written to his friend the Earl of Arundel.

> My very good Lord,
>
> I was likely to have had the fortune of Caius Plinius the elder, who lost his life by trying an experiment about the burning of the mountain Vesuvius. For I was also desirous to try an experiment or two, touching the conservation and induration of bodies. As for the experiment itself, it succeeded excellently well; but in the journey (between London and Highgate) I was taken with such a fit of casting [vomiting] as I knew not whether it was the stone, or some surfeit, or cold, or indeed a touch of them all three. But when I came to your Lordship's house, I was not able to go back, and therefore was forced to take up my lodging here, where your house-keeper is very careful and diligent about me; which I assure myself your Lordship will not only pardon towards him, but think the better of him for it. For indeed your Lordship's house was happy to me; and I kiss your noble hands for the welcome which I am sure you give me to it, etc.
>
> I know how unfit it is for me to write to your Lordship with any other hand than mine own; but in troth my fingers are so disjointed with this fit of sickness, that I cannot steadily hold a pen [LL7.550].

If Bacon had dated this letter and if he had not referred to Pliny's death from an experiment, much of the speculation about it would not have been necessary. These two factors, combined with the fact that Bacon did die not long thereafter, make speculation inevitable.

Some weather-eyed commentators have doubted the presence of snow so late in the year in southern England. We know that Bacon died on April 9, 1626. Spedding assumed that at "the end of March …

he took advantage of an unseasonable fall of snow to try whether it would preserve flesh from putrefaction" (LL7.549). The "end of March" is not specific; we must assume the sufficiency of snow needed for his experiment. When he wrote the letter, the housekeeper was taking care of him sometime prior to April 9, when he died. It is entirely possible that Bacon lived longer than the two or three days Hobbes allowed him after the onset of his chill. His "disjointed fingers" have also drawn much comment. Possibly they foretold further deterioration, but Bacon certainly did not consider himself to be suffering death throes. His decision "to try an experiment or two" suggests that he intended to go out again.

Bacon's final experiment and death have fostered the revisionist urge. One pair of scholarly biographers who did much valuable research overreached when they tried strenuously to prove that Bacon died of opium.[2] History is often full of holes that historians must somehow fill, and speculation can be very elaborate, but it seems better to stick with facts reported by competent people whenever possible. Bacon seems to have died after an experiment. Whether Bacon deserves to be called a scientist or not, science for him was fun, and not trivial fun, for it sprung from and energized the search for knowledge. Seeking knowledge can be hard work, but Bacon deemed it a great pleasure. Even as an old and recently sick man—and it is easy to forget that sixty-five was then very old and that physicians had neither remedies for age nor useful geriatric insights—he was ready to rush out into the snow and anticipate (a few centuries ahead of the time when it could be successfully practiced) the work of Clarence Birdseye.

It seems unlikely that any other important philosopher of Bacon's time was interested in refrigeration (a topic enormously important to us, although we do not think about it much because we know we have it when and where we want it). In *Sylva Sylvarum*, published the year after Bacon's death, we can see a reference to "artificial freezing" that probably reflects his appreciation of the work of a Dutch inventor, Cornelis Drebbel, who served King James for a while and who had devised a method of chilling the air that astounded the king and a group of his nobles (W5.77). In his *New Atlantis*, refrigeration, as we noted, is one of the practices of the busy experimenters in Salomon's House.

Fifteen months after his death Bacon's executors had still not executed his will, much of which his debts surely rendered inapplicable. Gorhambury, of course, remained a valuable property. Some wry verses appeared in Blackbourne's 1730 edition of Bacon's works, but apparently dated from 1658. In them we can see, even before Pope's nasty couplet, the condescension of this "good man" that has lumbered down through the centuries.

> Now Verulam, good man, is in his grave,
> I muse who shall his House and Title have;
> That spacious—specious—precious refectorie.
> Which cost a world of wealth (so saith the story);
> Those pebble-paved brookes, empaled lakes [lakes made pale],
> Thick clad with countless sholes of ducks and drakes [LL7.551].

Sir Thomas Meautys, long Bacon's trusted secretary, and Sir Robert Rich eventually administered the will. Meautys, who married a daughter of Bacon's older half-brother Nathaniel, had the use of the estate. After renting it for some years, Meautys lived at Gorhambury from 1642 to 1649.[3] Thereafter it passed to Sir Harbottle Grimston, who in 1660 was chosen speaker of the House of Commons. Grimston had no plans for the now-deteriorating estate. Verulam, the house that Francis Bacon built, was demolished and "sold about 1665 or 1666 by Sir Harbottle Grimston, Baronet, to two carpenters for four hundred pounds," wrote Aubrey.[4] Indignities continued to rain down on Bacon. Aubrey's final remark: "This October 1681, it rang over all St. Albans that ... Grimston ... had removed the Coffin of this most renowned Lord Chancellor to make room for his own to lie in the vault there at St. Michael's Church."[5] The body of this distinguished man could not even rest in company with his mother's, as he had wished. The removal has been verified in Daniel Coquilette's book about Bacon's judicial career.

However his writings are classified, Bacon is best known as a writer. Let us consider judgments of Bacon by two renowned writers, one a contemporary and one a younger man who established a strong relationship with him. Each represented an important school of poetry in the early seventeenth century. Ben Jonson, who praised Bacon in verse at his elevation to the peerage and poetically fathered the Cavalier poets of the seventeenth century, described him thus in his *Discoveries*: "Yet there appeared in my time one noble speaker, who was full of gravity in his speaking.... No man ever spoke more neatly, more pressly [precisely], more weightily, or suffered less emptiness, less idleness, in what he uttered.... He commanded when he spoke; and had his judges angry and pleased at his devotion. No man had their affections more in his power. The fear of every man that heard him was that he should make an end."[6]

If Jonson preferred Bacon's oratorical skill, George Herbert, who probably met Bacon when he was accompanying King James on a progress at Cambridge, saw him as a profound voice for nature and philosophy. Archbishop Thomas Tenison, a seventeenth-century Bacon editor, named Herbert as one of the men who translated Bacon's expanded version of *The Advancement of Learning* into Latin (W2.80). In 1625, Bacon wrote a dedicatory letter to his "very good friend, Mr. George Herbert" which begins: "The pains that it pleased you to take about some of my writings I cannot forget; which did put me in mind to dedicate to you this poor exercise [of seven verse translations of Psalms].... So, with signification of my love and acknowledgment, I ever rest, Your affectionate friend, Fr. St. Albans."[7]

Herbert surely recognized that Bacon's free-wheeling versions of the Psalms were undistinguished, but Bacon surely hoped to express his respect for a great young poet. Herbert no doubt accepted these offerings uncritically, but he wrote a Latin poem about Bacon, a man he saw as an "evergreen of elegance/And of profundity, Nature's cosmographer,/ Philosophy's store, trustee / Of speculation and experiment," among other fine things.[8]

The most elaborate tribute to Bacon from a poet came from a great Romantic poet in his important critical treatise *A Defence of Poetry*. It is hardly surprising that Shelley, a contemplator of nature, should value the work of another contemplator, even though Bacon never attempted any lyrical celebration of the natural features he observed so discretely. "Lord Bacon was a poet. His language has a sweet and majestic rhythm, which satisfies the sense, no less than the almost superhuman wisdom of his philosophy satisfies the intellect; it is a strain which distends, and then bursts the circumference of the hearer's mind, and pours itself forth together with it into the universal element with which it has perpetual sympathy."

Shelley's tribute rounds out a triad of major poets to a writer who practiced prose almost exclusively. The terms they use—*speaker, rhythm, cosmographer, philosophy*—show some of Bacon's diversity. He and the work he did are difficult to classify, and it is a shame that so many later writers in classifying him have failed to recognize his richness. Bacon has been quoted enough in these pages to illustrate his marshaling and mastery of the English language in his guises as speaker, judge, essayist, naturalist, and advocate of learning. His literary capability surfaces even in literary forms that he practiced rarely or only occasionally, such as Utopian fiction, biography, poetry, or natural history.

It is more difficult yet to classify his thought when he was in the mode of the advancement of learning (a mode from which he seldom strays far). Few people call him a scientist today, although he seems entitled to be called a herald of science. By claiming a command of induction, sometimes seeming to bless himself as its virtual originator, he subjected himself to adverse criticism. Although some of his critics have questioned his competence, he seems to have understood the inductive process well. It is useful to remember that such terms as *hypothesis* and *representative* postdated Bacon. Curiously, the *Oxford English Dictionary* finds *hypothesis* first used in a phrase by Bacon's friend the Earl of Essex, in this clause: "If I be commanded to set down the hypothesis or to descend into particulars." As a word used "to account for known facts, *esp.* in the sciences ... [as] a starting point for further investigation" it does not appear until 1646. *Representative* meaning "typical of a class" does not show up until 1788, and *typical* itself, meaning "of or pertaining to a type of representative specimen," dates from 1850.

C. M. Broad argued as far back as 1926 in a Bacon tercentenary that the man could not distinguish between a merely prejudiced investigation and one guided by sound principles of induction.[9] Others have disagreed. Although Antonio Pérez-Ramos concedes that "there is no science in the modern sense which has developed in a purely

195

Baconian manner," he argues that "the patterns of reasoning whereby hypotheses are reached constitute in themselves a crucial and defining trait of Baconian induction."[10] These patterns involve experiments which not only test hypotheses but lead to ways of refining them. Another scholar holds that "Francis Bacon helped to shape the scientific enterprise as the collection of materials, and the inductive discovery of general features and principles."[11] It is difficult, however, to defend Bacon as both curious about a vast display of natural objects and greatly concerned with particulars. We know today what Bacon had to learn as he went along in an era when it was becoming apparent that one person's mind could not assimilate the bulk of human learning: an investigator can exhaust the particularities of only a few subjects.

If Bacon is not a scientist, he cannot logically be blamed, as he once was, for propelling us into a habit of exploiting nature and bringing about nasty consequences likely to destroy us. He loved nature, and while humans may be hard on what they love, most frequently they do not destroy it. He was most emphatically a scholar, and that raises an issue that Bacon recognized. Should he have been more often the scholar rather than the busy participant in public life? He faced, to a greater extent than scholars do today, the practical necessity of making a living. Other than dwell at one of the few great universities that might promote the works of an illustrious professor—places whose programs Bacon considered out of date—one had to look for a Maecenas, a great patron, and even King James, more cultivated than most leaders of his time, proved a disappointing patron. Arguably, Bacon could not have prospered, could not have survived economically, as a full-time scholar; he had to use his skills and energies in public life.

But that explanation is not sufficient. Bacon *loved* public life; he was temperamentally drawn to dividing his time between his studies and the political and judicial works he could adroitly perform. Even when James and the Duke of Buckingham came to view him as too much of a nuisance to retain at Court, Bacon continued to desire the active, as well as the contemplative, life. Some critics have talked about his "two lives"; but he had only a double-edged one in which to exercise his varied talents. From 1607 to 1613, for instance, Bacon's public life involved important functions in all three of the governmental powers that we try to separate: executive, legislative, and judicial. He advised the king, who occasionally, at least, followed his advice. Gifted as a speaker, psychologically apt, and eager to promote conjunction between monarchical power and the needs of the monarch's subjects, he proved to be one of the great Parliamentarians of his time. As for his work in the judiciary, he boasted to the House of Lords at his trial of making "two thousand decrees and orders in a year" (LL7.216), and he never tired of proposing a digest of English law, a perhaps impossible task that he was probably more competent than any Englishman up to his time to attempt.

Over this public period he continued to exercise his scheme for the reform of knowledge generally. Information about when he did his scholarly work is scattered and only suggestive. *The New Organon* appeared right at the end of the period between his first important judicial appointment in 1607 and his last year as Lord Chancellor, 1620, but he had been planning *The Great Instauration*, the larger work of which it is a part, as early as the beginning of that period. Had it satisfied him at any point in that period, he would have published it. As a matter of fact it still did not satisfy him in 1620. We don't know when he wrote most of his essays, but it seems likely that he worked on a number of them during those late public years which gave him such topics as "Of Revenge" and "Of Simulation and Dissimulation," although the edition containing them did not reach print until 1625.

Two works published just before and just after the end of his life illustrate continuing and contrasting tendencies. We have seen how the essays combine his goals of probing and testing ideas, on the one hand, and advising his readers magisterially on the other. They also exemplify his investigative and moral imperatives. Like Machiavelli, to whom he often alludes, he is more interested in what people do than what their consciences tell them to do, but he is also a moralist. One scholar has shown that his essays on health, sickness, beauty, deformity, sovereignty, nobility, riches, want, magistracy, privateness, prosperity, adversity, and fortune expand his treatment of these topics in his survey of learning in *The Advancement of Knowledge*, published back in 1605.[12]

His *New Atlantis* is a visionary work that also supports his philosophical predilections. It depicts a world where men are busy in a manner more mechanical and vocational than scientific—that is, in a manner much practiced in the twenty-first century, and designed less to under-stand the world than to make life better than it has been, frankly, as good as it can be. The men in Bacon's laboratory work *on* and *with* nature. They busy themselves with what Bacon finds little time to do, despite his fondness for experiments. The Jew, Joabin, who guides the visitors around, and the great father figure who explains the working of Solomon's House are philosophers committed to social progress.

If Bacon can be designated with one word, the word is *investigator.* He knew that understanding nature is a preliminary—a triage, in fact—to employing it. Bacon displays an attachment to the natural world that would surely have prevented him from the incessant misuse of nature practiced by many of his would-be followers. Students of his philosophy should see him as a gardener—not just a man who made gardens for himself but who made them for the inhabitants of and visitors to Gray's Inn. They should see him as a man who looked not only upon but into nature, especially in the limited number of natural histories that he accomplished. As an investigator of nature, he sought not just concepts but ingredients.

Bacon remained a man who, despite an imagination that often cen-tered on the sea and the land, desired to be at home. As a man of law he maintained a long and close association with Gray's Inn. When dis-coursing on judicial duties and judicial obligations, he was not speaking merely "from the bench," and when he was contemplating the revision of laws, he was not merely sounding off "at Court," for he continued to live for long stretches among lawyers, and when he lived there he worked at making the Inn more habitable and beautiful. Except for the times he spent, especially the summer months, in his country home only about twenty miles from London, he remained in town, close to workplaces that were, in the cases of both York House and Gray's Inn, also home-places. When banned for a time from the "verge," he was a tremendously unhappy man.

We have little information about his consorts with writers, but of course a number of writers had connections with the Inns of Court, and Bacon stayed in touch with writers old and new through their works. As an orator, he studied Cicero, whom he resembled in several ways; as a naturalist he maintained close relations with Pliny; as an essayist he may never have met Montaigne, but he joined him in testing and evaluating his own experience in his own way. The company one keeps tells much about a person, and Bacon kept company with the finest writers.

It may be appropriate to conclude with some of the closing words of Bacon's plan for the *Instauratio Magna, The Great Instauration.* He intended a work of six parts and yet did not even attempt the last three of them. The plan is a poignant document, for he remained generally healthy and capable, as it turned out, of several more productive years; yet, he judged the work a failure. Because he considered the parts that he had completed or at least begun "subservient and ministrant" to the sixth part, *The New Philosophy, or Active Science,* which he realized would never be written, they are steps to a downfall.

Yet what he says about that impossible sixth part is wise and invigorating. He is not writing scientifically but philosophically and even religiously (although I am omitting his sincere and eloquent prayer at the end). Whether we agree with his religious conviction or not, do we not agree with his hope for humanity? He speaks of the junction of knowledge and power, the twin contemplative and active principles to which he devoted his life, the bond I have called its double edge. Individually we cannot all successfully combine these two principles, but we can certainly hope that humanity will combine them.

Some passages in the quotation below have already appeared, but here we can see how they fit into his conclusion about this great but impracticable work. We can also hear the "sweet and majestic rhythm" praised by Shelley and other features of the style which Bacon called magistral.

> The sixth part of my work (to which the rest is subservient and ministrant) discloses and sets forth that philosophy which by the legitimate, chaste, and severe course of inquiry which I have explained and provided is at length developed and established. The completion however of this last part is a thing both above my strength and beyond my hopes. I have made a beginning of the work—a beginning, as I hope, not unimportant:—the fortune of the human race will give the issue;—such an issue, it may be, as in the present condition of things and men's minds cannot easily be conceived or imagined. For the matter in hand is no mere felicity of speculation, but the real business and fortunes of the human race, and all power of

operation. For man is but the servant and interpreter of nature: what he does and what he knows is only what he has observed of nature's order in fact or in thought; beyond this he knows nothing and can do nothing. For the chain of causes cannot by any force be loosed or broken, nor can nature be commanded except by being obeyed. And so those twin objects, human Knowledge and human Power, do really meet in one, and it is from ignorance of causes that operation fails.

And all depends on keeping the eye steadily fixed upon the facts of nature and so receiving their images simply as they are [W8.52–53].

Chapter Notes

Introduction

1. Francis Bacon, *Francis Bacon: The Major Works,* ed. Brian Vickers (Oxford: Oxford University Press, 2008), 582.

2. John Aubrey, *Aubrey's Brief Lives,* ed. Oliver Lawson Dick (Boston: David Godine, 1999), 9.

3. Ibid., 11.

4. Nieves Mathews, *The History of a Character Assassination* (New Haven: Yale University Press, 1996).

5. Joel J. Epstein, *Francis Bacon: A Political Biography* (Athens: Ohio University Press, 1977), 134.

Chapter 1

1. Robert Tittler, *Nicholas Bacon: The Making of a Tudor Statesman* (Athens: Ohio University Press, 1976), 60.

2. Lisa Jardine and Alan Stewart, *Hostage to Fortune: The Troubled Life of Francis Bacon* (New York: Hill and Wang, 1999), 2.

3. C. S. Lewis, *English Literature in the Sixteenth Century Excluding Drama* (Oxford: Clarendon Press, 1954), 307.

4. Tittler, 66–67.

5. Ibid., 139.

6. Ibid., 147.

7. Jardine and Stewart, 56.

8. Ibid., 57.

9. Tittler, 192.

10. Jardine and Stewart, 60.

11. William Ralph Douthwaite, *Gray's Inn, Its History Associations, Compiled from Original and Unpublished Documents* (London, 1886), xii.

12. Ibid., 28.

13. Ibid., 167.

14. Ibid., 90.

15. Ibid., 91.

16. Emma Rhatigan, "'The Sinful History of Mine Own Youth': John Donne Preaches at Lincoln's Inn" in Jayne Elisabeth Archer et al., *The Intellectual and Cultural World of the Early Modern Inns of Court* (Manchester: Manchester University Press, 2011), 90.

17. G. B. Harrison, *Elizabethan Plays and Players* (Ann Arbor: University of Michigan Press, 1956), 23.

18. Andrée Hope, *Chronicles of an Old Inn: Or, A Few Words About Gray's Inn* (London: Chapman and Hall, 1887), 27.

19. Ibid., 27–28.

20. Douthwaite, 208.

Chapter 2

1. Douthwaite, 2.

2. See particularly Richard C. McCoy, "Law Sports and the Night of Errors: Shakespeare at the Inns of Court" in Jayne Elizabeth Archer et al., *The In-*

tellectual and Cultural World of the Early Modern Inns of Court (Manchester: Manchester University Press, 2011), 286–301.

3. Douthwaite, 229.

4. McCoy's article, cited above, has examined this episode in considerable detail.

Chapter 3

1. G. B. Harrison, The Life and Death of Robert Devereux, Earl of Essex (New York: Henry Holt, 1937), 194.

2. Ibid., 249.

3. Peter Ackroyd, Shakespeare: The Biography (New York: Doubleday, 2005), 278.

4. Harrison, Life and Death, 277.

5. John Bruce, ed., Correspondence of King James VI of Scotland with Sir Robert Cecil and Others in England (Westminster, 1861), vii.

Chapter 4

1. The Geneva Bible: A Facsimile of the 1560 Edition (Madison: University of Wisconsin Press, 1969), 21.

2. Ludovico Ariosto, Ariosto's Orlando Furioso: Selections from the Translation of Sir John Harrington, ed. Rudolf Gottfriend (Bloomington: Indian University Press, 1963), 306.

3. Dermit Cox, "The Book of Proverbs" in The Oxford Companion to the Bible, ed. Bruce M. Metzger and Michael D. Coogan (New York: Oxford University Press, 1993), 625.

4. Baldassare Castiglione, Il Cortegiano (The Book of the Courtier), trans. Charles Singleton (Garden City, NY: Doubleday Anchor, 1959), 43–44.

5. Dudley Carleton, Dudley Carleton to John Chamberlain, 1603–1624, Jacobean Letters, ed. Maurice Lee (New Brunswick, NJ: Rutgers University Press, 1972), 84.

6. Robert Richard Pearce, A History of the Inns of Court (London, 1848), 325–26.

7. Douthwaite, 79.

Chapter 6

1. Catherine Drinker Bowen, The Lion and the Throne: The Life and Times of Sir Edward Coke (Boston: Little, Brown, 1956), 351.

2. T. Wakeman, ed., Report of a Speech of James the First in the Star-Chamber ... by E. Wakeman (London, 1848).

Chapter 7

1. Laura Norsworthy, The Lady of Bleeding Heart Yard: Lady Elizabeth Hatton, 1578–1646 (New York: Harcourt, Brace, 1936), 43.

2. Ibid., 49.

3. Quoted by Rosalind Niblett, Roman Verulamium (St. Albans: St. Albans District Council, 2000), 2.

4. Ibid.

5. William J. Thoms, ed., A Survey of London, Written in the Year 1598 by John Stow (London: Whittaker, Ave Maria Lane, 1842), 167–68.

6. Aubrey, 11.

7. Quoted by Jardine and Stewart, 464.

Chapter 8

1. Ben Jonson, The Complete Poems, ed. George Parfitt (New York: Penguin, 1975), 198.

2. Aubrey, 13.

3. Paula Henderson, "Sir Francis Bacon's Essay 'Of Gardens' in Context,"

Garden History 36, no. 1 (Spring 2008), 165.

4. Aubrey, 13.

5. Ibid., 12.

6. Dante, *Inferno* Canto 26, 106–109 (London: J. M. Dent, 1932), 293. The translator is John Aitken Carlyle, brother of Thomas Carlyle. It was used as the most accurate translation of this passage of Dante's Italian that I could find.

7. The discussion which follows is based on Aphorisms 39–52, his early, imperfect, but highly influential exercise in epistemology—a study not so designated until the middle of the nineteenth century.

8. Perez Zagorin, *Francis Bacon* (Princeton: Princeton University Press, 1998), chapter 3 in particular, methodically examines Bacon's understanding of nature and its laws.

9. Bowen, *The Lion and the Throne*, 424.

Chapter 9

1. Robert C. Johnson, "Francis Bacon and Lionel Cranfield," *Huntington Library Quarterly* 23.4 (1960), 307.

2. Ibid., 320.

3. Daniel R. Coquillette, *Francis Bacon: Jurists* (Edinburgh, 1992). His findings have been summarized in a more easily available book, Brian Vickers, ed., *Francis Bacon: The Major Works* (New York: Oxford University Press, 2008), 695–702.

4. Elizabeth McClure Thomson, ed., *The Chamberlain Letters* (Toronto: Longmans Canada Limited, 1966), 263.

5. Paul Murray Kendall, *The Art of Biography* (London: George Allen & Unwin, 1965), 94.

6. Zagorin, 213–220.

Chapter 10

1. Jardine and Stewart, 488.

2. Margery Purver, *The Royal Society: Concept and Creation* (Cambridge: M.I.T. Press, 1967), 45.

3. Zagorin, 106.

Chapter 11

1. Michel de Montaigne, *The Complete Essays of Montaigne*, trans. Donald M. Frame (Stanford: Stanford University Press, 1958), p. 505. Here Montaigne writes, "Lying is an ugly vice, which an ancient paints in most shameful colors when he says it is giving evidence of contempt for God, and at the same time fear of men." Thus Montaigne himself was quoting, the original author being Plutarch.

2. Montaigne, 135–36.

3. Douthwaite, 183.

4. Ibid., 185.

5. Charles Lamb, *The Complete Works and Letters* (New York: The Modern Library, 1935), 121–22.

6. Brian Vickers, *Francis Bacon and Renaissance Prose* (Cambridge: Cambridge University Press, 1968), 175.

7. F. P. Wilson, *The Plague in Shakespeare's London* (New York: Oxford University Press, 1963), 136–37.

Chapter 12

1. Aubrey, 16.

2. Jardine and Stewart, 504–509.

3. Ibid., 518.

4. Aubrey, 13.

5. Ibid., 16.

6. Ian Donaldson, *Ben Jonson: A Life* (New York: Oxford University Press, 2011), 379.

7. George Herbert, *The Complete English Works*, ed. Ann Pasternak Slater

(New York: Alfred A. Knopf, 1974), 348.

8. George Herbert, *The Latin Poetry of George Herbert*, ed. Mark McCloskey and Paul R. Murphy (Athens: Ohio University Press, 1965), 167. This passage was translated by McCloskey.

9. C. M. Broad, *The Philosophy of Francis Bacon: An Address Delivered at Cambridge on the Occasion of the Bacon Tercentenary, 5 October 1926* (www.ditext.com/broad.bacon), p. 23.

10. Antonio Perez-Ramos, *Francis Bacon's Idea of Science and the Maker's Knowledge Tradition* (Oxford: Oxford University Press, 1988), pp. 290, 261.

11. Nancy K. Frankenberry, *The Faith of Scientists in Their Own Words* (Princeton: Princeton University Press, 2008), p. 64.

12. R. S. Crane, "The Relation of Bacon's Essays in His Program for the Advancement of Learning" in Brian Vickers, ed., *Essential Articles for the Study of Francis Bacon* (Hamden, Connecticut, 1968), pp. 272-292.

Bibliography

Ackroyd, Peter. *Shakespeare: The Biography*. New York: Doubleday, 2005.

Archer, Jayne Elisabeth, Elizabeth Goldring, and Sarah Knight, eds. *The Intellectual and Cultural World of the Early Modern Inns of Court*. Manchester: Manchester University Press, 2011.

Ariosto. *Orlando Furioso. Selections from the Translation of Sir John Harington*. Edited by Rudolf Gottfriend. Bloomington: Indiana University Press, 1963.

Aubrey, John. *Aubrey's Brief Lives*. Edited by Oliver Lawson Dick. Boston: David R. Godine, 1996.

Bacon, Francis. *Francis Bacon: The Major Works*. Edited by Brian Vickers. Oxford: Oxford University Press, 2008.

_____. *The Works of Francis Bacon*. Edited by James Spedding, Robert Leslie Ellis, and Douglas Denon Heath. London, 1857–59.

Bowen, Catherine Drinker. *Francis Bacon: The Temper of a Man*. Boston: Little, Brown, 1963.

_____. *The Lion and the Throne: The Life and Times of Sir Edward Coke*. Boston: Little, Brown, 1956.

Broad, C. M. *The Philosophy of Francis Bacon: An Address Delivered at Cambridge on the Occasion of the Bacon Tercentenary*. 5 October 1926. www.ditext.com/broad/bacon.htm.

Bruce, John, ed. *Correspondence of King James VI of Scotland and Sir Robert Cecil and Others in England*. Westminster, 1861.

Carlton, Dudley. *Dudley Carleton to John Chamberlain, 1603–1624: Jacobean Letters*. Edited by Maurice Lee. New Brunswick, NJ: Rutgers University Press, 1972.

Castiglione, Baldassare. *Il Cortegiano (The Book of the Courtier)*. Translated by CharlesSingleton. Garden City, N.Y.: Doubleday Anchor, 1959.

Coquilette, Daniel R. *Francis Bacon: Jurists*. Edinburgh, 1992.

Donaldson, Ian. *Ben Jonson: A Life*. Oxford: Oxford University Press, 2011.

Douthwaite, William Ralph. *Gray's Inn: Its History & Associations Compiled from Original and Unpublished Manuscripts*. London: Reeves and Turner, 1886.

Epstein, Joel. *Francis Bacon: A Political Biography*. Athens: Ohio University Press, 1977.

_____. "Francis Bacon and the Issue of Union, 1603–1608." *Huntington Library Quarterly* (February 1970): 121–132.

Frankenberry, Nancy K. *The Faith of Scientists in Their Own Words*. Princeton: Princeton University Press, 2008.

The Geneva Bible: A Facsimile of the

1560 Edition. Introduction by Lloyd E. Berry. Madison: University of Wisconsin Press, 1969.

Harrison, G. B. *Elizabethan Plays and Players.* Ann Arbor: University of Michigan Press, 1956.

_____. *The Life and Death of Robert Devereux, Earl of Essex.* New York: Henry Holt, 1937.

Harrison, J. L. "Bacon's View of Rhetoric, Poetry, and the Imagination." *Huntington Library Quarterly* 20 (1937): 107–125.

Henderson, Paula. "Sir Francis Bacon's Essay 'Of Gardens' in Context." *Garden History* 36, no. 1 (Spring 2008): 59–84.

_____. "Sir Francis Bacon's Water Gardens at Gorhambury." *Garden History* 20.2 (Autumn 1992): 116–131.

Hobhouse, Henry. *Seeds of Change: Five Plants That Transformed Mankind.* New York: Harper and Row, 1986.

Hope, Andrée. *Chronicles of an Old Inn: Or, A Few Words About Gray's Inn.* London: Chapman, and Hall, 1887.

Jardine, Lisa, and Alan Stewart. *Hostage to Fortune: The Troubled Life of Francis Bacon.* New York: Hill and Wang, 1999.

Johnson, Robert C. "Francis Bacon and Lionel Cranfield." *Huntington Library Quarterly* 23, no. 4 (1960): 301–320.

Jonson, Ben. *The Complete Poems.* Edited by George Parfitt. New York: Penguin, 1975.

Kendall, Paul Murray. *The Art of Biography.* London: George Allen & Unwin, 1965.

Lamb, Charles. *The Complete Works and Letters.* New York: The Modern Library, 1935.

Lewis, C. S. *English Literature in the Sixteenth Century Excluding Drama.* Oxford: Clarendon Press, 1954.

Mathews, Nieves. *Francis Bacon: The History of a Character Assassination.* New Haven: Yale University Press, 1996.

Matthews, Toby. *A Collection of Letters.* London, 1660.

Metzger, Bruce M., and Michael D. Coogan, eds. *The Oxford Companion to the Bible.* Oxford: Oxford University Press, 1993.

Montaigne, Michel de. *The Complete Essays of Montaigne.* Translated by Donald Frame. Stanford: Stanford University Press, 1958.

Niblett, Rosalind. *Roman Verulamium.* St. Albans: St. Albans District Council, 2000.

Norsworthy, Laura. *The Lady of Bleeding Heart Yard: Lady Elizabeth Hatton, 1578–1646.* New York: Harcourt, Brace, 1936.

Pearce, Robert Richard. *A History of the Inns of Court.* London, 1848.

Perez-Ramos, Antonio. *Francis Bacon's Idea of Science and the Maker's Knowledge Tradition.* Oxford: Oxford University Press, 1988.

Pesic, Peter. "Proteus Unbound: Francis Bacon's Successors and the Defense of Experiment." *Studies in Philology* 98, no. 4 (Autumn 2001): 428–456.

_____. "Wrestling with Proteus: Francis Bacon and the 'Torture' of Nature." *Isis* 90, no. 1 (March 1999): 81–94.

Prest, Wilfrid R. *The Inns of Court under Elizabeth I and the Early Stuarts, 1590–1640.* London: Longman, 1972.

Purver, Margery. *The Royal Society: Concept and Creation.* Cambridge: M.I.T. Press, 1967.

Rees, Graham. "Reflections on the Reputation of Francis Bacon's Philosophy." *Huntington Library Quarterly* 65, nos. 3/4 (2002): 379–394.

Scarth, Alwyn. *Vulcan's Fury: Men Against the Volcano.* Hong Kong, 1999.

Sessions, William. *Francis Bacon Revisited.* New York: Twayne, 1996.

Shakespeare, William. *The Complete Works of William Shakespeare.* Edited by David Bevington. 5th ed. New York: Longman, 2004.

Smith, Sebastian. *Southern Winds: Escaping to the Heart of the Mediterranean.* New York: Penguin, 2004.

Spedding, James, ed. *The Letters and Life of Francis Bacon.* 7 vols. London, 1861–1874.

Stow, John. *A Survey of London, Written in the Year 1598 by John Stow.* Edited by William J. Toms. London, 1842.

Syfret, R. H. "The Origins of the Royal Society." *Records of the Royal Society of London* 5 (1918): 75–137.

Thomson, Elizabeth McClure, ed. *The Chamberlain Letters: A Selection.* Toronto: Longmans Canada Ltd., 1955.

Tittler, Robert. *Nicholas Bacon 1510–1579: The Making of a Tudor Statesman.* Athens: Ohio University Press, 1976.

Vickers, Brian. *Francis Bacon and Renaissance Prose.* Cambridge: Cambridge University Press, 1968.

_____, ed. *Essential Articles for the Study of Francis Bacon.* Hamden, CT, 1968.

Index

Index

Index